Not a New Problem

Not a New Problem

Violence in the Lives of Disabled Women

Edited by
Michelle Owen, Diane Hiebert-Murphy, and Janice Ristock

Foreword by Emily Ternette

Understanding Violence Series

Published by
RESOLVE (MANITOBA)
&
FERNWOOD PUBLISHING
HALIFAX & WINNIPEG

Editing: Jessica Antony
Cover design: John van der Woude Design
Printed and bound in Canada

Published by Resolve (Manitoba) and Fernwood Publishing
32 Oceanvista Lane, Black Point, Nova Scotia, B0J 1B0
and 748 Broadway Avenue, Winnipeg, Manitoba, R3G 0X3
www.fernwoodpublishing.ca

Fernwood Publishing Company Limited gratefully acknowledges the financial support of the Government of Canada, the Canada Council for the Arts, the Manitoba Department of Culture, Heritage and Tourism under the Manitoba Publishers Marketing Assistance Program and the Province of Manitoba, through the Book Publishing Tax Credit, for our publishing program. We are pleased to work in partnership with the Province of Nova Scotia to develop and promote our creative industries for the benefit of all Nova Scotians.

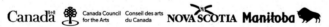

ISBN 9781773630779

Cataloguing in Publication data is available from Library and Archives Canada.

Contents

For Patricia Joan Kelln (1954–2017)

About the Authors

Josée Boulanger is a PhD candidate in Rehabilitation Sciences at the University of Ottawa and co-Director of the Creative Co-Lab. Her interests lie in using participatory visual methods to work with people who have cognitive and communication disabilities. Boulanger worked with members of the People First self-advocacy movement to co-create *The Freedom Tour*, a documentary film featuring institutional survivors from Western Canada.

Mary Bunch is a Faculty Lecturer at the Institute for Gender, Sexuality, and Feminist Studies at McGill University. She received her PhD in Theory and Criticism from the University of Western Ontario. Bunch's research interests include disability, queer, and feminist theory.

Linda DeRiviere is Associate Professor of Public Policy and Public Administration in the Department of Political Science at the University of Winnipeg. Her research interests focus on gender and labour market policies, including public policies in the area of domestic violence.

Ian Ford is a social worker living in Ottawa. Specializing in the area of disability, Ian works as a disability counsellor at Algonquin College and sits on the board of the Ontario Association of Social Workers (Eastern Branch). Ian has also worked as an advocate addressing men's roles in ending violence against women.

nancy viva davis halifax was born on the North Shore of New Brunswick on Mi'gma'gi territory. She lives as a guest on stolen traditional territories of the Haudenosaunee Nation, the Métis, and, most recently, the territory of the Mississaugas of the Credit River. halifax is oriented toward body/s, illness, disability, and difference with a commitment to imagine and articulate what *flickers at the threshold.*

Roy Hanes is Associate Professor in the School of Social Work at Carleton University. His primary areas of teaching, research, practice and advocacy for the past forty years have been with people with disabilities. He is a founding member of the Canadian Disability Studies Association and of the Persons with Disabilities Caucus of the Canadian Association for Social Work Education, and he is also the co-founder of the minor in Disability Studies at Carleton University.

Susan L. Hardie is the Executive Director of the Canadian Centre on Disability Studies (CCDS). She has worked for over three decades in various capacities in the cross-disability field inclusive of mental health. Dr. Hardie draws on community, professional and academic knowledges to inform her work, which is grounded in intersectionality, inclusion, and reflexivity.

Diane Hiebert-Murphy is Professor in the Faculty of Social Work and the Psychological Service Centre at the University of Manitoba. Her research addresses power and relationship satisfaction in high-conflict couples, women's risk for intimate partner violence, couples therapy for partner abuse, and family-centered practice in childhood disability services. Since 1998 she has operated the Couples Project, a provincially funded service/training/research program that offers group and conjoint counselling to couples in high-conflict relationships.

Liza Kim Jackson was born on the west coast of Turtle Island on unceded Coast Salish territories of Scottish/English settler ancestry. Working creatively in the low-income and homelessness community, she joins a long tradition of survival and resistance to colonial capitalism as a system of violence.

Pat Kelln was a well-known advocate in the British Columbian anti-violence and disabled women's communities. She was the spokesperson for Pacific DAWN (DisAbled Women's Network) and founder of the Vancouver Shoe Memorial, an annual public display designed to bring awareness to the issue of murdered women. Pat Kelln died in January 2017 — this chapter was her last project.

Christine Kelly is Assistant Professor in Community Health Sciences at the University of Manitoba. She uses qualitative methods to explore the politics of care, aging, and Canadian disability movements. Kelly is co-editor of *Mobilizing Metaphor: Art, Culture and Disability Activism in Canada* (UBC Press 2016) and author of *Disability Politics and Care: The Challenge of Direct Funding* (UBC Press 2016). She presently leads a study on directly funded home care in Canada.

Karen March is a sociologist and Associate Professor who holds the position of Director of the Pauline Jewett Institute of Women's and Gender Studies. She teaches courses on the family, qualitative methodology, and adoption. She was active in setting up the Disability Studies minor at Carleton University.

Fran Odette is a lecturer at George Brown College in Toronto where she teaches in the Assaulted Women and Children's Counsellor Advocate Program. She focuses on programing related to violence against women with a focus on gender and disability. In 2016–2017 Odette was President of the Canadian Disability Studies Association.

Michelle Owen is Professor in Women's and Gender Studies and Coordinator of the Disability Studies Program at the University of Winnipeg. Her research and teaching interests include disability, chronic illness, gender, sexuality, and violence. She co-edited *Working Bodies: Chronic Illness in the Canadian Workplace* (McGill-Queens University Press 2014) with Sharon Dale Stone and Valorie Crooks.

Stephanie Parent has a Master's of Public Health from Simon Fraser University and has worked in the health care sector for the past decade. She worked with Pat Kelln to help Pacific DAWN implement the "What Women Want" survey. Parent currently works as an evaluation specialist at Providence Health Care and as a project manager for a non-profit organization.

Janice Ristock is Professor in Women's and Gender Studies in the Faculty of Arts at the University of Manitoba. Her scholarly work reflects an overarching focus on community well-being and social justice, with a particular focus on the intersecting areas of gender and sexuality, interpersonal violence, and homophobia and stigma.

Natalie Spagnuolo is a PhD candidate in Critical Disability Studies at York University, and is involved in disability advocacy at the local and national levels. She is co-director of the Creative Co-Lab and helps lead Memory Witness and Hope, a participatory, multi-modal project in which English- and French-speaking survivors of regional centres access supports to share their stories with peers and the community at large.

Emily Ternette lives with a disability and has been active in the disability movement for over twenty-five years. She worked with the Manitoba League of Persons with Disabilites (MLPD), a human rights advocacy organization, for seventeen years. She is also past co-chair of DisAbled Women's Network (DAWN) Manitoba, a provincial women's organization that advocates for the rights of women with disabilities in the province.

Laura Track is a lawyer with the B.C. Human Rights Clinic at the Community Legal Assistance Society. She has also worked as a staff lawyer with the West Coast Women's Legal Education and Action Fund (West Coast LEAF). There, Track's work focused on law and policy reform to advance women's equality before and under the law.

Jane Ursel is Professor of Sociology at the University of Manitoba and the founding director of RESOLVE, a tri-provincial research network with centres at the Universities of Manitoba, Regina and Calgary. She is currently involved in three major studies: a local study of the criminal justice processing of all sexual assaults reported to police in the City of Winnipeg in the years 2015 and 2016; a longitudinal study of the Winnipeg Family Violence Court; and the Canadian Domestic Homicide Prevention Initiative for Vulnerable Populations (in which she is a co-investigator).

Heather Willis has a BA in Disability Studies from Ryerson University and a post-graduate diploma in Disability Studies from the University of Leeds. She is the first Accessibility Coordinator at Ryerson University and was the recipient of the Alan Shepard Equity, Diversity and Inclusion Award in 2014.

Karen K. Yoshida is Professor in the Department of Physical Therapy at the University of Toronto. Her PhD is in Community Health with an emphasis in the sociology of health and disability. She has been teaching and conducting research within a disability studies partnership framework over the past thirty years.

Foreword

Thriving After Trauma

Emily Ternette

I was born in 1953 with spina bifida. At that time, doctors didn't know much about the condition and the majority of babies with spina bifida died. However, a doctor in Winnipeg performed life-saving surgery on me, and I have been able to live a relatively "normal" life.

My first memories of my father are of him holding my hand and walking with me when I was about five or six. He would repeat over and over, "Heel, toe, heel, toe." He was reminding me of the correct way to walk, and as a child — and especially as a child with a disability — I wanted to please my Dad, make him proud of me. From that experience, in my child's mind, I believed that if I walked "correctly" my father would love me. He was my hero.

I don't have many memories of my early childhood except the bullying that I experienced from Grades 1 to 7. It was around the age of 12 that I became afraid of my father and began to experience severe depression. My parents moved me to an all-girls school, which helped somewhat. However, the depression lingered and I was sent to a psychiatrist. And that's when the nightmare really began.

When the psychiatrist failed to help me, I went to a service organization for people with disabilities. The social worker there connected me with a psychologist that had just been hired. He was young, seemed empathetic and after a couple of sessions he gave me a hug. Before long, we were kissing and then having sex. I thought that he loved me. I had no idea that what he was doing was sexual abuse until years later when I, once again, went into therapy because I was still depressed. During the years that I was seeing the psychologist I had a number of short-term relationships. I could never understand why they didn't last.

In 1985, I answered an ad in the newspaper that was asking for someone to help with a television show on community television. I applied, and met the man that eventually would become my husband. In 1990, after his father died, we decided to move in together. My best friend at the time was helping me set up our new apartment when suddenly I just sat down and said to her "I think something happened to me." Emotional memories came flooding back of my father sexually violating me. I have never recovered memories with pictures — like a movie in your head — but I couldn't stop crying. My friend validated me not just by being there to bear witness, but also by telling me that my father had tried to molest her as well. When I told my partner he first reacted with anger and wanted to confront my father. I talked him out of it, convincing him that it was my issue and I needed to deal with this in my own way, in my own time.

I never did confront my father about the abuse. I was afraid of him until the day that he died. However, I did confront the psychologist that I saw for so many years. His response was that he didn't realize that it was wrong! That wasn't the response I was hoping for, but I was proud of myself that I challenged him.

I believe that those who abuse people with disabilities do so because we are seen as an easy target. Many of us aren't able to talk back or run away because of our disability. But what is even more insidious and disturbing in my mind is that abusers don't see people with disabilities, especially women, as having any value. So, in their minds it's okay to abuse us. It's also about power. Abusers feel powerful when they abuse someone whom they deem as "less" than them.

There is hope. Eventually, I found a counsellor who believed my story and helped me move forward in my life. When I first began my journey to look for help because of my depression, sexual abuse was never talked about. Thankfully, today we are much more open about the topic. Women with disabilities must tell their stories, too!

Chapter 1

Disability, Violence, and Social Change
An Introduction

Michelle Owen, Diane Hiebert-Murphy, and Janice Ristock

Violence in the lives of disabled women is, unfortunately, not a new problem. But it is a problem about which little has been written. This gap in our knowledge needs to be addressed, because women with disabilities are valuable members of our society whose experiences need to be brought to the forefront in our efforts to stop all forms of violence. Emily Ternette's account of violence and thriving at the beginning of this book is one important narrative of many. Without such knowledge, political action for social justice and for the prevention of violence is impossible.

Our intention is to address this knowledge gap, to bring greater awareness to an important and often hidden issue, as well as to open up discussions about necessary services, policies, and social justice responses. This edited collection is meant for use not only by those who study the issue or have experiential knowledge — students, practitioners, service providers, community organizations, activists, disabled women — but also by anyone interested in learning more about the issue. It is important to note that this is obviously not an easy topic, and there are some descriptions of violence in the chapters that may be difficult to read. But it is our hope that increased knowledge will lead to social change.

Disability and Women

The authors in this book use key terms such as "women," "violence," and "disability" in a broad sense, based primarily on self-definition. If a person identifies as a woman, for instance, we follow their lead. Similarly, the meaning of violence is grounded in a person's perception that they have been harmed. Related terms that fall under the umbrella include "abuse," "assault," "harassment," "domestic violence," "family violence," and "intimate partner violence" (IPV). We have not limited the book to considering one type of violence because a wide range of violence is experienced by women in general and disabled women in particular. We avoid disempowering words like "victim" and "suffer."

The term "disability" may be defined in many ways. Consider the example of a person using a wheelchair who cannot enter a building. In the medical model, this person's "disability" is firmly attached to the body itself. The model assumes that the person's legs do not work "normally" and must be cured; if the legs cannot be fixed, then the person is the problem. The social model of disability reverses this relationship so that societal obstacles (such as architecture, lack of resources, stigma) are the problems to be fixed, not the individual. Hence, the person using a wheelchair who cannot enter a building is disabled by the lack of ramps and automatic doors, not by their body. The building itself is the disability. We use the social model that locates disability in the environment rather than in the body (Barnes and Mercer 2003), although there is slippage. It is sometimes difficult, and problematic, to eradicate bodies and diagnoses from discussions of disability.

Thus, the social model of disability has its limitations; it is, for example, challenged by chronic illness, insofar as even extensive environmental accommodations may not be enough to ease the pain associated with such illness (Wendell 1996). Despite these drawbacks, however, the social model is a useful tool and much better than its oppressive predecessors. From this perspective, disabled people are no longer regarded as flawed humans to be pitied, but as members of an oppressed group who have rights. People with disabilities are empowered as a political and social group capable of collective action. In addition to material problems such as lack of accessibility and scarce resources, disabled people struggle with ableism, the belief that "normal" bodies/minds are superior, and the prejudice against people who are "abnormal." In this sense, ableism is akin to sexism, heterosexism, classism, ageism, and racism.

Of course, disabled people also have multiple social positions, based on gender, sexuality, indigeneity, race, ethnicity, and class. Like other authors (such as Thiara, Hague, and Mullender 2011), we use an intersectional framework together with a social model of disability. People with disabilities are not a homogeneous group; they have different experiences based on gender, disability/chronic illness, and violence, as well as a variety of other identities and histories (Driedger and Owen 2008). For example, an Indigenous mother with diabetes who is subjected to IPV brings with her the legacy of colonialism and the horrific impact of residential schools. What's more, she might live on reserve or reside in a city, have a good job or be living on social assistance, have a same-sex partner or be a lone parent. So while disability can be a powerful connection, it is crucial to recognize intersections and the differences they make to experiences of violence.

You may have noticed that we sometimes use the term "women with disabilities" and other times "disabled women." (And, except when referencing the work of others, we do not use terms like "impairment" or "activity limitations," which are grounded in the bio-medical model.) Language is important. In North America, the phrase "people with disabilities" has been shaped by a people-first approach to language: the person comes first and disability is secondary. A person is described as *having* cerebral palsy or as a person *with* schizophrenia. This powerful people-first concept has been challenged in recent years by activists and scholars influenced by the social model of disability on the grounds that the phrase "people with disabilities" suggests that disability is bio-medical and resides in or is somehow attached to the body.

By contrast, the phrase "disabled people" suggests that people are disabled by external forces. From this perspective, buildings and attitudes and policies are disabling, not bodies. A person *is* disabled, they do not *have* a disability. This phraseology has the additional advantage of being the norm in British disability studies and disability activism, which have a longer history than is the case in Canada and the U.S. We find merit in both language constructions and use them interchangeably. The advantages of this choice include not alienating one side of the debate or the other, making our work familiar to a variety of audiences nationally and internationally, and including critics who recognize the benefits of the social model while maintaining that chronic illness and disability can still be an embodied experience. Using both "people with disabilities" and "disabled people," we hope, serves to destabilize the perception of disability, which is rich and diverse and organic.

Violence Against Women and Disability

According to the most recent national post-census inquiry, the 2012 Canadian Survey on Disability (CSD), one in seven people 15 years or older is disabled (Statistics Canada 2015) — a total of 3.8 million individuals, or almost 14 percent of the Canadian population, not including children. Overall, more women report being disabled than men (14.9 percent vs. 12.5 percent), and Canadians report more disability as they age (Statistics Canada 2015). Among those aged 15 to 24, women and men have very similar rates of disability (4.3 percent vs. 4.5 percent), but among those 75 years and older, the prevalence of disability for women rises to 44.5 percent compared with 39.8 percent for men.

However, these statistics do not tell the whole story. The actual number of adults in Canada living with disabilities is likely higher than reported. A number of Canadians, including those living in institutions and on Indigenous reserves, did not even receive the survey. Those who did were asked to report on disabilities that limited their daily activities. In other words, if a person filled out the survey on a day when they did not feel that their activities were affected, they would not report being disabled. Similarly, if their disability was accommodated to the extent that they did not feel an impact on their daily life, they would not be included in the CSD total. The limitations of this data aside, it must be recognized that our country includes over two million disabled women.

Violence against all women and girls is a significant social problem. The Canadian Women's Foundation (2018: 1) states that "half of all women in Canada have experienced at least one incident of physical or sexual violence since the age of 16" and that "approximately every six days, a woman in Canada is killed by her intimate partner" (2). According to police data, in 2011 about 173,600 women aged 15 years and older were victims of violent crime (Statistics Canada 2013). Since not all violence is reported, moreover, the actual numbers are certainly higher. Of the cases that did come to the attention of the officials, men were responsible for 83 percent of the violence; 45 percent of perpetrators were intimate partners of the victims (Statistics Canada 2013). Despite alarming evidence of the danger to Canadian women, there are not enough services to keep them safe. It is estimated that every night 3,491 women and their 2,724 children sleep in shelters, and another 300 are turned away (Statistics Canada 2013). An unknown number of these women are disabled.

The risk for experiencing violence is greater for some groups of women. For example, being Indigenous puts women at increased risk: Indigenous women are killed at six times the rate of non-Indigenous women (Canadian Women's Foundation 2018: 7). The Royal Canadian Mounted Police (RCMP) reports 1,181 cases of missing or murdered Indigenous women in Canada between 1980 and 2012 (Canadian Women's Foundation 2018). This figure has been critiqued as conservative by those working in the area who believe that the true number may be more than double (Canadian Women's Foundation 2018). Women with disabilities have also been identified as a group of women particularly at risk for violence. This was our motivation for putting this collection together.

Information from the 2014 General Social Survey on Victimization confirms that disability puts all Canadians at a higher risk of experiencing violence (Cotter 2018). Overall, disabled people were twice as likely as non-disabled people to experience violent crime. In particular, people with cognitive disabilities or mental health-related disabilities are victimized nearly four times more often than their non-disabled counterparts. At the time of the survey, 40 percent of Canadians with disabilities reported that they had been abused physically or sexually by an adult before they were 15, with even higher rates for women than men. By comparison, about a quarter (27 percent) of non-disabled Canadians were abused as children. Approximately one in five respondents (22 percent of women and 21 percent of men) indicated that they had been abused by a current or former intimate partner emotionally, financially, physically, or sexually. This is two times the rate of the non-disabled Canadian population. The survey also found that while women and men with disabilities reported similar rates of spousal violence, the impact on disabled women was more severe. Women with disabilities reported sexual assault at twice the rate of women without disabilities. Disabled people — especially disabled women — were more likely to use formal support services (61 percent) than non-disabled people.

It is important to note that inside Canada and beyond, much of the literature pertaining to violence and women (disabled and non-disabled) focuses on the domestic sphere. Disabled women have been identified as particularly vulnerable to experiencing violence in the context of families (Brownridge 2009). One problem with this focus on the domestic is that women with disabilities also experience forms of violence related specifically to disability, such as abuse by caregivers (Nixon 2009). Sometimes caregivers are hired; sometimes they are partners. The fact that violence from caregivers occurs in the home as well as in institutions disrupts how we commonly think about the boundaries of what is "domestic" (Nixon 2009). Moreover, disabled women are more likely to live alone than women without disabilities and less likely to be partnered or have children. According to Statistics Canada (2009), while 27.7 percent of non-disabled women live with a spouse and children, only about half that proportion of women with disabilities (14.6 percent) report the same. For these reasons, disabled women may be misrepresented in the domestic violence literature or left out altogether (Barranti and Yuen 2008).

Current literature on women and disability addresses five key issues: the higher prevalence of violence among disabled women, factors that account for increased vulnerability, the types of violence disabled women experience, the impact of violence, and gaps in services to address the problem. It is difficult to conduct research on violence experienced by women with disabilities. They may be afraid to communicate, unable to communicate, prevented from communicating, and/or not supported if they do communicate. Consequently, estimates of prevalence are likely an underrepresentation of the extent of the problem. Notwithstanding these challenges, most authors contend that the risk for violence is higher for disabled women than it is for women without disabilities (Rich 2014; Cohen et al. 2005). This is in line with the data released in 2018 from the General Social Survey on Victimization (Cotter 2018). Research suggests that women with disabilities are twice as likely to experience interpersonal violence (Barranti and Yuen 2008), with estimates that range from 40 percent of women with disabilities in this country having experienced some sort of violence to a prediction that 60 percent of disabled Canadian women are likely to experience violence at some point in their lives (DAWN Canada 2017a).

What factors account for the vulnerability of women with disabilities to violence? DAWN/RAFH (DisAbled Women's Network Canada-Réseau d'Action des Femmes Handicapées du Canada) is a leader in the field, and has been conducting research on violence in the lives of women with disabilities for the last three decades. Bonnie Brayton, National Executive Director of DAWN Canada, shares her story of being sexually abused in a video clip on the organization's website (DAWN Canada 2017b). Like Ternette, Brayton experienced violence as a child from someone in her family whom she trusted. This was a frightening experience, and she still feels the impact as an adult. Fortunately, Brayton was able to tell someone what was happening and they took action. She emphasizes that communicating her experience to someone who believed her was crucial. Another woman, Lilly, writes about being invisibly disabled and surviving domestic abuse (DAWN Canada 2017c). She did not get the support she needed, which led her to feel that she deserved to be abused. As these stories highlight, being young, having disabilities and chronic illnesses, and being isolated all increase the risk that women will experience violence.

As is the case with non-disabled women, many aspects of women's lives (including their age, sexuality, indigeneity, racialization, ethnicity, and class) intersect to produce vulnerability for violence. Some factors are distinctive to the experience of women with disabilities, who routinely experience violence both within and outside the family. In addition to spouses and intimate partners, disabled women are abused by other family members, health care providers, caregivers such as personal attendants, social workers, doctors, nurses, and institutional or residential staff, and strangers (Barranti and Yuen 2008; Carman 2006; Rajan 2013). At the core of violence towards disabled women is the power differential that results from being female and having disabilities and/or chronic illnesses in an able-bodied patriarchal context. Nixon (2009) asserts that the construction of disabled women as passive and nonsexual may make them more vulnerable to violence. Women with disabilities are socially marginalized and made invisible (Barranti and Yuen 2008; Forte et al. 2005). They may be isolated with few resources and little education (Barrett et al. 2009). Economic and physical dependence on others may increase the vulnerability of women with disabilities to violence (Cohen et al. 2005). Women with disabilities who have experienced interpersonal violence are also less likely to have good health, health insurance, or a doctor than disabled women who have not experienced interpersonal violence (Barrett et al. 2009). The common thread is the dependency of disabled women. Increased dependency places them at greater risk of abuse not only from partners or caregivers, but also from medical professionals (Nixon 2009).

When violence occurs, disabled women face even more obstacles to reporting violence and abuse than non-disabled women. For example, a blind woman might not be able to find information about shelters on the Internet, while a deaf woman may have difficulty making a call for help. Cognitive or multiple disabilities may increase the risk of experiencing abuse, as well as making it less likely that violence will be reported by them than it is by those with less severe or no disabilities (Hahn et al. 2014). Finally, disabled women have reported feeling as though they were not believed when reporting abuse (Rajan 2013).

The Rajan report (2013) explores the reasons women with disabilities may be unable or unwilling to leave an abusive situation. They may lack the financial resources to leave or need the support their abuser provides; they may not know how to leave, where to go to access the necessary services, or even that they are experiencing abuse. Cohen et al. (2005) suggest that women with disabilities tend to be older and have lower incomes and less education than those without activity limitations. Disabled women may find it difficult to leave an abuser, upon whom they may be dependent for financial support, housing, and personal care (Forte et al. 2005). As a result of these challenges, women with disabilities may not get the help they need and be forced to stay in an abusive situation longer than a woman without disabilities (Barranti and Yuen 2008).

Women with disabilities often experience multiple types of violence. Most of the participants involved in the DAWN research reported more than one type of violence, and in the majority of focus groups, disabled women highlighted psychological, verbal, and financial abuse, as well as abuse by individuals and organizations that are supposed to offer assistance (Rajan 2013). The latter includes health care, shelters, the legal system, social workers, and the police. Physical and sexual abuse and racism were also named by the participants. Violence may take the form of preventing the use of medical devices such as respirators, withholding medication, or not allowing a woman to use her wheelchair or cane (Rajan 2013). According to Barranti and Yuen (2008), disability-specific abuse may include intentionally withholding access to food, water, medications, and adequate hygiene practices, or damaging assistive devices. Withholding care is also common when intimate partners act as caregivers (Hahn et al. 2014), and women with disabilities may be left in physical discomfort or kept in isolation (Nixon 2009). According to Barrett et al. (2009), disabled women are twice as likely as women without disabilities to be forced to have sex with an intimate partner. Rich (2014) observes that the threat of institutionalization may also be used as a form of violence.

Previous research has been largely based on surveys with, and reflections by, older women with disabilities. Owen (2014), drawing instead on interviews she conducted with disabled girls and young women about violence, identifies psychological abuse and neglect as the most often cited types of violence. Covert and subtle forms of violence were common, and included name-calling, bullying, belittling, lack of care, and disempowerment. The participants in this study reported rates of sexual and physical abuse in keeping with the literature, with over two-thirds of women with disabilities experiencing physical or sexual assault when they were young.

A particularly revealing Canadian instance of violence against a disabled young person is the murder of 12-year-old Tracy Latimer in 1993 (Enns 1999). Unfortunately, the Canadian public, as well as the judiciary, was sympathetic to Tracey's father, Robert Latimer. Ending Tracey's life was viewed as mercy killing or "compassionate homicide" rather than as an incident of violence against disabled people.

The effects of violence on disabled women are many and varied. Even if they are not disabled, women who have experienced interpersonal violence are more likely than those who have not experienced violence to have poor physical and mental health (Barrett et al. 2009; Dienemann et al. 2000; Forte et al. 2005). Dienemann et al. (2000) contend that there are many negative mental and physical health consequences for women who experience intimate partner abuse. Depression, according to Karakurt, Smith, and Whiting (2014: 2), is one of the most harmful consequences, and "can eventually lead to suicidal ideation or suicide attempts." Women who are disabled, particularly those with activity limitations, are more likely than those without to experience severe forms of physical abuse, suggesting that they may be particularly at risk for negative consequences (Cohen et al. 2005). Indeed, disability itself may result from abuse (Rajan 2013).

Research has also examined services to address violence experienced by women with disabilities and questioned the adequacy of current services to respond to their needs. Barranti and Yuen (2008) argue that there is a large gap in the research on interpersonal violence, that this research neglects women with disabilities, and that — in part as a result of this neglect — services for victims of domestic violence are often physically and programmatically inaccessible to women with disabilities. According to the 2011 DAWN report (Rajan 2013), disabled women feel that service providers lack respect and compassion, and have little training or knowledge for working with women with disabilities. The report identifies a number of changes needed to improve the service delivery system for disabled women, including the need for sensitive and skilled counsellors as well as financial assistance for those seeking services. The unique needs of disabled women from various cultural backgrounds have also been discussed. According to Lightfoot and Williams (2009), women with disabilities and of differing racial backgrounds have distinct experiences of domestic violence that require unique strategies of prevention and support. Racialized women with disabilities experience increased discrimination and oppression, while differing cultural attitudes toward disabilities can impact both domestic abuse and access to services. As a result, generic services and support for women experiencing violence are often not appropriate for the unique needs of disabled women within minority cultural groups.

Sections and Chapters

A review of the literature reveals the limits of what is currently known about violence against disabled women in Canada. As a result, some sources appear in several of the following chapters, and there is overlap in the literature that is reviewed. Moreover, a number of significant topics are woven throughout the book: issues faced by Indigenous women, intimate partner violence, mothering, childhood abuse, depression, and poverty. The chapters in this collection extend understanding by exploring the many forms of violence that disabled Canadian women experience and the barriers they encounter when they seek services. In doing so, many of the authors offer a critique of current policy and offer suggestions for change. Despite the difficulty of the topic, the message is hopeful: social change is possible.

The first section focuses on violence in and because of relationships. In

Chapter Two, "Mothering with Disabilities: Violence and Equality Rights," Laura Track examines discrimination against disabled mothers and the impact of violence. She notes that parents with disabilities, especially mothers, routinely confront attitudinal barriers. This chapter includes a discussion of the findings from the project "Mothering with Disabilities," sponsored by West Coast Women's Legal Education and Action Fund (West Coast LEAF). Track concludes that the state is legally obligated to protect disabled mothers, who have equality rights.

Chapter Three, "The Healing Journey: Women with Disabilities and Intimate Partner Violence," by Michelle Owen and Jane Ursel, is based on the findings from a tri-provincial research project. The goal of The Healing Journey study was to document the efforts women make to secure a safe and violence-free life for themselves and their families. Owen and Ursel point to the complicated relationship that exists between disability and IPV. The authors explore four unexpected findings about the lives of Indigenous and non-Indigenous disabled women who have experienced IPV. Owen and Ursel's analysis of the prevalence of depression and childhood abuse helps to fill a knowledge gap.

In Chapter Four, "Out of the Closet: Intimate Partner Violence as a Cause of Disabilities," Roy Hanes, Karen March, and Ian Ford focus on the long-term damage resulting from IPV. Little work has been done in this area, but they speculate that for some older women, dementia and related disorders may be a result of concussions and traumatic brain injuries caused by IPV. The authors' goal is to raise awareness about this issue and stimulate conversation and research.

In the second section, the focus broadens from the familial to the structural — violence that is embedded in the fabric of society. Chapter Five, by Natalie Spagnuolo and Josée Boulanger, is entitled "An 'Unconscious Terrain of Habits': Structural Violence against Women Labelled with Intellectual Disabilities." The authors contend that understanding the legal system, especially as it pertains to people labelled with intellectual disabilities, as well as recognizing societal beliefs about competence, is crucial to understanding the type of violence that is experienced. Sadly, violence against women who are labelled with intellectual disabilities is often met with indifference. Narratives are employed in this chapter as a way to illustrate and personalize the workings of structural violence.

Linda DeRiviere continues this theme in Chapter Six, "A Crisis of

Poverty: Economic Disparities, Disabled Women, and Abuse." She also draws on The Healing Journey study, using the data to demonstrate how IPV contributes to disabled women's vulnerability to living in poverty. Women who have been abused have lower incomes and reduced employment opportunities. Moreover, IPV has a negative impact on women's chronic health conditions and/or disabilities.

Chapter Seven, by Liza Kim Jackson and nancy viva davis halifax, is a departure from the more traditional narratives of the rest of the book. They advise the reader to go slowly as they implement "crip artist praxis" to describe their project in "Making Homelessness Harder: Possibilities for Radical Re-Orientation." The focus of this chapter is the systemic violence, homelessness, and, especially, poverty experienced by women with disabilities living in a capitalist economy. The narratives they recount were gathered by the Red Wagon Collective in Toronto.

In the third section, the emphasis shifts to services, action, and policy. In Chapter Eight, "Home Care: Gendered Violence in Independent Living Attendant Services," Christine Kelly critiques the concept of "care" in the context of disabled people hiring and managing their own attendants. Drawing on her study of the Ontario Direct Funding program, which is administered by an Independent Living organization, she explores themes related to abuse and violence. Kelly concludes that "care" is a complicated concept that has the potential to be both transformative and oppressive.

Chapter Nine, "Taking Action: Gender-Based Violence, Disability, and the Social Determinants of Health," by Karen Yoshida, Mary Bunch, Fran Odette, Susan Hardie, and Heather Willis, contains a review of the health literature on violence against disabled women and the findings of a community-academic study. The purpose of this research was to consult with disabled women across Canada about health issues using message boards and chat rooms. The authors conclude by discussing the circumstances that would make life safer for disabled women, as well as proposing a process for intervention.

"'What Women Want': Pacific DAWN Talks to Women with DisAbilities about Escaping Violence," by Pat Kelln and Stephanie Parent, is the final chapter. It describes a community-based project designed to investigate what types of services are actually required by women with disabilities who experience abuse. Members of Pacific DAWN set out to go beyond surveys that query non-disabled personnel about accessibility. They developed their own survey, which gathered demographic information about women with disabilities and asked them crucial questions about services. The goal of this research is to guide activism and impact government as well as non-governmental services.

We hope that through this collection you are inspired to gain even more knowledge, continue the work you may already be doing, or perhaps even take action.

References

Barnes, Colin, and Geof Mercer. 2003. *Disability*. Cambridge, U.K.: Polity Press.

Barranti, Chrystal C.R., and Francis K.O. Yuen. 2008. "Intimate Partner Violence and Women with Disabilities: Toward Bringing Visibility to an Unrecognized Population." *Journal of Social Work in Disability & Rehabilitation*, 7, 2.

Barrett, K.A., B. O'Day, A. Roche and B.L. Carlson. 2009. "Intimate Partner Violence, Health Status, and Health Care Access among Women with Disabilities." *Women's Health Issues*, 19, 2.

Brownridge, D.A. 2009. *Violence against Women: Vulnerable Populations*. New York: Routledge.

Canadian Women's Foundation. 2018. "Fact Sheet: Moving Women out of Violence." <canadianwomen.org/wp-content/uploads/2017/09/FactSheet-VAWandDV_Feb_2018-Update.pdf>.

Carman, Linda. 2006. "Partner Abuse in Physically Disabled Women: A Proposed Model for Understanding Intimate Partner Violence." *Perspectives in Psychiatric Care*, 42, 2.

Cohen, Marsha M., Tonia Forte, Janice Du Mont, Ilene Hyman and Sarah Romans. 2005. "Intimate Partner Violence Among Canadian Women with Activity Limitations." *Journal of Epidemiology and Community Health*, 59, 10.

Cotter, Adam. 2018. *Violent Victimization of Women with Disabilities, 2014*. Ottawa: Statistics Canada.

DAWN Canada. 2017a. "Women with Disabilities and Violence." <dawncanada.net/issues/issues/fact-sheets-2/violence/>.

___. 2017b. <dawncanada.net/?videos=bonnies-story-of-abuse>.

___. 2017c. <dawncanada.net/issues/issues/we-can-tell-and-we-will-tell-2/womens-stories-of-abuse/>.

Dienemann, J., E. Boyle, W. Resnick, N. Wiederhorn and J.C. Campbell. 2000. "Intimate Partner Abuse among Women Diagnosed with Depression." *Issues in Mental Health Nursing*, 21, 5.

Driedger, Diane, and Michelle Owen (eds.). 2008. *Dissonant Disabilities: Women with Chronic Illnesses Explore Their Lives*. Toronto: Canadian Scholars' Press Inc./Women's Press.

Enns, Ruth. 1999. *A Voice Unheard: The Latimer Case and People with Disabilities*. Halifax and Winnipeg: Fernwood Publishing.

Forte, T., M.M. Cohen, J. Du Mont, I. Hyman and S. Romans. 2005. "Psychological and

Physical Sequelae of Intimate Partner Violence among Women with Limitations in Their Activities of Daily Living." *Archives of Women's Mental Health,* 8, 4.

Hahn, Josephine W., Marie C. McCormick, Jay G. Silverman, Elise B. Robinson and Karestan C. Koenen. 2014. "Examining the Impact of Disability Status on Intimate Partner Violence Victimization in a Population Sample." *Journal of Interpersonal Violence,* 29, 17.

Karakurt, Gunner, Douglas Smith and Jason Whiting. 2014. "Impact of Intimate Partner Violence on Women's Mental Health." *Journal of Family Violence,* 29, 7.

Lightfoot, Elizabeth, and Oliver Williams. 2009. "The Intersection of Disability, Diversity, and Domestic Violence: Results of National Focus Groups." *Journal of Aggression, Maltreatment & Trauma,* 18, 2.

Nixon, Jennifer. 2009. "Domestic Violence and Women with Disabilities: Locating the Issue on the Periphery of Social Movements." *Disability & Society,* 24, 1.

Owen, Michelle. 2014. "Researching the Experiences of Girls and Young Women with Disabilities: 'A Victim of Subtle Abuse Rather Frequently.'" In Helene Berman and Yasmin Jiwani (eds.), *Faces of Violence in the Lives of Girls.* London: Althouse Press.

Rajan, Doris. 2013. "Women with Disabilities and Abuse: Access to Supports." Montreal: dawn/rafh Canada. <dawncanada.net/main/wp-content/uploads/2013/08/Women-with-Disabilities-and-Abuse-Access-to-Supports.pdf>.

Rich, Karen. 2014. "'My Body Came between Us': Accounts of Partner-Abused Women with Physical Disabilities." *Affilia,* 29, 4.

Statistics Canada. 2009. "Canadian Community Health Survey." <statcan.gc.ca/pub/89-503-x/2010001/article/11545/tbl/tb1004-eng.htm>.

____. 2013. "Measuring Violence against Women: Statistical trends: Highlights." <statcan.gc.ca/pub/85-002-x/2013001/article/11766/hl-fs-eng.htm>.

____. 2015. "Canadian Survey on Disability, 2012." <statcan.gc.ca/pub/89-654-x/89-654-x2015001-eng.htm>.

Thiara, Ravi K., Gill Hague and Audrey Mullender. 2011. "Losing Out on Both Counts: Disabled Women and Domestic Violence." *Disability & Society,* 26, 6.

Wendell, Susan. 1996. *The Rejected Body: Feminist Philosophical Reflections on Disability.* New York: Routledge.

Section 1

Violence in Relationships

Chapter 2

Mothering with Disabilities
Violence and Equality Rights[1]

Laura Track

In 2012, a Mississauga woman gave birth to a healthy baby boy she and her partner named William. Within hours, however, the Peel Children's Aid Society was threatening to remove William from his parents — both of whom have cerebral palsy, a disorder that limits their motor capabilities and affects their speech — unless they secured round-the-clock care from an "able-bodied attendant" (CBC News 2012). The social worker ruled that the couple's physical disabilities made them unfit parents and obtained a warrant to remove the child from the home. It was only after disability advocates and supporters of the parents intervened and promised their assistance that the Society backed down.

Dominant discourses about mothers and motherhood feature able-bodied women who are mature, white, heterosexual, cisgender, married, and economically secure (Filax and Taylor 2014). Disabled mothers exist outside of these norms and challenge mainstream conceptions of the "good mother"; disabled mothers who are also poor, non-white, lesbian, trans, single, and/or young face additional stigmatization and discrimination (Filax and Taylor 2014).

Parents with disabilities are regularly subject to the discriminatory attitudes of a disabling society. When discriminatory attitudes are held by people with the power to intervene in families' lives, and when discriminatory views underlie entire systems that impact disabled people's ability to parent — as they did in William's case — the results can be devastating. Too often, child welfare workers jump to conclusions that parents with disabilities will be unable to adequately care for their child; judges, lawyers, medical professionals, and parenting assessors may exhibit similar biases in family law disputes. These are the very professionals best positioned to offer the support that disabled parents may need to provide for their children's best interests. Too often, however, these professionals act on assumptions and stereotypes to deem disabled parents "unfit" and to separate children from their disabled parents, rather than undertaking an assessment of the family's unique strengths, needs, and challenges, and offering appropriate supports and services. This constitutes discrimination against disabled mothers and their children that may be contrary to human rights, constitutional rights, and international human rights law; it also has tremendous negative consequences for children, families, and entire communities.

Historical Context and the Ideology of Motherhood

Discrimination against disabled mothers has deep historical roots. While societal attitudes towards women and people with disabilities have shifted from one era to the next, women with disabilities have generally been regarded by the mainstream as unsuited for motherhood (Blackford 1993). Nowhere is this clearer than in the eugenics movement, which led to legislation in many provinces that allowed for the forced and involuntary sterilization of women deemed "mentally defective" (Blackford 1993). British Columbia's Sexual Sterilization Act, for example, was not repealed until 1972.

While non-therapeutic and non-consensual surgical sterilization of disabled women was rejected by the Supreme Court of Canada more than thirty years ago as a "grave intrusion on a person's rights" that could never be justified (*E (Mrs) v Eve*, [1986] 2 SCR 388 at para 86) and such blatantly discriminatory laws are no longer on the books, prohibitions on disabled women's fertility still abound. Disabled women are routinely denied access to assisted reproductive technologies on the basis that their disability makes them unfit for parenthood (Basson 1998). In one example from the United States, a disabled woman seeking motherhood through donor insemination was required to write a ten-page essay on how she would take care of her baby; this was not required of women without a disability (Collins 1999). In another U.S. case, a blind woman was refused access to assisted reproductive technologies because, according to the fertility clinic, she posed a "direct threat" to the safety of her yet-to-be-conceived child (Colorado Cross-Disability Coalition 2009). Her appeal of the clinic's decision was denied by the courts.

Feminist researchers and scholars have pointed out the many ways in which the "ideology of motherhood" divides women on the basis of their social characteristics into "good mothers," who are socially encouraged and supported to become mothers and raise children, and "bad mothers," who are discouraged from bearing and raising children (see, for example, Iyer 1997). Disabled mothers, it seems, are inherently suspect. They must fight stereotypes, myths, and biases about their capacity to parent; they often face hostility and discrimination regarding their choice to parent and shaming due to their needs for additional support. Indigenous women — both disabled and not — have endured gross levels of state violence and intrusion into their families' lives for generations and are particularly vulnerable to the "bad mother" label.

Compounding the disadvantage experienced by mothers with disabilities are neoliberal economic policies that have undermined the economic and social security of people with low incomes, particularly women. A person with a disability in Canada is twice as likely as the rest of the population to be poor, and women with disabilities are more likely than their male counterparts to live below the low-income cut-off (Council of Canadians with Disabilities n.d.). Poverty negatively affects the health and well-being of women with disabilities and hinders their ability to improve their life conditions. Poverty also leaves women with disabilities — as it does women generally — vulnerable to violence, exploitation, and coercion (Sampson 2003). Drastic cuts to social services and supports, including income assistance, legal aid, and social housing programs, have reinforced and exacerbated existing inequalities. Disabled Indigenous, racialized, queer, and trans women, who experience higher levels of poverty due to historic and ongoing oppression and discrimination, have been additionally disadvantaged by government cuts and clawbacks (see, for example, MacDonald and Wilson 2013).

Under the *Canadian Charter of Rights and Freedoms*, all levels of government have a legal obligation to uphold the equality rights of women, mothers, and people with disabilities, and human rights law requires that disabilities be accommodated in the provision of services. Moreover, Canada is signatory to the *United Nations Convention on the Rights of Persons with Disabilities* (UNCRPD), which requires states to protect the rights of disabled parents, provide supports to disabled parents to assist them in child rearing, and ensure children are not separated from their parents based on a disability (Article 23). Our research shows that these legal obligations are not being consistently met.

West Coast LEAF's "Mothering with Disabilities" Project

This chapter is an adaptation of a 2014 research report by the West Coast Women's Legal Education and Action Fund (West Coast LEAF), a Vancouver-based non-profit legal organization that works to end discrimination against women using equality rights litigation, law reform, and public legal education. The chapter explores some of the legal and policy issues affecting mothers with disabilities, and the ways in which violence — both individual experiences of male violence and the deeper structural violence of alienating, inaccessible, and discriminatory child protection and family law systems — intersect with and contribute to those legal and policy issues.

West Coast LEAF employs a participatory approach to law reform work; it seeks to ground recommendations for reform in the lived experiences of the women whose lives are most directly impacted by the laws and policies being analyzed. The insights and recommendations here reflect the experiences of disabled mothers themselves, who know best how law and policy can better support their equal rights as parents.

The overarching conclusion of our research is that disabled mothers face distinct legal challenges stemming from barriers associated with both their gender and their disability, and that all levels of government are complicit in the infringement of their legal equality rights. The legal systems and institutions that should be supporting them, particularly the child protection and family court systems, are failing to ensure that mothers with disabilities have the resources and supports they need to provide for their children, as well as failing to support disabled mothers' efforts to keep themselves and their children safe from male violence and abuse. Biases and stereotypes held by child protection workers, health care professionals, and society more generally about the capacity of disabled women to parent mean that the equality rights of disabled mothers are routinely violated, with devastating impacts on mothers, children, and communities.

West Coast LEAF's "Mothering with Disabilities" project explored the ways in which Canadian law and policy fall short when it comes to protecting the equality rights of mothers and prospective mothers with disabilities. We sought to expose some of the myths, biases, and stereotypes that influence institutional decisions impacting mothers with disabilities, and to explore the law's potential to help mothers with disabilities fight discrimination and faulty assumptions made about them. Our report, *Able Mothers: The Intersection of Parenting, Disability and the Law* (Track 2014), included a series of recommendations to strengthen and improve laws and policies to ensure greater respect for the dignity, equality, autonomy, and legal rights of mothers with disabilities.

To inform our project and ensure that its analysis was attentive to the diverse experiences of women with disabilities, we consulted a broad range of women with disabilities, as well as several advocates and service providers who work with disabled women. Our recommendations were informed by the stories and experiences of disabled mothers, who are the experts on their own experience and often have a clear vision of what systemic changes are needed to improve their lives.

We spoke to a total of twenty-five mothers for this project. Eleven of the women were white/Caucasian, nine were Indigenous, three were of South Asian origin, and two were of Central/South American origin.

Participants reported a wide range of disabilities. Most women reported having more than one disability. Every participant reported some form of mental illness, with depression being the most common. Eleven of the twenty-five women reported addiction issues. The majority also discussed the impact of male violence and historic trauma on their mental and physical health.

Key Issues

Male Violence and Social Support Exclusion

Our findings converged around two key themes: women's experiences of male violence and the ways in which this violence contributed to their disabling conditions; and women's experiences of discrimination and exclusion from the systems that should support them, particularly within the child protection and family law systems. This systemic discrimination included biased assessments and decisions regarding their capacity to parent and a lack of institutional supports to help them escape the violence in their lives and provide for the best interests of their children.

Male Violence and its Disabling Impact

Notably, all but four of our participants disclosed that they had been subject to abuse and violence in their lives, most by a male intimate partner and one by a parent. Canada-wide, research has shown that women with activity limitations are approximately twice as likely to experience intimate partner violence as women without activity limitations (Cohen et al. 2005). Women with disabilities are twice as likely to report severe physical violence (being beaten, kicked, bitten, or hit) and three times as likely to report being forced into sexual activity (being threatened, held down, or hurt) (Brownridge 2006).

Disabled women's vulnerability to abuse is increased by the social context of their disability, including poverty, inaccessible environments, social devaluation, discrimination, and social exclusion (Powers et al. 2009). These factors are particularly prevalent in the lives of Indigenous women, who are three times more likely to be victims of violence than non-Indigenous women and more than twice as likely to be victims of spousal violence (Brennan 2011). Abuse within intimate relationships may be exacerbated for Indigenous women by poverty, the history of colonization, and the cultural legacy of mistreatment and abuse in residential schools. Poverty overlapped with experiences of violence for all the Indigenous women and most non-Indigenous women in our sample.

In the past decade, researchers and service providers have increasingly focused on the connections between male violence against women and women's mental wellness and substance use (Haskell 2010). The stress and fear caused by male violence can lead to chronic health problems for women, including mental illness and substance use issues. For example, at one B.C. addictions treatment facility, 86 percent of women seeking treatment had experienced some form of violence during their lives (Poole 2007). In other studies, up to 83 percent of women accessing services for mental health issues have reported experiencing violence at some point during their lives (Firsten 1991).

Substance use is often a means of coping with experiences of violence (Ad Hoc Working Group on Women, Mental Health and Addiction in Canada 2006). Research conducted with women accessing transition houses in B.C. found that coping with violence and trauma was the primary reason women gave for using alcohol (B.C. Centre of Excellence for Women's Health 2004). After accessing the support of the transition houses, women generally used alcohol less frequently.

Many of our participants reported both mental health and substance use issues, and many also reported that violence had led to both their addiction and their mental health challenges:

> I went through abuse growing up from an alcoholic boyfriend of my mom's, and so I grew up hating life, hating myself, and not feeling like I would get anywhere. I started using drugs when I was 15 years old, and successfully stayed productive that way. (A mother now in recovery)
>
> And it's an ongoing life for me, because of the abuse that happened. The reasons why I did what I did were the addictions. (A mother who lost custody of her three children)
>
> My experiences would have been different if courts listened to me, if they realized the impact of his violence on me, if they better understood my trauma and depression and connected me with support folks rather than punishing me for it. (An immigrant mother)

The experience of the immigrant mother underscores a particularly critical point: with support, rather than punishment, the majority of the women we interviewed felt they could have parented their child effectively. However, the support they required to escape the violence and provide for their child's best interests was not available to them, and it was often poverty, not their disability, that most undermined their capacity to parent.

Child Protection: A Duty to Support?

Child protection in British Columbia is governed by the Child, Family and Community Services Act (the CFCSA or the Act). Among the Act's guiding principles are supporting families to care for children in the home, improving services for Indigenous families, using apprehension only as a last resort, and reunifying children and parents as quickly as possible when a temporary removal is necessary. The Act also highlights the necessity of supporting families to remain together, stating: "if, with available support services, a family can provide a safe and nurturing environment for a child, support services should be provided" (section 2(c)). This is also a requirement of the UNCRPD, which states, "States Parties shall render appropriate assistance to persons with disabilities in the performance of their child-rearing responsibilities" (Article 23(2)).

The legislation clearly imposes a duty on government to provide supports to parents, including parents with disabilities, to assist them to provide a safe and nurturing home for their children. However, our research shows that disabled mothers are not receiving the supports they need, and are losing their children to the child protection system as a result. Making matters worse, the system is itself critically underfunded and failing to provide adequate resources to kids in care (B.C. Representative for Children and Youth 2014b).

Mothers Experiencing Spousal Violence

Under the CFCSA, a child is in need of protection if the child has been or is likely to be physically or emotionally harmed by a parent, sexually abused or exploited, or neglected (section 13). Amendments to the CFCSA passed in March 2014 state that a child can be emotionally harmed by exposure to domestic violence in the home, and that the likelihood of physical harm to a child increases when the child is living in a situation where domestic violence is present (sections 13(1)(e)(ii) and 13(1.2)). Without the services necessary to help women flee their abusers, including accessible transition houses and affordable housing, transit, childcare, and legal assistance, these provisions will deprive women of custody of their children in situations where they are being abused by their partners.

Women in our sample reported feeling that abuse they were experiencing was being held against them by child protection workers, but that they were not being offered meaningful options to help keep themselves and their children safe. They also reported being held responsible by social workers for the impact of their spouse's violence on their children. One participant told us:

> After the violent incident, social workers became involved in my case again. They blamed me for not protecting my daughter from his abuse. He was not held accountable for anything. They coerced me into signing a voluntary care agreement by saying the baby is not safe with me at this point. They then placed her in a foster home for two-and-a-half months. (An Indigenous mother)

The child protection system should be supporting disabled mothers to flee spousal violence, not using the existence of violence in their relationships as grounds to remove their children. Yet, many women report that fleeing an abuser would result in poverty and homelessness for them and their children. Inadequate social assistance rates, a lack of accessible housing (including transition housing), and the restrictions on legal aid mean that many women with disabilities feel trapped in abusive situations, with few options for keeping themselves and their children safe.

Addiction Issues

> With [the Ministry of Children and Families] it was like "you're a bad parent. You have addiction issues, you don't get your kid." (An Indigenous mother)

Disabling addictions are prevalent in the child protection context. In a 2002 survey of B.C. child protection workers, staff estimated that 70 percent of their child protection cases included substance use issues on the part of the mother (B.C. Representative for Children and Youth 2014a). Substance use disorders were the most common reason for child welfare officials to become involved in the lives of the mothers we interviewed. Nine participants shared that their substance use disorders had resulted in the removal of their children. Two participants voluntarily placed their children in care because they knew that neither they nor their partners could parent the child because of their struggle with substance abuse. Other participants also knew that their substance abuse was undermining their ability to parent, but did not know where to turn. Most of the participants with substance use disorders had turned to alcohol and drugs as a way of coping with trauma, depression, and anxiety.

Several of our participants emphasized the need for services and supports to help mothers address addiction issues without losing custody of their children. Mothers with substance use disorders face a lose-lose scenario: either they seek help for their addictions and risk losing custody of their children; or they keep quiet so as not to draw attention to themselves and their families and struggle with their addictions on their own, without the benefit of treatment and support. Neither situation supports the best interests of the children.

How to manage parental addiction issues is addressed in a policy of the Ministry of Children and Family Development (MCFD); however, an investigation by B.C.'s Representative for Children and Youth found that only one in ten of the workers assigned to a case involving parental substance abuse had any formal training on how to work with families challenged by addiction, and only one of the workers had ever heard of the policy (B.C. Representative for Children and Youth 2014a). MCFD has no budget dedicated to train workers on this issue. This lack of training can result in poor outcomes for families, as parents with addiction issues may be less likely to co-operate and work with a social worker who lacks empathy and an understanding of substance abuse.

There is a huge need for supports for mothers and pregnant women with drug and alcohol addictions. However, despite the great demand for treatment, the vast majority of pregnant women and mothers seeking assistance to overcome drug dependency cannot obtain the help they need. Drug treatment programs routinely deny admission to pregnant women because they lack the resources and facilities to accommodate them, and the few that will treat pregnant women often have long wait lists (Kines 2012). Moreover, most drug and alcohol treatment centres cannot accommodate a child to stay with their mother while she gets help for substance abuse. As a result, mothers face a choice: either place their children with other family members or in foster care in order to get the help they need; or delay treatment for fear of losing their children. Neither is a good option for children, who can experience trauma both from being removed from their parent and from remaining in a situation where they are exposed to substance abuse.

Fear of losing their children is one of the major barriers that discourage women from accessing treatment for their addictions. Research indicates that allowing mothers to keep custody of their children while seeking treatment for their addictions results in more women seeking out such treatment (Lester, Andreozzi, and Appiah 2005). In addition, women who are working to manage and overcome their addictions may be better able to take care of their children than the overburdened and underfunded foster care system, especially when these mothers are provided with the material supports they need.

Family Law: Providing for Children's Best Interests

It is not just the child protection system in which discriminatory attitudes about disabled parents' capacity to care for their children play out, and in which poverty, violence, ableism, and sexism intersect to deprive disabled mothers of their rights as parents. In the context of family law, too, judges, lawyers, and parenting assessors, among others, may demonstrate similarly biased thinking in their decisions impacting disabled mothers and their children.

Under B.C.'s Family Law Act, a judge deciding a custody dispute is to consider only the best interests of the children involved. While the law suggests a number of factors to take into account, assessing the best interests of the child will always be a subjective determination, and in applying this standard, decision makers may, due to their own experiences or biases, invoke a normative and idealized image of parenting in a white, middle-class, non-disabled, heterosexual, two-parent family. A woman who deviates from this normative model of motherhood, whether due to her race, sexuality, gender identity, class, single-parent status, disability, or a combination of factors, risks being viewed negatively regardless of her actual history of caregiving for the child (Boyd 2002). Moreover, the high cost of legal representation and severe underfunding of legal aid mean that many disabled mothers will be left to navigate the legal process on their own, without the benefit of legal representation or advice on how to successfully advocate for themselves and their children.

Violence and the Best Interests of Children

To determine the best interests of the child, the Family Law Act directs the courts to consider the impacts of family violence on the child. Family violence, as defined in the Act, includes physical, sexual, emotional, and psychological abuse, including intimidation, harassment, coercion, and threats (section 1). In assessing the impact of family violence on the best interests of the child, a court must consider the nature, seriousness, and frequency of the violence and the harm it has done to the child's physical, psychological, and emotional safety and well-being (section 38).

Violence and abuse were common themes for the women we spoke to who had gone through a family law case. One mother who had lost custody of her child to a man who had abused her expressed frustration and despair that the courts had not taken the violence seriously and did not consider the effects of the violence on her mental health. Another mother highlighted how losing custody of her child had negatively impacted her mental health and had exacerbated her challenges.

> There is a failure of the courts, lawyers, [and the] legal and child protection system to provide a trauma-informed response to mothers who have been living in an abusive relationship. (A social worker)

Disabled mothers face distinct barriers to reporting violence and fleeing their abusers. Because of the unique situation of disabled mothers, they may have built a unique and adapted home environment in which to live and parent their children (Smith n.d.). For example, a woman with a mobility disability may have an adapted crib that can be lowered if she uses a wheelchair, or lifts to help her raise and lower her children into the bath. A woman who is blind or low vision will memorize her home, and it will be clear of obstructions. Leaving an abusive but adapted home can take away a disabled woman's independence and leave her vulnerable to losing custody of her children.

There are other barriers as well. Although women with disabilities experience high rates of domestic violence, many transition houses are unable to accommodate their needs. In a recent survey conducted by the B.C. Society of Transition Houses, 71 percent of shelters were found to be accessible to women with reduced mobility (B.C. Society of Transition Houses 2013). In another nation-wide survey of transition houses, many shelters commented that they were willing to accommodate disabled women and their children, but were restricted by finances, with several shelters reporting that funding was a huge barrier to making their spaces more accessible (Smith n.d.). While many shelters do their best to accommodate the needs of disabled mothers and their children fleeing violence, this gap in services for vulnerable women is deeply concerning.

> Many disabled women don't even try to access a transition house as they know their needs will not be met ... Transition houses are simply not funded to provide accessibility to women who have disabilities. Thus, with the best of intentions, the transition house doors are shut on these women. (Manager of a transition house)

Parenting Assessments

In custody cases, bias on the part of parenting assessors can also contribute to unjust and unequal outcomes for mothers with disabilities. Parenting assessors — generally psychologists, social workers, or family justice counsellors — conduct interviews with parents involved in custody disputes and make recommendations to the court about appropriate custody arrangements. These reports are given substantial weight by the courts. However, West Coast LEAF has documented concerns about bias and a failure to consider issues of violence on the part of some psychologists charged with preparing these assessments (Rahman and Track 2012). Given their importance as a tool for judges in making critical decisions about the best interests of children, it is essential that they be accurate, comprehensive, unbiased, and sensitively prepared.

Other research confirms that there are good reasons to fear this standard is not being met. A study of Ontario professionals involved in preparing these assessments suggested that deeply held personal biases may influence their work, and few of them were aware of how their own attitudes and experiences might impact their assessments and recommendations (Caplan and Wilson 1990). One particularly troubling finding from the Ontario study was that less than one-third of assessors agreed with the statement that adults rarely lie when they say their ex-spouse has sexually assaulted or hit them. These results suggest that when a woman discloses abuse to a parenting assessor, there is a very good chance that the assessor will not believe she is telling the truth. When this disregard for her experience is reflected in the assessor's report, either by ignoring it or using it to suggest she is lying in an effort to prevent her ex-husband from seeing the child, the resulting custody and access order from the court is highly unlikely to adequately protect the mother's safety or the child's best interests.

Four of our participants had undergone parenting assessments during a custody dispute. All four had concerns about how the assessments were prepared, but one in particular stood out for the way in which the mother's disability — multiple sclerosis — was portrayed, and the way in which her physical limitations were not accommodated:

> I did an extensive, and I'm not exaggerating, 700 questions where you would fill the bubbles … And my caregiver would write the bubbles, right? I would give the question and she would bubble it. And [the psychologist] said no, there should be no one helping you, so I had to redo it again. And that was 2009, almost five years ago and my hands worked much better, but it was so draining, because they were trying to pinpoint your personality type and all that. And so, I trusted her that she was going to assess me properly, you know? She came to my house, assessed my medical equipment, my home, my personality, my relationship to my son, the caregiver's relationship. It was basically like: come in to my underwear drawer and take a look … We were outside and playing tic-tac-toe on the chalkboard, and I couldn't do it very well with my hand. And she had written all of this stuff in the report. Oh, and my medical equipment, because I have a conversion in my van, you know, you push a button and the ramp comes out, and she said that that was dangerous for my son. He is 11 now, but he was 6 then. He knew the equipment since he was 2 or 3. He knows all of the equipment in the house, you know? He knows all of the things and how to use them, but then it was turned around to say that my disability equipment was dangerous and that my caregivers do everything.

West Coast LEAF has made recommendations to improve the qualifications and training of professionals who conduct parenting assessments and better ensure that violence is taken seriously and appropriately reported (Rahman and Track 2012). In April 2014, the B.C. government moved to amend the province's family law legislation to provide for the creation of regulations prescribing minimum standards for professionals who prepare parenting assessments. Under the newly created section 245.1, the Lieutenant Governor in Council may make regulations respecting these assessments and the training, experience, and other qualifications and practice standards those preparing them must meet. However, while the government indicated that it would be consulting with the family law bar, the College of Psychologists, and the College of Social Workers to develop these regulations, it is unclear if these consultations have taken place, and the amendment is not yet in force. Moreover, there was no mention of consultations involving anti-violence workers, women-serving organizations, or disability advocates. These consultations will be critical if women's diverse experiences of violence, particularly the experiences of disabled women, are to be adequately captured and reflected in new regulations.

Access to Justice and Legal Aid

> You can have the best laws, but if one does not have access to justice, it does not matter. (Advocacy service provider)

B.C. faces a critical lack of legal aid services. In 2002, massive cuts eliminated coverage for poverty law services and drastically curtailed family law services. The lack of legal aid for family law issues disproportionately impacts women, who are more likely to be economically disadvantaged by the breakdown of a marriage and are more likely to need legal assistance in these kinds of cases (Brewin and Stephens 2004). Given their high rates of poverty, women with disabilities are even less likely to be able to afford to retain a lawyer on their own, and may be additionally marginalized and isolated due to their disability. Moreover, given the high rates of domestic violence against women with disabilities, their need for access to legal advice about their rights is particularly critical to keeping themselves and their children safe.

Six participants in our research had accessed or attempted to access legal aid. Two had very positive experiences of being assisted by legal aid lawyers. The other four participants had less positive experiences. One was approved for legal aid, but her coverage ran out before her trial. Another made slightly over the income cut-off and was refused coverage. She described the impact:

Interviewer: "And did you feel heard at the court?"

Participant: "No, because I didn't have a lawyer. That's another thing. People should have a lawyer if they get assaulted." (A mother who experienced domestic abuse)

Service providers expressed significant concerns about the lack of legal aid and its impact on women, particularly women with disabilities. They pointed out that many mothers are representing themselves in custody trials, fighting against abusive spouses, and trying to keep their children safe without the benefit of legal advice or assistance. They also spoke to the need to ensure that legal aid intake workers are well trained to receive and process applications from women with disabilities and that accessibility needs are considered. These needs include accessible court forms, which are lengthy, complex, and inaccessible to women with low vision or for whom filling out a form by hand is physically challenging or impossible.

I never have a good experience with legal aid lawyers, you know. I think they don't solve the problem ... I applied but [didn't] qualify for legal aid the second time. I had no lawyer in court and I was in a five-day trial but it ended in three days as I could not take it anymore. (An immigrant mother)

Legal Reform to Support Disabled Mothers

Like all parents, disabled parents can't do it alone. It is common wisdom that raising a child takes a village — we all need support. Governments have a legal obligation under the CFCSA to provide the supports necessary so that children can remain with their parents when this is in their best interests. This is echoed by the UNCRPD. Fulfilling this obligation will require that governments provide resources and services — including adapted parenting equipment, accessible and affordable housing, and adequate legal aid and financial assistance — to mothers with disabilities.

Equality for mothers with disabilities will also require that the people making decisions that impact disabled mothers' lives, including parenting assessors, judges, and child protection workers, make those decisions based on a careful and individualized assessment of each mother's strengths, limitations, and needs for support, and not on the basis of myths and stereotypes about the capacity of disabled women to parent.

The legal rights of both children and their mothers — the rights of children to be raised in a supportive and loving environment, and the rights of mothers not to be discriminated against because of their perceived disabilities and not to be denied their right to parent when they are able to do so — demand nothing less.

Women with disabilities have a right to be treated fairly on the basis of their own unique strengths and skills. They have a right to sexual autonomy, reproductive freedom, and equality as mothers, without discrimination due to their disability. While there will be instances where a disability prevents a mother from parenting her child, most women with disabilities can be perfectly capable mothers when they have access to the right supports. When the social and environmental factors that function to disable them are removed — the physical barriers in their surroundings and the discriminatory attitudes of their communities, for example — their status as able mothers will be evident.

Notes

1. This chapter is adapted from West Coast LEAF's report "Able Mothers: The Intersection of Parenting, Disability and the Law" (September 2014). The author, who was then Legal Director at West Coast LEAF, is grateful to her collaborators on that project, particularly Shahnaz Rahman and Kasari Govender. Special thanks to the women who shared their stories to inform the report. The views expressed in this paper do not necessarily reflect the views of West Coast LEAF, and any errors are the author's alone. The full report can be accessed at <www.westcoastleaf.org>.

References

Ad Hoc Working Group on Women, Mental Health, Substance Use and Addictions. 2006. *Women, Mental Health, Mental Illness and Addiction in Canada: An Overview.* Canadian Women's Health Network.

Basson, R. 1998. "Sexual Health of Women with Disabilities." *Canadian Medical Association Journal,* 159.

B.C. Centre of Excellence for Women's Health. 2004. *Tracking Alcohol Use in Women Who Move through Domestic Violence Shelters.*

B.C. Representative for Children and Youth. 2014a. *Children at Risk: The Case for a Better Response to Parental Addiction.* June, Victoria, B.C.

___. 2014b. *Not Fully Invested: A Follow-up Report on the Representative's Past Recommendations to Help Vulnerable Children in B.C.* October, Victoria, B.C.

B.C. Society of Transition Houses. 2013. *Shelter Voices: A Day in the Life of B.C.'s Transition Housing Programs for Women and Children Fleeing Violence.*

Blackford, K.A. 1993. "Erasing Mothers with Disabilities though Canadian

Family-Related Policy." *Disability, Handicap & Society,* 8, 3.

Boyd, S. 2002. *Child Custody, Law and Women's Work.* Don Mills, ON: Oxford University Press Canada.

Brennan, S. 2011. *Violent Victimization of Aboriginal Women in the Canadian Provinces, 2009.* Statistics Canada. <statcan.gc.ca/pub/85-002-x/2011001/article/11439-eng.pdf>.

Brewin, A., and L. Stephens. 2004. *Legal Aid Denied: Women and the Cuts to Legal Services in B.C.* West Coast LEAF and the Canadian Centre for Policy Alternatives.

Brownridge, D.A. 2006. "Partner Violence against Women with Disabilities: Prevalence, Risk, and Explanations." *Violence Against Women,* 12, 9.

Caplan, P.J., and J. Wilson. 1990. "Assessing the Child Custody Assessors." *Review of Family Law,* 27, 3.

CBC News. 2012. "Disabled Parents Fight to Keep Newborn at Home." 1 May.

Cohen, M.M., T. Forte, J. Du Mont, I. Hyman and S. Romans. 2005. "Intimate Partner Violence among Canadian Women with Activity Limitations." *Journal of Epidemiology and Community Health.* 59, 10.

Collins, C. 1999. "Reproductive Technologies for Women with Physical Disabilities." *Sexuality and Disability* 17, 4.

Colorado Cross-Disability Coalition. 2009. "Rocky Mountain Women's Health Care." <ccdconline.org/ legal-case/07-28-2009/rocky-mountain-womens-health-care>.

Council of Canadians with Disabilities. n.d. *Rights of Persons with Disabilities in Canada.* Briefing Notes.

Firsten, T. 1991. "Violence in the Lives of Women on Psychiatric Wards." *Canadian Women's Studies/Les Cahiers de la Femme,* 11, 4.

Filax, G., and D. Taylor. 2014. "Introduction." In G. Filax and D. Taylor (eds.), *Disabled Mothers: Stories and Scholarship by and about Mothers with Disabilities.* Bradford, ON: Demeter Press.

Haskell, R. 2010. *Reducing Barriers to Support: Discussion Paper on Violence against Women, Mental Wellness and Substance Use.* Vancouver, BC: B.C. Society of Transition Houses.

Iyer, N. 1997. "Some Mothers Are Better Than Others: A Re-examination of Maternity Benefits." In S. Boyd (ed.), *Challenging the Public/Private Divide: Feminism, Law, and Public Policy.* University of Toronto.

Kines, L. 2012. "Province Urged to Treat Addicted Parents without Separating Them from the Children" *Times Colonist,* November 30.

Lester, B.M., L. Andreozzi, and L. Appiah. 2005. "Substance Use during Pregnancy: Time for Policy to Catch up with Research." *Harm Reduction Journal,* 1.

MacDonald, D., and D. Wilson. 2013. *Poverty or Prosperity: Indigenous Children in Canada.* Canadian Centre for Policy Alternatives and Save the Children.

Poole, N. 2007. "Interconnections among Women's Health, Violence and Substance Use: Findings from the Aurora Centre." In N. Poole and L. Greaves (eds.), *Highs and Lows: Canadian Perspectives on Women and Substance Use.* Toronto, ON: Center for Addictions and Mental Health.

Powers, L.E., P. Renker, S. Robinson-Whelen, M. Oschwald, R. Hughes, P. Swank and M.A. Curry. 2009. "Interpersonal Violence against Women with Disabilities:

Analysis of Safety Promoting Behaviours." *Violence against Women,* 15, 9.

Rahman, S., and L. Track. 2012. *Troubling Assessments: Custody and Access Reports and Their Equality Implications for B.C. Women.* Vancouver, BC: West Coast LEAF.

Sampson, F. 2003. "Globalization and the Inequality of Women with Disabilities." *Journal of Law & Equality,* 2.

Smith, J. n.d. "Disabled Mothering: Building a Safe and Accessible Community." DisAbled Women's Network. <http://www.dawncanada.net/issues/issues/mothering/disabled-mothering/>.

Track, L. 2014. Able Mothers: The Intersection of Parenting, Disability and the Law. Vancouver, BC: West Coast LEAF.

Chapter 3

The Healing Journey
Women with Disabilities and Intimate Partner Violence

Michelle Owen and Jane Ursel

The relationship between disability/chronic illness and intimate partner violence (IPV) is complex and needs to be examined in depth. Abuse can cause and exacerbate a disability, and it can increase women's vulnerability to violence and control. This chapter aims to address the gap in knowledge with the findings from the Healing Journey research project. Disability is more than difficulties with mobility and activity limitations, so we implemented an expanded definition based on self-identification for the purpose of this study. The result was that many more participants than expected identified as being disabled, particularly with high reports of chronic depression. A substantial number of these women attributed their disability to abuse, and they were much more likely to report experiences of childhood abuse than women without disabilities. Another unexpected finding in this study was that disabled women were accessing shelters and other services in greater numbers than women without disabilities. Unfortunately, not all of the services our respondents required were accessible, especially those with mental health issues and addictions.

The Healing Journey Project

In 2004, academics and their community partners in the three Prairie provinces of Canada (Manitoba, Saskatchewan, and Alberta) undertook an ambitious study of women who had experienced IPV. The title of the project, "The Healing Journey," refers to the fact that all of these women were on a journey; it did not presume that everyone would reach the desired end during our study.[1]

Women were recruited from shelters and other services in Alberta, Manitoba, and Saskatchewan. The sampling strategy emphasized heterogeneity and aimed to include women living in rural and northern regions, women with disabilities, lesbian women, Indigenous women, and women from diverse ethnic backgrounds. The study incorporated a longitudinal design based on an ecological model that examines women's experiences for a period of 4.5 years as they sought a violence-free life for themselves and their children.

One year prior to recruitment the tri-provincial research team conducted twenty-six focus groups in nine communities with service providers and experiential women (women who embody and live marginalized identities) to canvass their advice about recruitment, maintenance of participants, and strategies to deal with attrition. In total, 186 women participated in focus groups (March and September 2004). In Manitoba there were thirteen focus groups involving seventy-three women; in Alberta there were seven focus groups involving sixty-three women; and in Saskatchewan there were six focus groups involving fifty women. Overall, 24 percent of the women identified as Indigenous, 11 percent as immigrant, 4 percent as lesbian, and 3 percent as women with disabilities.

It is important to note that early in the study the researchers were concerned about the representation of marginalized women based on focus group participation. The principal investigator, Jane Ursel, brought women with disabilities together to discuss the low numbers of disabled women (3 percent) in the pilot. As a result, Colleen Watters and Michelle Owen were brought in to recruit, conduct interviews with, and help to retain this population. Although both Watters and Owen identify as women with disabilities and have many connections with other disabled women, recruitment was no easy task. They began by sending information about the project to the major disability organizations in Winnipeg. In addition they spoke to disabled women and used snowballing techniques. The latter method depends on participants telling others about the project. Despite their efforts, only six women who identified as disabled and who had experienced IPV were interviewed in Winnipeg as part of this targeted effort. We knew from our past research experiences that getting women to identify as disabled is a challenge, and that it is often difficult for women with disabilities to get ready for interviews, meet, communicate, maintain energy, manage emotional topics, take time out from other activities, and so on. Adding IPV to the mix complicated and intensified the process.

From 2006 to 2010, participants responded to two structured surveys in alternating order approximately once every six months for a total of seven waves of interviews. Survey 1 contained two components: history and demography, including experiences with violence and abuse and a series of questions on general functioning and service utilization. Survey 2 covered health and parenting. In addition, in the sixth wave of interviews only, a detailed income and employment history questionnaire was administered to facilitate a cost-analysis study (DeRiviere 2014).

All of our questionnaires were highly structured, but we wanted women to have an opportunity to tell us their story their own way. We asked each of our participants whether she would be willing to do an open-ended interview. From this inquiry we generated a smaller subsample of approximately thirty women in each province who were selected for qualitative interviews in which participants were invited to talk about their experiences in an open-ended format. We had a total of ninety-three open-ended interviews, which ranged from two to four hours long and provided a very rich history of these women's lives.

The intent of the Healing Journey study was to develop a clearer understanding of the life trajectories of women who had experienced IPV. We wanted to know what factors and experiences in women's lives were associated with escaping or ending intimate partner violence, and what factors and experiences keep women trapped in abusive relationships. Our goal was to recruit and maintain two hundred women in each province, for a total sample size of six hundred participants. However, we were well aware that women with a history of abuse often lead precarious and mobile lives; thus each province oversampled to give us a total of 665 women at Wave 1.

Participants were drawn from thirty-eight different cities and communities throughout the three Prairie provinces, with 31 percent of the sample living outside major cities and 15 percent living in northern communities. Women ranged in age from 18 to 80, with the majority clustered in the age group 26–49, with the average age of 36. Our decision to recruit women primarily from agencies and services was important for two reasons: first, we wanted to interview women who had used services to assess the most effective components of those services; and second, we needed to interview women in safe places where counselling was on site if required.

As a result, these recruitment decisions introduced a number of biases in our sample. We were successful in recruiting participants from a variety of ethnic backgrounds; however, in each province, Indigenous women, broadly defined as First Nations, Indigenous, or Métis, were over- represented. Overall, Indigenous women constituted 47 percent of participants; however, this varied by province (Manitoba at 59 percent, Saskatchewan at 54 percent, and Alberta at 30 percent). The number of women with disabilities was also disproportionately high, as will be discussed. Ultimately there were more similarities than differences between disabled and non-disabled women in terms of Indigenous heritage, age, and sexuality. Another characteristic of our participants was that half of the women we interviewed had an annual income lower than $15,000. Most of the participants (91 percent) were mothers, and of the women we interviewed who had children, approximately half had families of one or two children; however, there were a significant number of women who had large families of five or more children.

Disability and IPV

Canadian women with disabilities experience more IPV than women without disabilities (DAWN 2014; Brownridge 2006). While it is difficult for any woman in an abusive relationship to find resources and obtain help (Barrett and St. Pierre 2011), disabled women have additional challenges related to their disabilities and chronic illnesses (DAWN 2014). The intersection of disability with race, indigeneity, ethnicity, class, sexuality, and age results in increased vulnerability to violence and more barriers to leaving (Owen 2014a; Owen 2014b; Renooy 2002, Block and Keys 2002). More research needs to be conducted on disability and intersectionality and the implications for IPV (Valentine 2001). There is not much research or writing that specifically addresses IPV in the lives of women with disabilities. While there is a small but growing body of work about the impact of violence and abuse on disabled women, IPV is often not separated out or highlighted. One explanation for this is that women with disabilities are not commonly regarded as sexual beings or as people in intimate relationships (DAWN 2014). As well, disabled women encounter significant barriers to reporting all types of violence, including IPV, and in seeking refuge in shelters (DAWN 2014).

Many sources contend that women with disabilities are subject to higher rates of overall violence and abuse than women without disabilities (CRIAW 2002; DAWN 2014; Roeher 1995). As is the case for non-disabled women, violence against disabled women is usually perpetrated by someone close to them. Women with disabilities are at higher risk for abuse because many depend on a wide variety of people, including family, attendants, interpreters, drivers, medical staff, neighbours, and friends. Moreover, according to the Canadian Research Institute for the Advancement of Women (CRIAW 2002: 6), "Violence is a major cause of injury to women, ranging from cuts and bruises to permanent disability and death." Women who are physically or sexually abused as adults or children are at a greater risk of a variety of health problems, including chronic pain, anxiety, and depression (CRIAW 2002).

DisAbled Women's Network (DAWN) has been a leader in research on violence against women with disabilities. At its first national meeting in 1985, violence against women was identified as a priority issue. *Beating the Odds: Violence and Women with Disabilities* reported that 40 percent of respondents indicated that they had been raped, abused, or assaulted, and 64 percent had been verbally assaulted (Ridington 1989). In 1995 DAWN Toronto characterized violence against women and girls with disabilities as a crisis (Ridington 1989). According to its data, one out of every three women with disabilities in Canada experience physical or sexual assault as adults compared to about one-quarter of women without disabilities (Ridington 1989). Today, DAWN Canada continues to investigate violence against women with disabilities with a project entitled "Without a Voice: Women with DisAbilities and Victimization" (2014).

In 1992 DAWN Canada surveyed the accessibility of shelters for disabled women. It found that many shelters were not manageable for women with mobility disabilities, and women with mental health issues were not accepted (Smith 2009). Since that time DAWN Canada has conducted a National Accessibility and Accommodation Survey. The findings indicate that although the situation has improved over the past two decades, there is still work to be done. While many of the shelters surveyed are partially physically accessible, 10 percent reported not being able to accommodate women with mental health issues. Overall, 97 percent of shelters indicated that they had accommodated disabled women, while 45 percent of shelters reported having to turn women with disabilities away. The major reasons given for not being able to help disabled women were inaccessible common areas, an inability to provide personal support, lack of services for deaf women, and, most significantly, an inability to deal with mental illness. Ten percent of the shelters surveyed had declined services to women in this latter group (Smith 2009).

The 2014 YWCA Canada report, *Saying Yes: Effective Practices in Sheltering Abused Women with Mental Health and Addiction Issues*, provides much-needed information about women with disabilities that are hidden or "invisible" (Bopp 2014). The purpose of the YWCA study was to document, test, and disseminate the policies and strategies that shelters across the country have developed to accommodate women with mental health and addiction issues. The report states, "Many women with mental health and addiction issues who experience violence face very restricted access to shelters and transitional housing for abused women. This leaves women with these particular disabilities at substantial risk of homelessness and their needs remaining unaddressed" (Bopp 2014: 1). A large part of the problem is that shelters have zero-tolerance policies for drugs and alcohol, and women with mental health issues have traditionally been referred elsewhere. Two recommendations from the YWCA study that are particularly relevant for this chapter are stretching the eligibility criteria for receiving services and working with women with mental health and addiction issues (Bopp 2014). Disabled women encounter violence from many people, not just intimate partners. Mental health issues can be a result of other disabilities and chronic illnesses, as well as violence. Addiction issues may be a way of self-medicating mental health issues, and may also worsen mental health.

Violence Against Women
Results in and Causes Disability

There are four significant findings from the Healing Journey project relevant to this chapter:

1. A large proportion of the participants identified as women with disabilities and chronic illnesses;
2. A substantial number of disabled women attributed their disability to abuse;
3. Women with disabilities were much more likely to experience childhood abuse than women without disabilities; and
4. Women with disabilities reported that they were accessing shelters and other services in greater numbers than women without disabilities.

Almost two-thirds of the participants (62.7 percent, or 416 out of 665 women interviewed) identified as having disabilities or chronic illnesses. These numbers took us by surprise. As previously mentioned, pre-interview focus groups had only a 3 percent participation rate by disabled women. Special recruitment was thus implemented to ensure that the experiences of women with disabilities who had experienced IPV were included in the research. We were obviously not anticipating that the majority of the women in the study would indicate that they were disabled and/or chronically ill. The unexpected participation of women with disabilities provided interesting opportunities for analysis.

To put these numbers in perspective, according to the 2012 Canadian Survey on Disability (CSD) almost 14 percent or 3.8 million Canadians 15 years and older report having a long-term condition or health problem that limits their daily activities (Statistics Canada 2012a). In every age group — except 15 to 24 years, where the rates were similar— more women than men (15 percent versus 13 percent) indicated that they experienced limitations due to disability or chronic illness (Statistics Canada 2012a). Prevalence of disability increases with age, and women live longer on average than men (Milan 2016). It is important to note that the CSD, like the earlier Participation and Activity Limitation Survey (PALS), only surveyed Canadians residing in private homes. This means that people living on reserves and in institutions were excluded. The numbers would certainly be higher if these populations, which include Indigenous peoples, seniors, and disabled adults, were included. However, the proportion of Canadians who report chronic illness and disability (14 percent), even though women have a higher prevalence, is vastly different from the percentage of women in the Healing Journey research who report chronic illness and disability (62.7 percent).

Participants described four major types of chronic illness and disability: psychological, physical, addiction-based, and intellectual. The most often identified type of disability was psychological, described in the study as "mental health problems or chronic mental health problems, or conditions that are presumed to be primarily psychological in nature." Depression was cited more than other conditions, including post-traumatic stress disorder (PTSD), and anxiety/panic attacks.

The second most reported type of disability was "chronic physical health problems, or reported conditions that are presumed to be primarily physical in nature," including "physical" disabilities. Many women identified as having multiple physical disabilities/conditions. Irritable Bowel Syndrome (IBS) and other bowel problems and joint/extremity problems were those most cited, as well as chronic fatigue/fatigue, asthma, thyroid problems, high blood pressure, hepatitis C, arthritis, back and joint pain, migraines, fibromyalgia, and Chronic Obstructive Pulmonary Disease (COPD).

The third category includes "addictions to alcohol, cigarettes and marijuana." Unfortunately, this category was not further broken down.

Intellectual disability includes "difficulties in cognitive functioning, or illnesses that are considered primarily development or neurological in nature, this includes learning difficulties and memory problems." This category was also not broken down. Examples are attention deficit hyperactivity disorder (ADHD), memory loss, fetal alcohol syndrome and fetal alcohol effects (FAS/FAE), and learning disabilities.

To draw another comparison with the wider population, Canadian women who identify as having activity limitations most often report disabilities related to pain, flexibility, or mobility (Statistics Canada 2012a). This is followed by mental health-related disabilities and disabilities related to dexterity, hearing, and seeing (Statistics Canada 2012a). Indigenous women are more likely to be diagnosed with at least one chronic condition than are non-Indigenous women and Indigenous men (Arriagada 2016). The numbers were highest for First Nations, Métis, and Inuit women living off reserve (Arriagada 2016). In the latest Aboriginal Peoples Survey

(APS), Indigenous women were most likely to report arthritis, followed by high blood pressure, asthma, mood disorders, and anxiety disorders (Statistics Canada 2012b).

In the Healing Journey project, depression was the most common health concern for women with disabilities, followed by bowel and joint problems. According to the Canadian Mental Health Association, one in five Canadians will experience depression at some point. "Mental illness," including depression, is the leading cause of disability in Canada and around the world. The World Health Organization (WHO) estimates that more than 300 million people worldwide experience depression, and that it is more pervasive in women than men (World Health Organization 2018).

But similar to other studies, including the CSD and APS, many participants reported having multiple conditions. We speculated that the high rate of disability/chronic illness might be attributed to the large proportion of Indigenous women who took part in the study. Although much more work needs to be done in this area, it is estimated that the disability rate of Indigenous peoples is two to three times higher than for non-Indigenous people due to factors such as chronic illness, lack of health care, racism, and poverty (Stienstra 2002). In the Healing Journey study, however, the numbers do not support this interpretation, with almost equal numbers of Indigenous and non-Indigenous women identifying as having disabilities and chronic illnesses.

Table 3-1 Disability and/or Long-Term Illness by Indigeneity

Disability	Indigenous		Non-Indigenous		Total #
	#	%	#	%	
Yes	221	63	194	62	415
No	122	35	106	34	228
Unsure	6	2	12	4	18
Total	349		312		661

The key to the high number of women with disabilities and chronic illnesses may be what is self-reported rather than diagnosed. In other words, our survey picked up women not previously identified as disabled. This could be attributed to the way we asked about disability and chronic illness. The Canadian Survey on Disability (2012) defines disability as difficulty and limitation resulting from a long-term condition or health problem. By contrast, we asked, "Do you have any disabilities and/or long-term illnesses?" and "If yes, what are they?" prior to asking about limitations. This was based on self-identification only, and no diagnosis was needed. The illness or disability did not have to limit activities. Moreover, we gave a wide range of examples. In this way, women who had not thought about something as a chronic illness or disability (depression being a good example) may have made the connection and claimed the identity for the first time. Depression is probably also common in women who have experienced IPV, although more research is needed in this area.

A significant number of women attributed their disability to their abuse history. Over a quarter (28.1 percent) of the women with disabilities who participated in the study indicated that their long-term illness or disability was a result of partner abuse. Disabled women described this connection in vivid terms: "[He] didn't want me taking anti-depressants, I felt crazy without them"; "[He] stole my meds to get high so [I] couldn't walk for four days once — that was the final straw"; "He has hit me in the face with the butt of a gun causing permanent eye damage"; "[He] raped me daily, gave me an STD."

Another 6.1 percent of the disabled participants said that their long-term illness or disability was caused by childhood abuse. In total, a third (34 percent) of the respondents from this population indicated that their long-term illness/disability was a result of IPV, either childhood abuse or partner abuse.

In addition, another 10.9 percent of women with disabilities were unsure whether their chronic illness or disability had been caused by IPV. Even leaving aside disabled women who were unsure, although we can speculate about them, it is significant that 34 percent of participants who reported disabilities and chronic illnesses made the connection to IPV, and that the most cited disability/chronic illness was depression. Violence and disability exist in a circular relationship. All people with disabilities are more vulnerable to violence and abuse, with disabled women being victimized more than disabled men (DAWN 2014; The Roeher Institute 1995). Violence and abuse are also known to cause disability (CRIAW 2002). This finding highlights the intertwined nature of violence and disability.

While some women indicate how abusive partners created long-term illnesses and disabilities, they also reported how their partners used their disabilities to further abuse and control them. One participant who indicated that she experienced depression and hearing loss reported that her partner "broke both hearing aids to stop me from being able to communicate with others." Another participant who has a degenerative disc stated that "every single time I needed medicine, he wouldn't allow it." She reported that he exerted this control through denying her any access to money: "I never had control of any money anyway, he'd check through my purse to make sure I didn't have any." One woman who had a spine injury and IBS reported, "He would make me walk to the hospital with my bad back to punish me." This was in addition to the daily terror she experienced: "He threatened to shoot my son. Held a machete to my face. Strangled me almost daily and threatened to kill my cat."

In many cases it was impossible to make the distinction between causing or exacerbating a disability or using a pre-existing disability as a means of control. A participant who lived with depression and addictions indicated that her partner "used my addiction to keep me around and keep me using. He could then use withdrawal to get what he wanted." Another participant who was an immigrant with a number of disabilities reported the following:

> [He] stabbed me once in the arm, once near my eye. Broke my hip. Tried to stab me another time but someone stopped him. Twisted my left shoulder. Hit my eye with a telephone because he heard women can call 911 if their husbands hurt them, my head was swollen for two months and I have a bit of vision loss.

The numbers of Indigenous women and non-Indigenous women who said that their disability or chronic illness was caused by abuse were very similar. However, indigeneity, disability, and abuse have a complex interaction. In Canada, Indigenous women experience higher rates of abuse, including childhood abuse, than non-Indigenous women, and also higher rates of disability.

There is a complex interaction between disability, indigeneity, and abuse. We found that women with disabilities had a much higher rate of reporting abuse in their childhood, as well as abuse as adults, than women without disabilities (this difference was statistically significant). Chart 3-1 illustrates that women with disabilities were two to three times more often abused as children than women without disabilities.

Further, we found that being disabled and abused had a leveling effect

Chart 3-1 Experience of Childhood Abuse Among Disabled Women and Non-Disabled Women

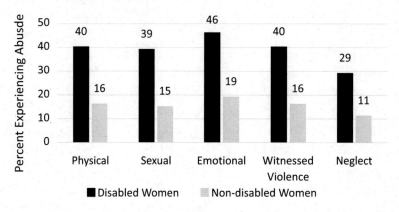

on the impact of ethnicity. The Healing Journey study and national studies have found that Indigenous women were much more likely to be abused as children than non-Indigenous women. However, when we compare among disabled women, the differences are substantially moderated. Chart 3-2 demonstrates that Indigenous women with disabilities are somewhat higher in reporting childhood abuse than non-Indigenous women with disabilities; however, the distinction is much less extreme than the differences in Chart 3-1. Further, these differences between Indigenous and non-Indigenous women with disabilities are not statistically significant.

Chart 3-2 Childhood Abuse Among Disabled Indigenous and Non-Indigenous Women

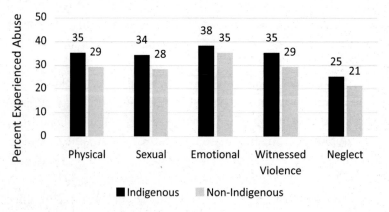

Service Use Among Women With and Without Disabilities

Women with long-term illnesses or disabilities were accessing social and legal services in greater numbers than women without disabilities. When asked how they felt about the experiences they had with social service agencies in general, non-disabled women who used these services were slightly happier with their experience than disabled women. However, the differences in satisfaction levels were not statistically significant.

The lower reported satisfaction level among women with disabilities was not surprising given what we know about systemic barriers such as accessibility issues, ableism, and the lack of knowledge about disabilities and chronic illnesses. If anything, one would expect the disparity to be wider. These figures suggest that social service agencies dealing with women with disabilities who have experienced IPV have improved since earlier studies. However, the YWCA study indicates room for improvement and the need for more information on IPV and disability to be available for service providers.

The majority of women with disabilities indicated that they had stayed in a battered women's shelter as an adult. Of these participants, Indigenous (49 percent) and non-Indigenous (51 percent) usage was similar. Interestingly, in this study, slightly more disabled women (65 percent) reported staying in a shelter compared to non-disabled women (61 percent), which is contrary to other research in this area. For example,

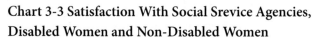

Chart 3-3 Satisfaction With Social Srevice Agencies, Disabled Women and Non-Disabled Women

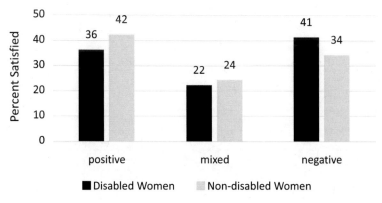

DAWN Canada's National Accessibility and Accommodation Survey found that, although many shelters are partially accessible to women with mobility challenges, they are unable to accommodate mental health disabilities (Smith 2009).

In the Healing Journey, disabled women reported using shelters and other services much more than one would expect based on other studies. One explanation is that we did not have a lot of participants with disabilities that limited mobility and would thus prevent access to some facilities. Depression was the most frequently reported disability. However, while women experiencing depression might not encounter physical barriers to shelter use, we know from both the DAWN study and the YWCA report that many such facilities are not equipped to deal with mental health challenges. It would be interesting to explore this further as mental health and depression are broad categories. We can speculate that women who are depressed may be more compliant than, for example, women who are living with schizophrenia. Nonetheless, our research has troubled the belief that services and shelters are not being used by women with disabilities.

In terms of engagement with justice system services, we see that disabled women had a higher utilization rate than non-disabled women. As in the social service assessments, we found that women with disabilities reported feeling slightly less positive about the way they were treated than women without disabilities. Table 3-2 illustrates the higher level of use of justice system services by women with disabilities and a moderately lower

Table 3-2 Women Reporting a Positive Experience of Staff in the Criminal Justice System by Presence or Absence of Disability

	Women With Disabilities		Women Without Disabilities		Total #
	#	%	#	%	
Justice Support Services	157	70	91	69	248
Lawyers	233	50	127	61	360
Prosecutors	137	50	75	53	212
Judges	189	58	86	57	275
Magistrates (JJP)	56	61	28	71	84
Probation Officers	66	64	29	62	95
Mediator	45	40	23	52	68

level of satisfaction in their experience with justice system personnel. As with the assessment of social services, the differences in satisfaction rates for disabled and non-disabled women are not statistically significant.

Disabled women rated their experience with judges and justice support services, such as victim services, quite positively, and their ratings were very similar to those of non-disabled women. Women with disabilities also had a slightly more positive assessment of probation officers than did women without disabilities. Among the professionals who disabled women rated less positively than did non-disabled women were lawyers, magistrates, and mediators. In these cases the differences in assessments were more dramatic, as women without disabilities were on average 10 percent more satisfied than women with disabilities.

The other critical component of the justice system is the police. Once again we find that disabled women utilized police services more frequently than non-disabled women.

Table 3-3 Involvement with Police
by Presence or Absence of Disability

	Women With Disabilities		Women Without Disabilities	
	#	%	#	%
Called police because of IPV	299	83	153	77
Other person called police because of IPV	209	58	91	46
Police arrested partner	164	52	87	53
Police escorted victim to shelter	83	26	29	18
Dual arrest	27	9	9	6
Police did not respond	39	12	11	8

In terms of police response to a call, the arrest of a woman's partner or ex-partner was similar for women with disabilities (52 percent) and women without disabilities (53 percent). There is a concern, however, that because of vulnerability disabled women may be less likely to identify their situation as abusive if police respond to a call. As one woman told us:

He never threatened to abuse anyone but me and once he used a telephone cord to whip me or use his belt. On one occasion he whipped me so hard that I was crying and someone called the cops, they came but I didn't complain about him as I was afraid of a confrontation with him afterwards … intimidated by the whole situation.

Police policy specifies that if there are reasonable and probable grounds that a crime occurred they must arrest. However, often the victim/complainant statement is the only or primary evidence. When women are too intimidated to state that they were abused, it is difficult to identify reasonable and probable grounds that a crime occurred in the absence of other evidence.

More women with disabilities (26 percent) than women without disabilities (18 percent) said the police escorted them to a shelter. Further, 74 percent of disabled women said they were granted a protection or prevention order if they applied for it, compared with 67 percent of non-disabled women. These differences may point to the fact that disabled women are perceived as more vulnerable and in need of greater assistance.

Of concern was the fact that more disabled women (12 percent) said that police did not respond when called compared to non-disabled women (7 percent). Further, more disabled women (9 percent) reported that the police arrested them as well as their partner or ex-partner than non-disabled women (6 percent). Both non-response to calls and dual arrests have a very negative effect on women's willingness to seek help. We are not sure why a difference would occur between women with and without disabilities, but this is a serious problem that merits further investigation.

Violence Against Disabled Women Cuts Both Ways

To reiterate, the intent of the Healing Journey study was to develop a clearer understanding of the life trajectories of women who experience IPV, and in this chapter we have focused on disabled women. We found that more women identify as having disabilities and chronic illnesses when they self-report and the terms are not defined by activity limitation. We also found that many women identify a link between their disability or chronic illness and the abuse they experienced either as a child or in their intimate partner relations. Finally, this study revealed that disabled women reported using social services and criminal justice services more frequently than non-disabled women. However, disabled women had a different experience of services, shelters, and the justice system than did non-disabled women. Interestingly, while disabled women were overall less positive in their assessment of the services they used, the differences in assessment were not large and were not statistically significant. The Healing Journey study revealed that women with disabilities are reaching out for help and are using services as much as — and, in some cases, more than — women without disabilities. Therefore, it is crucial that social policy and social services for women who experience IPV be rethought in terms of disability and chronic illness, especially depression.

The issue of accommodating disabled women in shelters has been written about for at least twenty-five years in the Canadian context. The message has been consistent, beginning with the DAWN survey of the accessibility of shelters for disabled women in 1992, through the DAWN National Accessibility and Accommodation Survey in 2008, and up to the YWCA Canada report in 2014. Shelters for women experiencing violence were not designed to accommodate women with disabilities. Despite this history and these ongoing challenges, disabled women are using shelters at a rate equal to or greater than non-disabled women. This indicates that shelters are an essential service for the safety of all abused women and highlights the increased necessity for these services to understand disability more broadly and accommodate the diverse and complex needs of women with disabilities.

Historically, there has been a tendency to think about disability in somewhat narrow terms and to equate disability with mobility challenges. But the issue is broader and is being expanded to encompass a range of chronic illnesses and disabilities, including mental health issues and addictions. The Healing Journey study has shown us how crucial it is to rethink disability using a broader lens. While mobility is important, it is only part of the story.

A revealing finding in this study is the fact that being a victim of interpersonal violence has a leveling effect. The differences we expected to find among abused women based on indigeneity or disability were either not present (for example, in the use of services by disabled and non-disabled women), or were much less pronounced (for example, the small differences between Indigenous and non-Indigenous women). This suggests that, for all women, regardless of indigeneity or disability, abuse has long-term debilitating effects. This reminds us of the high personal and social costs of domestic violence and the necessity of prioritizing accessible services.

Our findings have helped to fill a gap in the academic literature. We also hope that the Healing Journey research in general, and this analysis of disability and IPV in particular, will make a contribution to policy and services that will be accessible and responsive to the needs of all women experiencing IPV.

Note

1. This was a project of RESOLVE (Research and Education for Solutions to Violence and Abuse), a tri-provincial network of researchers and service providers working in the area of interpersonal violence. RESOLVE is funded by the Prairie Action Foundation (PAF). The Healing Journey was funded primarily by the Social Sciences and Humanities Research Council (SSHRC) Community-University Relations Alliances (CURA) program. Substantial additional funding was provided by PAF, the Alberta Heritage Foundation for Medical Research, and the Alberta Centre for Child, Family and Community Research.

References

Arriagada, Paula. 2016. "First Nations, Métis and Inuit Women." *Women in Canada: A Gender-Based Statistical Report*. Seventh edition. Ottawa: Statistics Canada.

Barrett, Betty Jo, and Melissa St. Pierre. 2011. "Variations in Women's Help Seeking in Response to Intimate Partner Violence: Findings from a Canadian Population-Based Study." *Violence against Women*, 17, 1.

Block, Pamela, and Christopher Keys. 2002. "Race, Poverty and Disability: Three Strikes and You're Out! Or Are You?" *Social Policy*, 33, 1.

Bopp, Judy. 2014. *Saying Yes: Effective Practices in Sheltering Abused Women with Mental Health and Addiction Issues*. Toronto: YWCA Canada.

Brownridge, D. 2006. "Partner Violence against Women With Disabilities: Prevalence, Risk, and Explanations." September. *Violence against Women*, 12, 9.

CRIAW (Canadian Research Institute for the Advancement of Women). 2002. *Violence against Women and Girls Fact Sheet*. Ottawa: CRIAW/ICREF.

DAWN (DisAbled Women's Network) Canada. 2014. "Factsheet: Women with Disabilities and Violence." <dawncanada.net/main/wp-content/uploads/2014/03/English-Violence-January-2014.pdf>.

DeRiviere, Linda. 2014. *The Healing Journey: Intimate Partner and its Implications in the Labour Market*. Halifax: Fernwood Publishing.

Milan, Anne. 2016. "Female Population." *Women in Canada: A Gender-Based Statistical Report*. Seventh edition. Ottawa: Statistics Canada. <statcan.gc.ca/pub/89-503-x/2015001/article/14152-eng.htm>.

Owen, Michelle. 2014a. "'Violence, Discrimination, and Prejudice': Theorizing the Experiences of Girls and Young Women with Disabilities." In Helene Berman and

Yasmin Jiwani (eds.), *Faces of Violence in the Lives of Girls*. London: Althouse Press.

____. 2014b. "Researching the Experiences of Girls and Young Women with Disabilities: 'A Victim of Subtle Abuse Rather Frequently.'" In Helene Berman and Yasmin Jiwani (eds.), *Faces of Violence in the Lives of Girls*. London: Althouse Press.

Renooy, L. 2002. *You Deserve to Be Safe: A Guide for Girls with Disabilities*. North Bay: DAWN Ontario. <dawn.thot.net/safe.html>.

Ridington, J. 1989. *Beating the Odds: Violence and Women with Disabilities*. Vancouver: DAWN Canada. <dawncanada.net/odds.html>.

Roeher Institute. 1995. *Harm's Way: The Many Faces of Violence and Abuse against Persons with Disabilities in Canada*. North York: The Roeher Institute.

Smith, Jewelles. 2009. "Bridging the Gaps: Survey Examines Accessibility at Women's Shelters." *Canadian Women's Health Network*, 11, 2 (Spring/Summer) <cwhn.ca/en/node/41613>.

____. 2012a. "Canadian Survey on Disability." <statcan.gc.ca/pub/89-654-x/89-654-x2015001-eng.htm>.

____. 2012b. "Aboriginal Peoples Survey." <23.statcan.gc.ca/imdb/p2SV.pl?Function=getSurvey&SDDS=3250&lang=en&db=imdb&adm=8&dis=2>.

Stienstra, D. 2002. *Intersections: Disability and Race/Ethnicity/Heritage/Languages/Religion*. Winnipeg, MB: Canadian Centre on Disability Studies. <disabilitystudies.ca/Documents/Research/Completed%20research/Intersection%20of%20disability/Intersection%20of%20disability.pdf>.

____. 2012. *About Canada: Disability Rights*. Halifax and Winnipeg: Fernwood Publishing.

Valentine, F. 2001. *Enabling Citizenship: Full Inclusion of Children with Disabilities and Their Parents*. Ottawa: Canadian Policy Research Networks.

World Health Organization. 2018. *Mental Disorders: Fact Sheet* <http://www.who.int/mediacentre/factsheets/fs396/en/>.

Chapter 4

Out of the Closet
Intimate Partner Violence as a Factor Contributing to Cognitive Disabilities

Roy Hanes, Karen March, and Ian Ford

In this chapter, we use the metaphor of the closet to highlight the need to pay attention to a hidden, often overlooked connection between long-term cognitive damage and injuries to the brain caused by intimate partner violence. The term intimate partner violence (IPV) "refers to acts of physical, sexual or emotional abuse by a current or former intimate partner whether cohabiting or not" (Wong, Choi et al. 2014: 6). Cognitive damage occurs when an injury to the brain affects a person's thinking, concentration, memory, emotions, and social behaviour in negative ways (Draper and Ponsford 2008). Specifically, we argue that women who experience blows to the head from IPV may exhibit symptoms of cognitive damage and memory loss, which in their later years are often misdiagnosed as consequences of the aging process, lifestyle, and nutrition. Proper diagnosis is important because it affects medical treatment plans and social service provision, as well as the family support offered to women with disabilities. We need to take the topic of the connection between IPV and cognitive damage out of the closet if we wish to enhance the quality of life for these women as they age.

In some ways, the following chapter resembles other chapters in this collection; in other ways, it is quite different. It is similar to chapters that focus on disabled women who have experienced IPV, while it differs in presenting IPV as a causal factor in the development of later-life disability. We argue that women who have been beaten and sustained head injuries may develop long-term cognitive problems, including dementia, as a result of that violence. (Dementia is a brain condition marked by increasing memory disorders, personality changes, and/or impaired reasoning as people begin to age [Draper and Ponsford 2008].)

Research on concussion and contact sports such as hockey and football reveals both short- and long-term associations between concussion caused by blows to the head and late-onset dementia for men (Daneshvar et al. 2011; McKee et al. 2009). For women, the more common type of violence that may lead to late-onset dementia is IPV. IPV is a global issue that affects 30 percent of women worldwide and cuts across class, race, ability, age, and religious, political, and national boundaries (Valera and Kucyi 2017). Indeed, IPV on a global scale is so pervasive that the World Health Organization (WHO) considers it an international social problem that infringes on the rights of all women and girls: "acts of violence against women are not isolated events but rather form a pattern of behaviour that violates the rights of women and girls, limits their participation in society, and damages their health and well-being" (WHO 2013: 2).

Considering the global extent of violence toward women and girls, and the potential for violence to cause serious impairments for this population, we feel that narrowly focused treatments based on medical model diagnoses — which attribute dementia to "poor lifestyle choices" or genetic predisposition — do not adequately address the social, political, economic, and cultural roots of IPV. Consequently, it is important to shift the diagnosis and treatment of women with dementia from a medical model to a social model wherein IPV is investigated as a possible contributor to the onset of dementia. This would be a radical shift, requiring political will, since contemporary ideology assumes a medical model. In the short term, researchers, academics, service providers, and policy developers need to consider the association between IPV and cognitive damage as part of their strategies for quality health care, social service provision, and family support for women. And for the long term, local, national, and international strategies need to be developed wherein IPV and impairments such as dementia and memory loss are addressed not solely as individual problems, but also as individual consequences of a much larger social problem.

Our interest in one potential cause of the cognitive disability of dementia led to an analysis of how marginalization and oppression occurs for abused women. The research on sports-related concussion and traumatic brain injury from IPV indicates that medical practitioners legitimize male athletes and youth as neurological patients and abused women as candidates for mental health counselling.

Entering the Closet: N's Dream Becomes a Nightmare

Our interest in the connection between IPV and long-term cognitive damage stems from personal contact with N, a woman who was diagnosed with dementia in her early 80s. While N could remember past events, recognize people, and hold short conversations, she possessed no memory of daily activities such as visits with family or friends, telephone conversations, or eating a meal. After diagnosis, N lived with her children until she died at the age of 88. Although they were pleased and willing to care for her, N's dementia placed stress on her family, medical agencies, and social service organizations, as well as on N.

Far too often, dementia such as that which N experienced is assumed to be the result of a variety of factors such as lifestyle, genetic predisposition, and/or past health issues. While such factors can never be totally ruled out, the assumption that they are the only factors can and should be challenged. N is a case in point. As a single mother who had raised four children on her own, N had always been an independent woman. She worked as a nurse until the age of 60 and participated actively in her community. She had been a non-drinker, and there was no history of dementia in her immediate family (parents, sister, or brother). N smoked, but so did her father and brother. Notably, however, N had been subjected to ten years of IPV.

Like most women who experience IPV, N had not expected that her marriage would turn into a living hell of beatings and years of psychological and emotional torment. The first beating came as a punch in the face within days of marriage. Subsequently, the physical abuse became a regular daily routine lasting for thirteen years, until she moved herself and her children out of the home. During her time with her husband, N suffered multiple assaults, including vicious punches and kicks to the head and other parts of her body. During the forty-five years after she left, she was not beaten. Knowing of her previous beatings to the head raised questions for us, however, about the connection between IPV, concussion, and later-life dementia. Could N's symptoms be a residual effect of the concussions she had experienced through IPV as a young woman rather than a part of her aging process? Were her symptoms indicative of a form of brain disease known as pugilistic dementia? As crass as it may seem, was N what Roberts et al. (1990) call "a punch-drunk wife"?

Hidden in the Closet: Cognitive Damage and Intimate Partner Violence

N's experience raises questions about IPV and later-life cognitive disability. Why, for example, had knowledge of her previous physical abuse by her husband not been considered as a part of either her assessment or treatment management plans? We believe this oversight occurred because the association between IPV and cognitive damage for women remains hidden in the closet. The topic of IPV appears rarely on the agenda of medical professionals and scientists examining the long-term effects of concussion, brain injury, and/or cognitive problems such as memory loss and dementia (Valera and Kucyi 2017). Organizations tackling IPV, such as women's groups and women's shelters, seldom feature cognitive impairment in their discussions or information material (Hunnicutt et al. 2017). This lack of attention to the association between IPV and cognitive damage, such as late-onset dementia, means many women may receive a misdiagnosis linked to the aging process, their genetic background, or a pre-existing disability, rather than a history of blows to the head.

The cognitive damage that women experience from IPV is a disturbing reality. In reviewing the literature, Wong, Choi et al. (2014: 6) report around 40 percent of IPV-related injuries involved "the head, neck or face (HNF) region … the most affected site … [being] … the prefrontal cortex, located in the frontal part of the head known to be responsible for cognitive functions such as perception, reasoning, judgment, problem solving and decision making." Often, however, the symptoms of confusion, difficulty in concentrating, memory loss, and cognitive slowing exhibited by women who have experienced IPV are diagnosed as the result of depression, anxiety, and post-traumatic stress disorder, rather than cognitive damage (Campbell et al. 2017). Such misdiagnosis leads to inappropriate treatment and inadequate support, which can hinder recovery and make both the short- and long-term impact of a brain injury worse (Draper and Ponsford 2008).

Concussions, Violence, and *Dementia Pugilistica*

Interest in the source, treatment, and management of cognitive damage brought on by blows to the head is not new. The diagnosis of *dementia pugilistica*, familiarly known by the term "punch- drunk syndrome," appeared in the 1920s when doctors noted that boxers who had experienced concussions could exhibit problems with memory, a lack of coordination, and symptoms similar to those of Parkinson's disease, such as tremors, slow movement, speech problems, and confusion (Martland 1928). Corsellis, Bruton, and Freeman-Browne added to that understanding in 1973 in a study in which they used brain-image scanning technology on fifteen retired boxers. These researchers labelled the cognitive damage found in the boxers chronic traumatic encephalopathy (CTE):

> The symptoms of CTE are insidious, first manifest by deteriorations in attention, concentration, and memory, as well as disorientation and confusion, and occasionally accompanied by dizziness and headaches. With progressive deterioration, additional symptoms, such as lack of insight, poor judgment, and overt dementia, become manifest. Severe cases are accompanied by a progressive slowing of muscular movements, a staggered, propulsive gait, impeded speech, tremors, vertigo, and deafness. (McKee et al. 2009: 2)

Today, the medical term CTE has supplanted *dementia pugilistica*. Recent research also indicates that CTE symptoms resemble the symptoms of other neurological diseases, such as Alzheimer's and post-traumatic stress disorder (PTSD), as well as mental health impairments such as anxiety and depression (McKee et al. 2009). About one-third of CTE cases are progressive and lead to permanent disability, such as speech difficulties, deafness, mobility disorders, seizures, and dementia (Blennow, Hardy, and Zetterberg 2012; Ling, Neal, and Revesz 2017). Despite medical advancements and technology, post-mortem examination of the brain is the only way to identify CTE (Esposito 2017). Diagnosis occurs mainly by looking for, assessing, and labelling patient symptoms and characteristics. This means misdiagnosis is highly likely (Campbell et al. 2017).

CTE, however, tends to be viewed as a male disease because most research concentrates on the short- and long-term consequences of concussion experienced in male-dominated contact sports such as boxing, ice hockey, football, soccer, and rugby (Daneshvar et al. 2011). A small body of work appears on children, adolescents, and young adults who experience sports-related concussions (Halstead and Walter 2010; Holmes et al. 2016). Those study findings indicate that age and gender are not major factors affecting concussion incidence or outcome; however, most study participants are male because the sports involved are still male-dominated (Purcell, Harvey, and Seabrook 2016).

The bulk of research on CTE takes a medical model approach, which views disability as a problem within the physical body and focuses on finding solutions to that problem through medical intervention. As a result, most research information on CTE considers the cause of cognitive damage, symptomology, risk screening, referral, and the recovery patterns of patients within one to two years post-injury (Draper and Ponsford 2008; Ling, Neal, and Revesz 2017). Long-term effects are rarely considered and are most often connected to sports-related head trauma. Complex social circumstances such as family environment or IPV receive minimal attention.

Peeking Through the Closet Door: A Social Model of Disability, Traumatic Brain Injury, and Intimate Partner Violence

The broader social, political, and cultural framework of patriarchy that contributes to men's control over women and society's implicit tolerance of IPV makes it imperative to have a disability lens that allows for a more multi-faceted approach than the medical model permits. A social model of disability believes that people with impairments are disabled by the societies in which they live (Hanes 2016). The conceptualization of disability as a social-political construct is found in the recent *United Nations Convention on the Rights of People with Disabilities*, which asserts that "disability is an evolving concept, and that disability results from the interaction between persons with impairments and attitudinal and environmental barriers that hinder full and effective participation in society on an equal basis with others" (United Nations Convention on the Rights of People with Disabilities 2006). The above definition represents a radical shift from a paradigm in which disability was linked to individual characteristics that deviated from a socially constructed notion of the acceptable human body and mind. Wendell (1989: 104) encapsulates the socially constructed nature of disability when she asserts:

> disability is not a biological given; like gender it is socially constructed from biological reality. Our culture idealizes the body and demands that we control it. Thus, although most people will be disabled at some time in their lives, the disabled are made "the other" who symbolize failure of control and the threat of pain, limitation, dependency and death.

Adherents to a social model of disability — disability activists as well as critical disability scholars — see oppression, exclusion, and discrimination as social actions rooted in an inability to accept "human variation" (Higgins 1992). They do not ignore health problems such as memory loss or dementia, nor do they oppose medical support or intervention for people who are impaired because of dementia. They do, however, reject the medicalization of *all* people labelled as disabled and, whenever and wherever possible, challenge actions based on such medicalization. Thus, followers of the social model argue, for example, that society should ensure all options for support be provided to women with dementia and their family members. Similarly, social model theorists would advocate for an expansion of research into causes of dementia, and they would support challenges to patriarchy, which contributes to IPV, sexism, and ableism.

An effective challenge to exclusion and discrimination requires attending to the structural barriers that aggravate or intensify disability effects. Structural barriers fall within one of five categories: (1) attitude; (2) lack of social support; (3) incorrect information; (4) physical hindrances; and (5) lack of accommodation (Shakespeare 2013). Each structural barrier is multi-faceted and closely intertwined with other barriers, and often functions in undetected and unforeseen ways. Whether separate or in combination, structural barriers restrict the life choices of persons with disabilities and prevent them from participating fully in their society.

It is important to attend to structural barriers when discussing cognitive damage and IPV because these barriers influence how women with disabilities are assessed, cared for, supported, and accommodated by medical practitioners, social service agents, families, and the community at large. Studies indicate that, in the case of women with disabilities, medical practitioners assume that a visible disability is either the woman's primary presenting problem or the underlying cause of the presenting issues, and they overlook invisible and relatively unknown impairments (Banks 2010). For example, women who are assaulted through IPV are rarely examined for brain injuries and subsequent cognitive damage from the assault and are sent home from emergency units with referrals to shelters or counselling services with no medical follow-up (Campbell et al. 2017). In these situations, practitioners' attitudes influence the treatment provided, the type and accuracy of information collected, the access to support, and the kind of aftercare prescribed.

Medical research offers insufficient documentation on either the short- or long-term cognitive damage for women who experience IPV. In a review of 1,132 research articles, Kwako et al. (2011) found only six that examined the occurrence or outcome of brain impairment caused to women from blows to the head sustained in IPV, and three that documented strangulation. The most common symptoms reported in those articles were headaches, dizziness, and memory loss. Post-concussive syndrome was also frequent. Post-concussive syndrome is recognized through symptoms such as headaches, confusion, and depression. Interestingly, the Kwako et al. study found that the majority of women who experience IPV had their immune functioning compromised. The one qualitative study that was found but not included in the analysis "identified head injuries, depression and insomnia as outcomes commonly linked to IPV" (Kwako et al. 2011: 116).

A small body of work on traumatic brain injury has emerged recently in response to the need for a deeper understanding of cognitive damage in women who experience IPV (Banks 2007; Kwako et al. 2011; Murray et al. 2016; Campbell et al. 2017; Hunnicutt et al. 2017; Valera and Kucyi 2017). Traumatic brain injury (TBI) is "an alteration in brain function or other evidence of brain pathology, caused by an external force that may cause cognitive impairment" (Campbell et al. 2017: 1). It can occur through IPV "from being hit in the head with fists or objects; having one's head pushed against a hard object, such as a floor or a wall; violent shaking; or attempted asphyxiation" (Banks 2007: 290). These studies are important because they draw attention to a very different source of cognitive damage for women than that which tends to dominate research and media reports, such as sports-related TBI. It could be argued that TBI and CTE related to IPV for women are as common as TBI and CTE from sports-related injuries — or even more common.

A comparison of the research findings of TBI studies on women and IPV with the findings of concussion studies on athletes reveals a strong distinction in the assessment and treatment patterns of each population. Both bodies of work report a noticeable number of men, youth, and women who exhibit relatively minor responses to mild TBI, such as brief loss of consciousness, and do not seek medical assistance. Men and youth are more likely to be kept for observation in emergency rooms, whereas women are "sent home without adequate information regarding the risk for lasting neurological symptoms such as headache, dizziness or cognitive slowing" (Campbell et al. 2017: 1). Unlike concussed men and youth who receive follow-up referral to neurologists and occupational therapists, women who experience blows to the head from IPV tend to have their symptoms attributed to mental health issues and are advised to get counselling (Banks 2010). Moreover, the treatment protocols and follow-up plans provided for TBI focus on concussive sports situations rather than the life complexity of women who undergo IPV (Kwako et al. 2011).

This comparison reveals an underlying process of discrimination and exclusion in the assessment and treatment of women who experience TBI from IPV. Specifically, a gender bias exists insofar as medical practitioners pay less attention to the potential cognitive damage to women who experience IPV than to male athletes and youth who engage in sports. This finding is significant because quick assessment and treatment of mild TBI can minimize both short- and long-term cognitive impairment (Draper and Ponsford 2008). Furthermore, concussion studies indicate that if a second brain injury occurs, the initial cognitive damage can intensify and, in some cases, lead to death (Valera and Kucyi 2017). In fact, awareness of this possibility has led to the banning of athletes from participating in sports activities after they have experienced a blow to the head. Additionally, coaches and trainers receive instruction on concussion care and watch for post-concussive syndrome so they can initiate preventive action if deterioration occurs. Few women who undergo IPV have a support person who possesses the knowledge to monitor the warning signs of increased brain dysfunction (Murray et al. 2016). They also frequently return to households where they experience repeated blows to the head continuously over months and years if they do not leave their situation (Kwako et al. 2011).

To understand why the medical treatment of TBI exhibits gender bias, we need to consider the role of prejudice more generally. Prejudice involves forming an opinion without taking the time and care to judge a person or situation appropriately. It gains support from stereotypes, that is, preconceived understandings of how particular groups of people think, dress, eat, interact, and generally conduct their everyday lives. Prejudice can be conscious or unconscious, and it can be expressed in either positive or negative ways. Sexism may be thought of as a particular form of prejudice. It can be defined as "a differential valuing of one sex, usually the male sex, over the other" (Renzetti and Curran 2003: 9), and it affects all women. (When sexism interacts with other forms of prejudice, such as ableism, women with disabilities are doubly disadvantaged.)

Studies of brains from athletes such as boxers, football players, soccer players, and hockey players, wherein *dementia pugilistica* or what would subsequently be called CTE were found, have created a stereotype regarding the type of person most likely to sustain cognitive damage, the symptoms of that damage, and subsequently of the treatment procedures applied. That stereotypical image is of a male athlete who has a concussion. Significantly, athletes are generally viewed as being worthy of care, their injuries as accidental, and their medical treatment as a necessity for recovery. In contrast, the stereotypical image of a woman who experiences IPV is a negative one. She is seen as a victim who is weak, passive, psychologically disturbed, and in need of counselling rather than medical intervention (Banks 2007, 2010). The tendency of medical professions to overlook the possible cognitive damage for women who suffer TBI from IPV and to prescribe mental health therapy rather than neurological assessment becomes more understandable when we consider how the role of such stereotypes influences judgment.

Plichta (2004: 1296) notes there is "little movement in the health care system to routinely screen women for IPV." The lack of attention given to the connections between TBI, IPV, and short- or long-term cognitive damage for abused women indicates there is also little movement in the health care system to deal with the medical problems exhibited by this population (Zink et al. 2004). The complexities of sexism that place women in a secondary position in society and the stereotypical prejudices held against women who experience IPV intertwine to create a process of discrimination that excludes them as legitimate patients requiring full medical examination and appropriate referral (such as neurological referral) when they appear at doctors' offices or hospital emergency units.

Opening the Closet Door: Intimate Partner Abuse and Older Women

We know from research by clinical psychologists, social workers, and academics that significant numbers of women experience IPV. Largely absent from that body of work, however, are women over the age of 65 (McGarry, Ali, and Hinchliff 2016). One reason for this is that few older women seek help for IPV. For example, in a comparative study of 342,462 female clients who utilized the domestic violence services in Iowa over a five-year period, Lundy and Grossman (2009) found only 1 percent were 65 years of age and older. This small proportion was "more likely to be White, report more emotional and less physical abuse, be referred to services by a legal source, have special needs or disabilities, and receive fewer services, less service hours and fewer contacts than women under the age of 65" (Lundy and Grossman 2009: 297).

Three different perspectives emerge in the literature on this problem, each of which offers insight into different barriers that limit older women's access to IPV professional and peer-related support services and helps to explain the paucity of older women in research on IPV. Some researchers believe that older women do not seek assistance simply because IPV risks decrease as a couple ages (Band-Winterstein 2012, 2015). Husbands become less violent physically, are more likely to die before their wives, or become ill and more dependent on them for care. Adult children are more capable than younger children of intervening in abusive situations and of helping a woman move out of the home. Old age also brings with it a normal social and physical decline that decreases motivation to change one's life circumstances and increases anxiety over how to manage such changes. Moreover, many couples in long-standing relationships tend to form mutual narratives in which they reconstruct the abuse in less negative ways. In any case, whether it is because they face decreasing abuse over time or because they develop mechanisms for coping with abuse, the fact that that women are less likely to seek help for IPV as they age has unfortunate consequences, both for researchers trying to understand the full impact of IPV and for the care of IPV victims: it keeps possible connections between brain damage caused by earlier abuse and the dementia exhibited by older women in the closet.

Other researchers think that the paucity of women over 65 seeking help for IPV can be best explained by a process of mutual exclusion: older women do not seek assistance and social service agents do not identify them as a population in need of support (Zink et al. 2004; Straka and Montminy 2006; Lundy and Grossman 2009; McGarry, Ali, and Hinchliff 2016). From this perspective, interpretations of IPV as personal clash with interpretations of IPV as social. Older women who hold traditional values and who learned to be submissive to their husbands, to maintain privacy in family matters, to be loyal, and to show family solidarity, see the abuse they experience as a personal failing. By contrast, the shelter system, which emerged in an era of feminist activism in the 1970s, sees violence toward women as a "social problem related to the structure of society and unequal social, gender or power relations … requiring a response at two different levels: the social or political and the personal" (Lundy and Grossman 2009: 298). These different interpretations of interpersonal violence ultimately obstruct older women's use of IPV resources (Straka and Montminy 2006).

Other research focuses on various aspects of ageism, a form of discrimination directed at someone simply because they are old; ageism can involve making arbitrary decisions about people because of their age, and it can involve internalized images that the aged have of themselves. When older women have internalized negative attitudes about aging that affect their perception of self, these attitudes limit their ability to seek help or challenge family members, professionals, and others who may label their symptoms as merely a product of age. Clearly, ageism can affect an older person's physical and mental health and well-being in a number of ways (Kydd and Fleming 2015). Social service workers and health care providers can demonstrate disrespectful attitudes toward older patients by talking down to them, discounting complaints, or avoiding aggressive therapy because they perceive a woman as too frail or elderly (Chrisler, Barney, and Palantino 2016). These negative stereotypes and attitudes are unlikely to create a supportive environment that encourages an older woman who has a history of abuse to share this information with professionals. The "forced silence" linked to a lack of trust is likely to perpetuate a situation in which IPV is not considered when memory problems and signs of dementia begin to appear.

Entering the Closet: Consideration of IPV and Cognitive Disability in Older Women

Traditionally, IPV patients have not been considered candidates for neurological testing. The assessment of victims of IPV typically includes the treatment of cuts and bruises, X-rays, MRIS, ultrasounds, and tests to determine the extent of potential fractures and internal injuries, but rarely does it include brain and head scans. This tendency — due in part to gender stereotypes, which have associated serious head injuries with male-dominated sports activities — has meant that data on TBI caused by IPV are sparse. Exacerbating this gap in the research is the fact that, for various reasons, older women are disinclined to report their experiences with IPV. As a result, little knowledge exists on the association between IPV, TBI, and women's long-term cognitive impairment.

What we do know is that living with IPV has adverse health outcomes such as "headaches, insomnia, choking sensations, hyperventilation, gastrointestinal symptoms, and chest, back and pelvic pain" (Dutton et al. 2006: 957). Chronic, long-lasting effects include depression, anxiety, and PTSD (Cook, Dinnen, and O'Donnell 2011). Fedovskiy, Higgins and Paranjape (2008: 48) report that "women with IPV histories had approximately three times the odds of meeting criteria for PTSD as compared to women who did not endorse a history of IPV." The prevalence of PTSD in women who have been abused "ranges in studies from 31 percent to 84.4 percent," depending upon the severity and the extent of the violence (Dutton et al. 2006: 958). Though they are suggestive, these findings do not link adverse emotional and psychological outcomes to long-term cognitive problems or dementia. Wong, Fong et al. (2014) found a small body of research on the structural/physical brain injuries in women who have experienced IPV; most of these studies report post-concussive syndrome as well as neurological problems such as difficulties with memory and concentration. Valera and Bernbaum (2003) note that it is unclear whether such deficits are due to structural/physical brain injury or to the psychological distress brought on by the fear of another violent attack. A greater focus on concussion and post-concussive syndrome for women who experience TBI from IPV will clarify this situation. Many mental health difficulties and neurological impairments experienced from IPV are ongoing and worsen as women age (McGarry, Ali, and Hinchliff 2016). These symptoms may be a foreshadowing of future dementia in women who have experienced IPV and need close monitoring by medical practitioners, social service agents, and family alike.

Recent work on Alzheimer's disease hints at possible connections between women's abuse, TBI, and later-life onset dementia. For example, Leung, Thompson, and Weaver (2006: 1077) found "in a sample of 40 older women (average age 76) with probable Alzheimer's disease … 17.5 percent (n=7) reported spousal abuse with head trauma … often more than 30 years earlier." (Some of the women were reluctant to share information about IPV, but their children reported it.) For the most part, however, public awareness materials pertaining to dementia and related disorders focus not on IPV but overwhelmingly on factors such as diet, genetic predisposition, lifestyle, and alcohol and drug use.

It is up to people working in the fields of medicine, gerontology, social work, and psychology to investigate possible links between IPV and TBI, whether those links create long-term cognitive impairment in older women, and, if so, in what way. Numerous times in this chapter we have noted the limitations of research on the connection between IPV, head injury, and later-life onset of dementia. It may be that the symptoms of CTE, Alzheimer's disease, dementia, and related disorders match so closely that in terms of treatment modalities, specific diagnosis is of secondary importance. Moreover, one might argue that once the effects of CTE or TBI or dementia begin to appear, looking for causation is also of secondary importance. We believe, however, that more specific diagnosis — that is, one that distinguishes IPV from other possible causes of TBI and long-term cognitive impairment — would lead to better, more appropriate treatment. More important, we contend that further research into the linkages between IPV, head trauma, and brain injury can lead to prevention and more informed treatment strategies that minimize the disablement of future generations of women such as N.

Keeping the Closet Door Open: Using the Social Disability Model

Conceptualizing the onset of dementia from traumatic blows to the head through interpersonal violence within a framework of disability is a daunting yet important task. Effective analysis of an older woman's situation and appropriate medical diagnosis of her long-term cognitive damage require full consideration of IPV. In turn, IPV is part of a broader social, political, and cultural framework of patriarchy, which implicitly supports the domination of men over women and of non-disabled people over people with disabilities. For this reason, we incorporate a social model of disability as a means of linking discussions of IPV to a disability framework. Women who experience IPV encounter structural barriers that obstruct their access to social support and medical care at both the social and the individual level. Among the identifiable practices of discrimination that aggravate and intensify the negative effects of abuse are ageism and sexism.

Disability is a political identity that leads to marginalization and oppression because society determines both who is a disabled person and how to manage a disability. Additionally, older women represent a neglected population for social service support and medical provision. Shifting from a medical to a social disability model uncovers invisible social processes that support the oppression of abused women and the misdiagnosis of symptoms leading to cognitive disability, disclosing hidden links between gender, patriarchy, ageism, and disability.

The criticisms of the social model of disability are numerous and many of them are valid. In his influential critique of the social model of disability, Shakespeare (2013) notes that it originated within a group of white men with physical disabilities and has a history of exclusionary politics. The social model does not adequately address race, class, gender, or sexual orientation, nor does it acknowledge violence against disabled women and girls or IPV as a potential cause of impairment. A similar critique of the social model of disability is made by Withers (2012), who agrees it tends to exclude women and other minority populations such as LGBTQ2 and racialized persons with disabilities. As well, and again historically, the political and contextual grounding of the social model minimized the lived reality of impairment such as day-to-day pain that many people with disabilities experience (Hanes in Robertson and Larsen 2016). Shakespeare (2013) makes the important point that the social model does not speak for all disabled people as many do not identify as being disabled, nor do they identify as being part of a larger community of disabled persons. Others argue the model offers a materialist or class-based analysis of society wherein disability and ability interconnect with modes of production and reproduction. The connection between economy and the need for workers, according to Stone (1984), is at the very root of the distinction between disabled and non-disabled citizens found in the English Poor Laws of 1601. In addition, a materialist connotation of the social model is rooted in the works of Michael Oliver (1990), who argues that people with impairments are disabled by the society in which they live when it comes to accessing opportunities for self- growth, especially in terms of access to employment. Similarly, Withers' (2012) critique of the social model points out that it concentrates on people with disabilities being left out of the work force and problematic notions of labour. Despite these shortcomings, the social model offers a strong theoretical perspective for understanding the links between individual impairment and broader social, political, economic, and cultural realities that disable people with impairments. We highlight those links in the following sections of this chapter through our analysis of the lack of attention being paid to the association between IPV, the cognitive impairment of women, diagnosis, and prevention.

The strength of the model lies in its capacity to advance a critical analysis of disability wherein the personal and political merge. The social disability model provides insight into the gendered medicalization of disabled bodies (that is, male athletes versus abused women) and highlights the processes of ageism by which older women fail to gain appropriate social support, research, and medical treatment. We believe further use of the social model of disability can assist with alternative ways of conceptualizing the effects of IPV and balance the present temptation to situate IPV injuries and impairments solely within a medical context. In other words, investigation and treatment of the potential long-term neurological problems sustained by women through IPV require a paradigm shift wherein societal and cultural contexts as well as relationship or interpersonal issues between two people are considered. At a societal level, TBI, CTE, dementia, and related disorders of women who have been beaten and abused must be given the same attention that is presently being offered to professional athletes and their families. Moreover, the solutions for these health problems need to address the sexist and ageist attitudes that sustain male violence against women.

Conclusion

Possible connections between IPV and the onset of dementia challenge contemporary academic, professional, caregiver, and service provider ways of thinking about the effects of violence against women. The current focus is on the here and now rather than the long term. While timely provision of medical care is paramount, singular medical model approaches focusing on immediate concerns are limiting. Prevention, diagnosis, treatment, and research can, and must, expand beyond the confines of medicalizing violence against women to address the social and personal issues of IPV. By using the social model of disability and addressing the social as well as the personal issues of violence, we can bring attention to the often hidden and silent consequences of IPV for women of all ages.

Where we go from here is of utmost importance. Our intention in this chapter has not been to focus on the medical issues of IPV; it has been to convey how violence contributes to the disability of women, especially long-term cognitive damage such as dementia. Further initiatives must consider contextual issues such as male dominance, poverty, and race, as these contextual issues contribute significantly to how others assess and treat women who are or were victims of IPV and how women assess and seek treatment for themselves.

Placing oppressive notions of disability on the shoulders of women, after subjugating them to violence, undermines their humanity. In *The Will to Change*, bell hooks (2004: 59) urges men to address issues of patriarchy and violence against women: "no man who does not actively choose to work to change and challenge patriarchy escapes its impact. The most passive, kind, quiet man can come to violence if the seeds of patriarchal thinking have been embedded in his psyche." It is important to address these issues and bring men into a full conversation about ending violence against women and violence against people with disabilities. As we dive into the (largely uncharted) waters of men's role in ending violence against women, we must take an intersectional approach and incorporate broader understandings of disability. We must not scare male allies away from the conversation, but we must also be willing to speak the truth. The reality of violence against women and women with disabilities is horrifying. The reality is also that this issue is not just a women's issue, or an issue faced by people with disabilities; it is everyone's issue — precisely because IPV may be committed against women and perpetrated by men, but it is withstood and managed by a society with sexist and ableist attitudes.

We conclude with two important ways in which boys and men can be encouraged to challenge the normalization of violence, especially IPV, thereby reducing the potential for short- and long-term cognitive disability for women, such as dementia:

- Speak up — actively speak out against about violence, not in such a way as to be a hero, but in a way to make their voices heard. Men and boys should not accept ableist or sexist language. Such language promotes violence.
- Work in the helping professions — inspire men and boys to become nurses and social workers. Traditional gender roles urge men to choose professions that are currently male dominated. If men have more career options that encourage human connection, if they work with women and work with people with disabilities, we believe things can change.

Clearly, this is not an exhaustive list. It is a beginning. We encourage people to add to it. Violence against women and women with disabilities are serious issues that require all hands on deck — including men. The insidious state of violence toward women is borne of masculinity, male brutality, and patriarchy. Change is possible as more and more boys and men join the movement to address this violence. Indeed, it is a necessary step in the prevention of IPV and IPV-related disability.

References

Band-Winterstein, Tova. 2012. "Narratives of Aging in Intimate Partner Violence: The Double Lens of Violence and Old Age." *Journal of Aging Studies,* 26.

____. 2015. "Aging in the Shadow of Violence: A Phenomenological Conceptual Framework for Understanding Elderly Women Who Experienced Lifelong IPV."

Journal of Elder Abuse and Neglect, 27.

Banks, Martha E. 2007. "Overlooked but Critical: Traumatic Brain Injury as a Consequence of Interpersonal Violence." *Trauma, Violence and Abuse,* 8, 3.

___. 2010. "2009 Division Presidential Address: Feminist Psychology and Women with Disabilities: An Emerging Alliance." *Psychology of Women Quarterly* 34.

Blennow, Kaj, John Hardy, and Henrik Zetterberg. 2012. "The Neuropathology and Neurobiology of Traumatic Brain Injury." *Neuron,* 76.

Campbell, Jacquelyn C., Jocelyn C. Anderson, Akosoa McFadgion, Jessica Gill, Elizabeth Zink, Michelle Patch, Gloria Callwood and Doris Campbell. 2017. "The Effects of Intimate Partner Violence and Probable Traumatic Brain Injury on Central Nervous System Symptoms." *Journal of Women's Health,* 00 (Spring).

Chrisler, Joan, Angela Barney, and Brigida Palantino. 2016. "Ageism Can Be Hazardous to Women's Health: Ageism, Sexism, and Stereotypes of Older Women in the Healthcare System." *Journal of Social Issues,* 72, 1.

Cook, Joan M., Stephanie Dinnen, and Casey O'Donnell. 2011. "Older Women Survivors of Physical and Sexual Violence: A Systematic Review of the Quantitative Literature." *Journal of Women's Health,* 20, 7.

Corsellis, Jan, C.J. Brunton, and D. Freeman-Browne. 1973. "The Aftermath of Boxing." *Psychological Medicine,* 3.

Daneshvar, D.H., D.O. Riley, C.J. Nowinski, A.C. McKee, R.A. Stern, and R.C. Cantu. 2011. "Long Term Consequences: Effects on Normal Development Profile after Concussion." *Physical Medicine and Rehabilitation Clinics in North America,* 22, 4.

Draper, Kristy, and Jennie Ponsford. 2008. "Cognitive Functioning Ten Years Following Traumatic Brain Injury and Rehabilitation." *Neuropsychology,* 22, 5.

Dutton, Mary Ann, Bonnie L. Green, Stacey I. Kaltman, Darren M. Roesch, Thomas A. Zeffiro and Elizabeth D. Krause. 2006. "Intimate Partner Violence, PTSD, and Adverse Health Outcomes." *Journal of Interpersonal Violence,* 21, 7.

Esposito, Domenic P. 2017. "195 Chronic Traumatic Encephalopathy (CTE): Clinical and Pathological Insights." *Neurosurgery,* 64.

Fedovskiy, K., S. Higgins, and A. Paranjape. 2008. "Intimate Partner Violence: How Does It Impact Major Depressive Disorder and Post Traumatic Stress Disorder among Immigrant Latinas?" *Journal of Immigrant Minority Health,* 10.

Halstead, Mark E., and Kevin D. Walter. 2010. "Clinical Report: Sports-Related Concussion in Children and Adolescents." *Pediatrics,* 126, 3.

Hanes, Roy. 2016. "Critical Disability Theory Revisited: Developing a Post-Social Model of Disability." In Jeanette Robinson and Grant Larsen (eds.), *Disability and Social Change: A Progressive Canadian Approach.* Winnipeg: Fernwood Publishing.

Higgins, Paul. 1992. *Making Disability: Exploring the Social Transformation of Human Variation.* Springfield: Charles C. Thomas Publishers

Holmes, Laurens, Joshua Tworig, Joseph Casini, Isabel Morgan, Kathleen O'Brien, Patricia Oceanic, and Kirk Dabney. 2016. "Implication of Socio-Demographics on Cognitive-Related Symptoms in Sports Concussion Among Children." *Sports Medicine,* 2, 38.

hooks, bell. 2004. *The Will to Change.* Toronto: Ataria Books.

Hunnicutt, Gwen, Kristine Lundgren, Christine Murray, and Loreen Olson. 2017.

"The Intersection of Intimate Partner Violence and Traumatic Brain Injury: A Call for Interdisciplinary Research." *Journal of Family Violence, 7*, 5.

Kwako, Laura E., Nancy Glass, Jacquelyn Campbell, Kristal C. Melvin, Taura Barr, and Jessica M. Gill. 2011. "Traumatic Brain Injury in Intimate Partner Violence: A Critical Review of Outcomes and Mechanism." *Trauma, Violence and Abuse, 12*, 3.

Kydd, Angela, and Anne Fleming. 2015. "Ageism and Age Discrimination in Health Care: Fact or Fiction? A Narrative Review of the Literature." *Maturitas, 81.*

Leung, F.H., K. Thompson, and D.F. Weaver. 2006. "Evaluating Spousal Abuse as a Potential Risk Factor for Alzheimer's Disease: Rationale Needs and Challenges." *Neuroepidemiology, 27.*

Ling, H., J.W. Neal, and T. Revesz. 2017. "Evolving Concepts of Chronic Traumatic Encephalopathy as a Neuropathological Entity." *Neuropathology and Applied Neurobiology, 43.*

Lundy, Marta, and Susan F. Grossman. 2009. "Domestic Violence Service Users: A Comparison of Older and Younger Women." *Journal of Family Violence, 24.*

Martland, Harrison. 1928. "Punch Drunk." *Journal of the American Medical Association, 91*, 15.

McGarry, Julie, Parveen Ali, and Sharron Hinchliff. 2016. *Journal of Clincial Nursing,* 26.

McKee, Ann C., Robert C. Cantu, Christopher J. Nowinski, E Tessa Hedley-Whyte, Brandon E. Gavell, Andrew E. Budson, Veronica E. Santini, Hyo-Soon Lee, Caroline A. Kubilus, and Robert A. Stern. 2009. "Chronic Traumatic Encephalopathy in Athletes: Progressive Tauopathy After Repetitive Head Injury." *Journal of Neuropathology and Experimental Neurology, 8*, 7.

Murray, Christine E., Kristine Lundgren, Loreen N. Olson, and Gwen Hunnicutt. 2016. "Practice Update: What Professionals Who Are Not Brain Injury Specialists Need to Know About Intimate Partner Violence-Related Traumatic Brain Injury." *Trauma, Violence and Abuse, 17*, 3.

Oliver, M. 1990 *The Politics of Disablement.* London: Macmillan Press

Plichta, Stacey B. 2004. "Intimate Partner Violence and Physical Health Consequences: Policy and Practice Implications." *Journal of Interpersonal Violence, 19*, 11.

Purcell, Laura, Janice Harvey, and Jaimie A. Seabrook. 2016 "Patterns of Recovery Following Sport-Related Concussion in Children and Adolescents." *Clinical Pediatrics, 55*, 5.

Renzetti, Claire M., and Daniel J. Curran. 2003. *Women, Men and Society.* Toronto: Pearson Press.

Roberts, G.W., H.L. Witwell, P.R. Acland, and C.J. Brunton. 1990. "Dementia in a Punch-Drunk Wife." *Lancet, 14.*

Robertson, Jeanette, and Grant Larsen (eds.). 2016. *Disability and Social Change: A Progressive Canadian Approach.* Winnipeg: Fernwood Publishing.

Shakespeare, Thomas. 2013. "The Social Model of Disability." In L.J. Davis (ed.), *The Disabilities Studies Reader.* New York: Routledge.

Stone, Deborah. 1984. *The Disabled State.* Philadelphia: Temple University Press.

Straka, Silvia M., and Lyse Montminy. 2006. "Responding to the Needs of Older Women Experiencing Domestic Violence." *Violence Against Women, 12*, 3.

United Nations Convention on the Rights of People with Disabilities. 2006. <un. org/development/desa/disabilities/convention-on-the-rights-of-persons-with-disabilities/convention-on-the-rights-of-persons-with-disabilities-2.html>.

Valera, Eve M., and Howard Berenbaum. 2003. "Brain Injury in Battered Women." *Journal of Consulting and Clinical Psychology,* 71, 4.

Valera, Eve M., and Aaron Kucyi. 2017. "Brain Injury in Women Experiencing Intimate Partner-Violence: Neural Mechanistic Evidence of an 'Invisible' Trauma." *Brain Imaging and Behaviour,* 11.

Wendell, Susan. 1989. "Toward a Feminist Theory of Disability." *Hypatia,* 4, 2: 104–124.

who (World Health Organization). 2013. "Global and Regional Estimates of Violence Against Women: Prevalence and Health Effects of Intimate Partner Violence And Non-Partner Sexual Violence." <http://apps.who.int/iris/bitstream/handle/10665/85239/9789241564625_eng.pdf;jsessionid=F2E0608C25CBD5288 867F005B31FD692?sequence=1> retrieved June 5, 2018.

Withers, A. 2012. *Disability Politics and Theory.* Black Point, NS: Fernwood Publishing.

Wong, Janet Yuen-Ha, Anna Wai-Man Choi, Daniel Yee-Tak Fong, John Kit-Shing Wong, Chu-Leung Lau, and Chak-Wah Kam. 2014. "Patterns, Aetiology and Risk Factors of Intimate Partner Violence-Related Injuries to Head, Neck and Face in Chinese Women." bmc *Women's Health,* 14.

Wong, Janet Yuen-Ha, Daniel Yee-Tak Fong, Vincent Lai, and Agnes Tiwari. 2014. "Bridging Intimate Partner Violence and the Human Brain: A Literature Review." *Trauma, Violence and Abuse,* 15, 1.

Zink, Therese, Saundra Regan, Linda Goldenbar, Sephanie Pabst, and Barb Rinto. 2004. "Intimate Partner Violence: What Are Physicians' Perceptions?" *Journal of the American Board of Family Practice,* 17.

Structural Violence

Chapter 5

An "Unconscious Terrain of Habits"

Structural Violence against Women Labelled with Intellectual Disabilities

Natalie Spagnuolo and Josée Boulanger

We know that the most intense forms of disability violence are directed against certain groups of disabled people — including people labelled with intellectual disabilities or psychosocial disabilities, disabled people who are Indigenous or Black, and disabled people of colour — and that disabled women in particular are among the most frequent targets of gendered forms of violence (Report of the U.N. High Commission 2012). It is no coincidence that these women tend to be among the poorest people in any given society. In Canadian society, violence against women labelled with intellectual disabilities is intimately linked to attempts to contain and even eliminate people who are assumed to be economically unproductive and burdensome to society. As Nikolas Rose (2007: 3) explains, this fear of people who do not meet certain definitions of productivity legitimizes attempts to "manage the quality of the population, often coercively and sometimes murderously, in the name of the future of the race." In light of these practices, Hansen, Barnett, and Pritchard (2008) ask whether genetic counselling and prenatal testing can ever be considered as neutral practices offering simple choices to families. Such efforts to manage bodies that "do not fit" inform what are known as eugenic practices. Historically, these practices have included forced sterilization, murder/euthanasia, and confinement in asylums or total institutions such as the Huronia Regional Centre in Ontario, the Michener Centre in Alberta, and the Woodlands Institution in British Columbia.

Within this eugenic context, criminal acts of violence have been committed under the purview of medical mandates to "care for" and "support" women labelled with intellectual disabilities. In the history of Canadian eugenics, people labelled with intellectual differences often included Indigenous, racialized, immigrant, and poor women. This is because perceptions of "subnormal" intelligence often reflect and support racist as well as class-based assumptions about normal behaviour. All of these groups were, and in many ways still are, at risk of being viewed as mentally "defective," "unproductive," and "dependent" (see McLaren 1990; Gould 1981; Stephen 2007; Dyck 2013). In recent decades, after practices of forced sterilization quite literally went on trial in the very public case raised by the institutional survivor Leilani Muir (see Dyck 2013), media attention has highlighted atrocities committed against labelled women. Muir's case, however, is only one example taken from a historical record replete with incidents of forced confinement in institutions, sexual assault, forced labour, and forced sterilization, as well as with acts of survivorship and resistance by women labelled with intellectual disabilities. Largely due to the testimonies, activism, and public history work of women like Leilani Muir, Patricia Seth, Marie Slark, Cindy Scott, and Valerie Wolbert, to name only a few, the Canadian public is now more aware of the extent of this form of institutionalized violence. But much more work remains to be done to expose both historical and current forms of violence.

We refer to women as being *labelled with* intellectual disabilities, rather than as *having* intellectual disabilities, to reflect the terminology used by many self-advocacy movements and People First of Canada, an important national-level disability organization of people labelled with intellectual disabilities. The term *labelled with* works to highlight the role of perception and prejudice, as well as racism and classism, in assessing mental and intellectual impairments. Intelligence is a complex and dynamic quality that cannot be reduced to test results, as proponents of the IQ would have us believe. IQ testing has been widely criticized as a pseudo-scientific and deeply flawed methodology (see Gould 1981). Rather than rely on the results of such tests, we believe that an individual must self-identify and endorse medical assessments related to intellectual impairments in order for these to be valid. This is not to deny that individuals may experience real intellectual impairments and that they may identify as *having* intellectual disabilities. Our choice in terminology rejects medically *imposed* labels; nevertheless, we recognize and respect that individuals may feel that these labels accurately describe their own experiences and impairments, and that labels may thus be appropriate in some cases.

Subject-to-subject violence enacted by or against women labelled with an intellectual disability is often framed as the result of behavioural problems on the part of labelled women themselves; subject-to-subject violence enacted against women labelled with an intellectual disability is often framed as mercy killings committed by non-disabled people. By contrast, we stress the need to situate these visible, personal acts of violence within a wider context of structural violence. Structural violence can be understood as a form of violence that is not criminal in nature but "pervasive and corrosive" (Association for Community Living–Manitoba 2010: 212). Following Zizek (2008) and Farmer et al. (2006), we argue that violence is embedded in systems and can be traced to several sources: the very laws that govern services for people labelled with intellectual disabilities, the absence of laws that guarantee their entitlement to appropriate supports, and deeply held beliefs about competence. This broader context helps explain why, when the victims are labelled as having an intellectual disability, violence is often met with indifference.

Personal narratives based on lived experience allow us to appreciate how structural violence manifests itself in people's everyday lives. Furthermore, narratives remain an accessible and creative way to nourish a disturbance of everyday practices that are harmful but have been normalized through routines developed against a backdrop of ableist beliefs. These stories are an important vehicle for promoting social justice, especially among marginalized groups. According to Stone-Mediatore (2003: 184), the value of experience-based stories from marginal standpoints includes a daily experience with the obscured costs of social contradictions, a shifting in and out of cultural worlds, an engagement in activities that defy the dualisms and exclusions of received analytic categories, and a resistance to the social relations that ruling beliefs present as "natural."

These stories are examples of structural violence because they reflect "social arrangements that put individuals and populations in harm's way"

(Farmer et al. 2006: 1686). Some of the stories we explore were produced for *The Freedom Tour*, a documentary film by People First of Canada, a self-advocacy movement based in Winnipeg. Others were produced by the Self-Advocacy Federation based in Edmonton and the Respecting Rights Committee that works through Toronto's ARCH Disability Law Centre. We have selected stories of fiction and non-fiction, produced by and with women labelled with an intellectual disability, that reflect violent treatment arising mostly in current community support systems, such as group homes.

New Structures and New Discourses: The More Things Change, the More They Stay the Same

In Ontario, services for people labelled with intellectual disabilities have shifted from the Ministry of Health and Long Term Care to the Ministry of Community and Social Services. For many institutionalized women labelled with intellectual disabilities, violence is part of everyday life (see Malacrida 2015; People First of Canada 2008). Disability advocates argue that this violence is engendered by institutionalization and the mindset behind it. While much has improved as a result of hard work by self-advocates, families, and community advocates to shut down many of Canada's large institutions, there is strong evidence that a deficit model of intellectual disability continues to underpin the system that is meant to support people in the community.

A deficit approach locates the "problem" within the person's behaviour or way of being, suggesting that the injustices experienced by people labelled with intellectual disabilities — such as poverty and homelessness — are the inevitable result of their own natural or biological "deficiencies." Such an approach draws attention away from the social causes of marginalization and the violent arrangements that render these causes invisible. Instead, people labelled with intellectual disabilities who face oppression are blamed for their own predicament, while society's role is erased. People caught up in this system can feel frustrated, sad, and angry. Much to their dismay, they and their families often realize that the supports they receive function according to the same way of thinking upon which total institutions were designed and managed. For as Pat Worth, one of the founders of People First, is quoted as saying, "An institution is not just a place, it is the way people think" (Worth n.d.). Since the thinking that underpins these asylums and institutions has not been challenged, their closure has not put a stop to the violence they generated. The institutions that serve these women have, admittedly, changed in structure and mandate; support mandates are now — at least on paper — geared towards supporting self-determination and life in the community. Importantly, these mandates reflect international law such as the *United Nations Convention on the Rights of Persons with Disabilities* (UNCRPD), which was developed because of pressure exerted by disability rights advocates around the world. Nevertheless, despite these signs of institutional progress, much of the old way of thinking, as well as the violence and risks associated with this approach, remains in place.

In Ontario, the funding system for disability supports is split between two provincial ministries: the Ministry of Health and Long Term Care (MHLTC) and the Ministry of Community and Social Services (MCSS). In 1974, people labelled with intellectual disabilities began to receive supports primarily through MCSS, which is the less funded of the two ministries. People with other types of impairments (for example, people with physical impairments, psychosocial impairments, or impairments acquired after birth or as a result of aging) continue to receive supports and services through the MHLTC. One notable exception is the income support program known as the Ontario Disability Support Program (ODSP), passed in 1997 under an act by the same name. ODSP, provided to people with physical and cognitive impairments, is managed through MCSS. The decision to move what are known as "developmental services" from the Ministry of Health to Social Services was strongly influenced by trends inspired by Wolf Wolfensberger (1972) on normalization. This shift involves re-framing intellectual disability by de-emphasizing or rejecting narratives that position this status as a medical condition or problem. The effort to de-medicalize this impairment category consequently segregated developmental services into a different ministry.

Although the theoretical recognition that intellectual disability should not be considered a health-related illness is a welcomed change, the relocation of services and supports from the MHLTC to the MCSS has, in practice, largely failed to challenge a deficit or pathologizing approach. Those with labels continue to be viewed through a deficit model as being deficient in intellectual capacity, as well as cognitive, emotional, and other forms of functioning. Far from empowering them, the segregation of people labelled with intellectual disabilities from "mainstream" disability services has resulted in further marginalization and has made it more difficult to advocate across diagnostic boundaries. As a result, we take an approach to disability that can be described as interactional rather than strictly biomedical or social. Following Sen, Mitra, and other capabilities researchers, we understand disability as a "deprivation result[ing] from the interaction among the resources available to the person, personal characteristics (e.g., impairment, age, gender), and the environment" (Mitra 2006: 241). This perspective avoids one consequence of a view of intellectual disability as non-interactional: that a focus on an either a social or individual (biomedical) definition of intellectual disability can be used to refuse access to services and supports.

The move to MCSS-managed services has not improved the situation of persons labelled with disabilities. It has done little, for instance, to reduce the actual practice of over-prescribing medications. *The Atlas on the Primary Care of Adults with Developmental Disabilities in Ontario* reports that, among people labelled with intellectual disabilities, "one in five [are] receiving five or more medications concurrently. Older persons with developmental disabilities, women and those with high levels of morbidity were more likely to be dispensed multiple medications." The report goes on:

> the most commonly prescribed medications were for mental health or behavioural issues, with antipsychotic medications being prescribed most frequently. Approximately one in five adults prescribed antipsychotics were dispensed two antipsychotics concurrently, putting them at risk for adverse reactions, including death. (Lunsky, Klein-Geltink, and Yates 2013: 3)

Despite the move to MCSS, moreover, people with labels are congregated into group homes that are largely designed and managed by the same logic as total institutions, arrangements that borrow their organizational logic from dated medical systems. Finally, all services and supports offered through MCSS are accessed exclusively by obtaining a letter from a medical professional certifying eligibility.

House of Horrors, a short film produced by the Self-Advocacy Federation (2015a), tells of the mundane, regimented, medicalized, and paternalistic environment endured by three women labelled with intellectual disabilities. One of the women, who lives in the group home, responds sarcastically to staff monitoring, exclaiming, "Oh, oh, somebody's exhibiting behaviours of concern!" Meanwhile, a second staff person prepares medications for consumption, calling out, "B.O.C, medication time, medication time!" In this scene, a clear link is drawn between "behaviours of concern" and the distribution of meds. In a failed or misguided effort at community inclusion, the same staff member then announces that the group will be going shopping. However, as one of the women points out, they all live well below the poverty line and have no money to spend. This short film, although fictional, very clearly expresses the failure of an attempt to de-medicalize and to promote self-determination. As family members, advocates, and former support workers, our observations match this depiction: we have witnessed the use of medication and heavy sedation as a method to make people more compliant and thus easier to for staff to manage.

Who Decides Who is a(t) Risk? Creating Vulnerabilities

The 2008 Social Inclusion Act — the key piece of legislation governing access to resources for people with the intellectual disability label in Ontario via MCSS — undermines the right to self-determination by reinforcing the belief that this group of people is incompetent. In a report prepared for the Law Commission of Ontario, Joffe (2010: 20) exposes the Act's "discriminatory assumptions that all people with intellectual disabilities cannot understand information on their own; that they are not able to recognize when they may need assistance or support; and that others may be in a better position to determine what is in their best interests." By adopting such a deficit approach, interventions can exacerbate the disadvantages caused by a cognitive impairment. Feminist philosopher Catriona Mackenzie (2014: 47) provides a helpful explanation of the risks of labelling certain groups as incompetent and vulnerable:

> Interventions that target specific groups identified as vulnerable and subject them to restrictions or forms of surveillance not applied to the rest of the community, that treat persons who are so targeted as incompetent and deviant or that marginalize and

socially exclude them, that do not consult with members of those groups in the formulation of policy or engage their participation in its implementation and that are primarily focused on reducing perceived risks to society rather than concerned with fostering autonomy count as objectionably paternalistic.

Our collective response to disabled people's perceived and supposedly inherent vulnerability can be qualified as objectionably paternalistic. A wide range of practices illustrate this paternalism: guardianship and substitute decision making; a culture that normalizes the devaluation of non-normative bodies and pathologizes adaptive behaviours such as: self-stimulation; "behaviour management" through medication (especially antipsychotics, according to the 2013 *Atlas on Primary Care* — see Lunsky, Klein-Geltink and Yates, 2013); segregation in education through "distinct" classes; supervised congregated living arrangements according to label; discriminatory admissibility criteria for adapted transportation (ParaTranspo, for example) based on medical proof of physical impairment; admissibility for supported communication and augmentative and alternative communication through the Ottawa hospital based on medical proof of physical impairment; and the non-existence of a right to supports, resulting in young adults living in nursing homes, hospitals, and homeless shelters while they wait for supports to become available.

Impairments can cause varying degrees of disadvantage depending on the context. To avoid paternalism, "Responses to vulnerability should be guided by the value of autonomy" (Mackenzie 2014: 45). However, in Ontario, we have yet to recognize a right to supports and services for people labelled with an intellectual disability. Instead, we have a largely paternalistic system that is designed and redesigned without the meaningful participation of labelled people. This absence of participation can be understood as a logical consequence of a system that excludes people based on an assumption of incompetence, with little regard for autonomy. This paternalistic and divisive approach minimizes costs to private organizations, denying services that would support the self-determination of those labelled as "too vulnerable" while shifting responsibility to the person labelled with an intellectual disability and to their family. In this context, the labour undertaken by people with disabilities, and sometimes by their families and friends — labour that is required to go about their lives in this hostile and non-supportive environment — is exploited and unacknowledged. It is not recognized as work because such recognition would be costly and would require radically different social arrangements.

Psychological assessments and legal capacity tests in Canada and elsewhere deny decision-making authority to individuals who are not considered to be mentally "competent" or to fully comprehend the decision's context and its implications (ARCH Disability Law Centre 2014; Series 2015). Such was the experience of Valerie Wolbert, former president of People First of Canada in Winnipeg, who told her story in 2006 to an audience of self-advocates and supporters:

> I was declared incompetent. I was under the Public Trustee for about a year and a half. I didn't have any freedom. I had to ask permission for when I wanted to go on a trip to Israel. I didn't have any control, where I lived, my money. I had to prove to the psychologist that I was competent. (National Film Board 2008d)

Valerie's right to decide for herself was obstructed by the system. She had to use her own resources to "prove" that she was a capable person. She was successful — but so many others are not. People found to be legally incompetent may not have the same abilities or resources to challenge their status and to request help to practice supported decision making (SDM), which is recognized in the UNCRPD as a way to replace substitute decision making of the type that Valerie and many others have been and continue to be subjected to. Paternalistic and deficit-focused thinking towards people who are thought to be intellectually impaired persists as a means of justifying the removal of decision-making authority.

Paternalistic thinking also works to justify the ongoing confinement of people in Canadian provinces such as Nova Scotia. Barken's (2013) interviews with staff and managers from segregated facilities in Nova Scotia reveal that these employees are convinced of the protective role that institutions are playing, despite heavy criticism from the wider de-institutionalization movement. Nova Scotia is unfortunately not the only place in Canada that officially holds on to the belief that total institutions are the best places for people labelled with intellectual disabilities. In Alberta, the Michener Centre remains open, and promotional videos for the Centre appeal to the "inherent" vulnerability of residents and their supposed inability to cope with life in the wider community. By uprooting children and adults from their families and communities and by forcibly placing them under a public guardian or trustee, these provincially funded institutions exacerbate their residents' disadvantages by depriving them of their most basic rights, thus causing profound vulnerability. Although in today's service systems, people labelled with intellectual disabilities are not automatically placed under guardianship as a prerequisite for supports, their freedom to make choices is often undermined by staff and parents for "her own good." The videos *It's Your Money* and *It's Your Life*, produced by the Respecting Rights Committee of the ARCH Disability Law Centre in Toronto, show clearly how the money of labelled women is controlled by staff and their social life controlled by a parent who works through a group home staff member.

Reinforcing "Otherness" and Normalizing Violence

The kinds of labels discussed above justify and normalize marginalization and violence towards people labelled with intellectual disabilities, and this is so despite a shift from a biomedical approach to understanding disability as a social issue, which can be traced in policy statements. The problem is that these policy statements have failed to generate a genuine shift in thinking or practice. The new discourse on "community living" and "self-determination" has not dislodged the belief that people labelled with intellectual disabilities are radically and profoundly different from the rest of us. As disability communities have often explained, when services are underpinned by a deficit logic, an individual's diagnostic label can reductively attribute all her needs to her "intellectual disability." The moral value that is attached to brain normalcy means that when it comes to intellectual disability, other characteristics are more readily discounted. As Walmsley and Johnson (2003: 12) explain, "the label often overshadows individuality and even a person's humanity. The label of intellectual disability is all encompassing and so stigmatizing that the person's gender, religion, sexual orientation or cultural background is not even acknowledged as a component of their identity."

The importance of the "health" of the brain in determining a person's identity rests on a centuries-old belief about a mind/body split in which the active brain is considered to be a "pilot" or "processor" for a passive body. If the brain is believed to be damaged, then the person is thought to be damaged in her entirety. According to this logic, if a body part is believed to be impaired, not all is lost because the central processing unit — the brain — remains intact. By insisting on a hierarchic ranking of brain and body, we hyper-marginalize people labelled with intellectual impairments compared to other disabled people. One of the many results of this impairment hierarchy is an intensification of poverty. Based on the Participation and Activity Limitation Survey (PALS) of 2006, the Council for Canadians with Disabilities reports that people with any type of cognitive disability or communication disability have poverty rates of 22.3 percent and 24.1 percent compared to 15.2 percent for people with a mobility impairment or 10.3 percent for people with a hearing disability. Statistics Canada's 2012 Survey on Disability demonstrates that increasing "severity "of disability corresponds with increasing poverty. Severity is a concept used by Statistics Canada to identify people who experience high levels of what are referred to as activity limitations in terms of intensity and combined types of impairment (Statistics Canada 2012). Canadians, with what are considered to be the most severe disabilities, are at the bottom of the income ladder, with a total median income of $14,390, as opposed to Canadians without disabilities at the top of the ladder, with a median income of $31,160.

The story of Roberta Ann Silverson, a survivor of Valley View Centre, a former institution for people labelled with intellectual disabilities, shows that poverty is a key life condition for people labelled with intellectual disability (interview by Susie Wieszmann of People First of Canada in Winnipeg and Josée Boulanger). Roberta does work, but as a volunteer and, as she points out, "they don't pay volunteers." Her situation is typical of that of many people with labels who are not fairly compensated for their labour or given access to adequate financial resources. During the interview, when Susie asks her if she goes shopping in her neighbourhood, Roberta answers incredulously, "With what? Buttons!? … By the time I pay my bills, pay my rent, there's nothing left." Her response echoes the reaction of the woman portrayed in the *House of Horrors* video when the support worker suggests shopping as an outing for the residents.

Experiences of poverty and exploitative labour relations are consequences of negative assumptions about people labelled with intellectual disabilities and represent some of the ways in which they are not given fair treatment. The denial of fair treatment based on an assumption of incompetence extends to the loss of the most intimate forms of bodily integrity, such as reproductive power. Roberta, for example, disclosed her own forced sterilization in the interview. She tells us that her mother had Roberta's "tubes tied" when she was young. When asked if she knows why her mother made this decision, she explains, "She called me mental retarded." Roberta was fully aware of the injustice done to her as a young woman, but as a woman labelled as "retarded," she had very little credibility. As a result, she was denied the power to protect herself from the violence that was done to her. Despite what her mother and any medical or social work professionals may have believed at the time, Roberta rejects these assumptions and defends herself, explaining, "I'm just a slow learner."

Despite a cultural and economic context that largely devalues the lives of women and men labelled with intellectual disabilities, some support staff and agencies recognize and defend the inherent value of the people they support. For example, in a YouTube video, Diane Nabess and a support worker named Sue — a woman who first supported Diane when she began using Calgary Scope's services — describe their history together (NFB 2008a). They describe a mutually respectful relationship that is possible even in a negative broader context. Sue is keenly aware of that context when she talks about having to justify Diane's life to medical professionals who were ready to "pull the plug" when she was hospitalized for a serious illness. The exchange between Sue and the medical person expose the potential violent urges — in this case, euthanasia — that are sustained in a system that uses a scientific rationale to assess the value of disabled lives. According to Sue:

> the doctors said, "What does Diane do in her life?" And I'm like feeling like I am having to justify Diane's life so they will help her ... We have to really advocate for our clients. It's happened to a couple other of our clients too ... that we had to justify their life on this earth. (NFB 2008a)

Sue's story illustrates that the capacity to reject this medical devaluation is based on the ability and willingness to recognize a person's value beyond utilitarian and normative judgments.

However, acts of resistance carried out by labelled people sometimes carry heavy costs and can result in criminalization. Consider, for example, the case of Nichele Benn, a Nova Scotia woman who lived in a group home and was charged several times with assaulting staff. Tammy Hiltz, President of People First of Canada in King County, explains: "Basically, she didn't want to do what the staff wanted her to do and acted out and now she's being charged for it" (People First Nova Scotia 2014). With the support of the disability community's advocacy, Nichele's mother was able to have the charges dropped and more individualized supports made available to her daughter.

A Fragmented System: Managing Lives and Creating Divisions

The system of supports for women labelled with intellectual disabilities, to the extent that it exists, is very fragmented. The needs of these women are often kept apart from those of their "intellectually abled" counterparts and, given the low levels of funding that have been set aside for segregated "developmental" services, such as personal support workers, these needs and desires — indeed, these entitlements — often end up being erased. Underpinning such erasures and the overall segregation of services is a hierarchy of impairments premised on deep-seated fears about unruly minds and bodies. These fears create artificial divisions between people with physical disabilities, people who use mental health services, and people labelled with intellectual disabilities. As many disability activists have pointed out, the resulting fragmentation along diagnostic lines weakens the ability of disability communities to advocate collectively for the resources and supports that would offer a genuine opportunity to live in the community (see, for example, Russell 1998). These divisions entail symbolic violence that controls individuals, making them more manageable, rather than understanding, respecting, and supporting their needs. As the postcolonial theorist Fanon explains, "systems of compartments" that isolate and segregate populations express a violence of their own. It is by drawing attention to these divisions that we can "reveal the lines of force" that are actually required to sustain such compartments (Fanon 1963: 37–38).

Such fragmented support systems resemble an "intricate system of bureaus in which no men, neither one nor the best, neither the few nor the many, can be held responsible, and which could be properly called rule by Nobody" (Arendt 1970: 38). A compartmentalized system consists of never-ending wait lists, assessing, ranking — only to place the assessed person on yet another wait list. Such compartmentalization is systemic violence that slowly but surely erodes people's resources and their capacity to be resilient. In this situation, a person may begin to feel faced with a dead-end, with "no one left who could even be asked to answer for what is being done" (Arendt 1970: 38). This is precisely the invisible and objective violence conjured up by Zizek (2008).

Here we are reminded of the staff at the *House of Horrors* who propose outings (such as shopping) as a matter of routine rather than responding to or supporting the interests of residents. Staff are likely following proper group-home protocol, as laid out by upper management. On these frontlines of service provision, frustrated residents are denied access to anyone with decision-making power, and their criticism can be deflected and more easily ignored.

Death by Numbers, another short film by the Self-Advocacy Federation, is further illustrative of the systemic violence that is built into the use of labels and standard bureaucratic sorting exercises. In one scene, Marjorie goes to an agency in search of housing and employment supports. The worker, referring to her assessment, tells Marjorie, "It says here that you have an IQ of 71. That's one point off our cut-off." Marjorie insists that she needs some support. The worker suggests that there might be another way. She sifts through Marjorie's file, adds some numbers up, and announces: "The numbers tell me you're a seven." "Is that a good thing?" Marjorie asks. "It depends on how you look at it ... well, uh…" The worker yells out into the hallway to another employee, "Hey Sheila! We've got a seven here!" At this point Marjorie is losing her patience: "This is ridiculous! What is this? Michener?" The worker responds threateningly, "Now don't rock the boat or we'll put you down to a four!" This short film is the most telling of structural violence. It illustrates the oppressive social arrangements enacted through routine acts of bureaucratized social work practice.

Creating Crises and Managing Risks

Within the current services system, "risk" is a flexible term that can be applied to any context that involves any level of interaction between people with disabilities and those whose decision-making power is granted greater authority and legitimacy.

In group homes there is a deep tension between the risk management aims of the many agencies and private companies that shape government-funded housing and support industries on the one hand, and on the other, clients' needs for dignified support and autonomy. Petner-Arrey and Copeland (2014) argue that liability issues related to the protection of service providers and their economies are important factors that limit the ability of front-line staff to deliver flexible, individualized, and more appropriate forms of support. It is thus very easy to invoke "liability reasons" to justify violence. Disruptions to the cost of doing business and to the scheduled hours of work constitute risks often seen as requiring managing. Social service systems appear to be struggling to account for the very existence of people with real or perceived differences — such as people labelled with intellectual disabilities — whose ways of being are characterized as disruptive and treated as inconvenient or threatening. The statistical and monitoring tactics that are used to capture the size, age, and other characteristics of people labelled with intellectual disabilities are quite telling in this regard. It is not uncommon for government data to include references to people with intellectual disabilities living longer and thereby creating a crisis for the system. These explanations may begin with the causal statement, "because these people are living longer than they used to..." (Canada Mortgage and Housing Corporation 2006). Variations on this statement include the following: "Like the broader population, many people with developmental disabilities are living longer. At the same time ... this population tends to age more rapidly than the broader population" (Select Committee on Developmental Services 2014). In this view, the crisis is caused by people exceeding their expected lifespan. There are eugenic undertones to the suggestion that the individual is guilty of subverting nature and outliving the predictions of medical experts through the use of new medical technologies and other developments. The life expectancies of non-disabled individuals can be expected to interact with social environmental changes, including technological ones; however, when people labelled with intellectual disabilities benefit from such changes, they are singled out as creating a crisis through their very existence. The social services system simultaneously presents itself as a victim of these unexpected demographic changes, and as a hero seeking to minimize the unsettling social effects of the "crisis," using this position to absolve itself of responsibility for its unresponsiveness and for its role in creating the crisis in the first place.

Containing Sexuality

Related to concerns around lifespan is sexual reproduction among women labelled with intellectual disabilities. Protective or "best interest" arguments used to regulate the sexuality of women with these labels are based on prejudicial views that these people have only a limited understanding of their own sexual actions. Women living in institutionalized settings risk having their sexual preferences denied, and those under guardianship may undergo forced or coerced sterilization (see Dyck 2013; Malacrida 2015). Some women may be encouraged or forced to "consent" to sterilization by family members, a situation comparable to the treatment of women who are confined in total institutions and forcibly sterilized to minimize the detectability of their sexual exploitation (and, supposedly, to spare them the experience of pregnancy-by-rape) (see Ghosh 2015). As the link between sterilization and pregnancy demonstrates, a paternalistic logic that pretends to support the best interests of women with disabilities through such measures as preventing pregnancy and hiding one possible outcome of rape can readily support violent outcomes.

Mother Dearest, a film by the Self-Advocacy Federation, parodies the relationship between a mother and her disabled daughter. In the video, "mother dearest" tries to put a bib on her adult daughter, an effort to which she forcefully responds: "What the fuck Mom?!" The daughter, at age 30, resists her mother's infantilizing actions and succeeds in convincing her to allow her to date men. The daughter then announces that her boyfriend will be by at eight and asks if she can borrow ten bucks. Her mother asks, "For what?" and she answers, "Condoms and lube!" The scene ends with a shot of the mother gasping. As funny as this short film may be, the daughter's suggestion that maybe her mother would prefer she learn witchcraft and become a lesbian is disappointing. Here we see a hierarchy of sexual orientation clearly suggesting that lesbian relationships are deviant. This unfortunate comment reminds us that disability advocacy has to be aware of other categories of exclusion, while being attentive to how messages that empower one group may do so by inadvertently marginalizing others within the movement (that is, the many lesbian women who are also people with disabilities).

The exchange depicted in *Mother Dearest* is an example of successful self-advocacy. In real life, conversations by women labelled with intellectual disabilities concerning their right to have sex would not wrap up so neatly. By focusing our attention on structural violence, the film highlights acts of disempowerment that happen on a daily basis and that may otherwise fall under the radar. From a deficit point of view, people who have been labelled with intellectual disabilities are seen as inherently incompetent. Following this logic, these people do not make good decisions, and it is in their own interest that non-labelled people make these decisions on their behalf. Abuse of power in this context is more difficult to identify since it is assumed that the non-labelled staff person or parent knows better and is working in the person's best interest. Despite these "well-intentioned" assumptions, threats are commonplace: "Do you want your coffee this morning? Then go have your shower!" or "Stop using that language or you won't be going to the movies tonight." Home sharers may warn women who don't have a key to their own home that "If you get home after 9 p.m., the door will be locked." The absence of equality, on a moment-to-moment basis, may give us reason to pause and consider whose best interests are really being served.

Equality: Undoing the "Unconscious Terrain of Habits"

Over-medication, the denial of decision-making authority, segregation, poverty, and other control tactics — all manifestations of structural violence — are easily normalized and made invisible through their structural embeddedness. The belief that certain forms of difference — or perceived difference — are dangerous or risky facilitates maintaining social arrangements that are, in fact, violent. Issues are neutralized as funding problems and presented by government service agencies as unfortunate, rather than intended, outcomes. In official discourses, harmful effects are linked to supposedly uncontrollable issues of "system capacity" rather than to structural forms of violence that can and must be exposed and challenged. It is important to counter this glossing over of the issue by highlighting the deliberate, calculated nature of the impoverishment and degradation of people labelled with intellectual disabilities, as many disability activists have done. The forceful ways in which labelled women are pushed into poverty, and for the most part kept there, can be productively analyzed as a form of violence that deliberately structures the conditions that threaten the very material survival of these women.

The real risks, as we have discussed and illustrated through stories by women labelled with intellectual disabilities, are the violent interactions and conditions that are structured through faulty support systems. Fostering security, by contrast, requires meeting people's individualized needs. We have noticed that when a person's needs are viewed as being high, they are more likely to go unmet; as well, their income is often lower and their exposure to violence is much higher. Unfortunately, these conditions are not unique to people labelled with intellectual disabilities. Dominant models of delivering disability supports are characterized by inflexible management techniques, which cut across many impairment classifications (see Chouinard and Crooks 2005). The failure to provide dignified, individualized support, rather than containment, is an issue particularly concerning to people labelled with intellectual disabilities, who often do not hold the keys to their own homes and whose legal capacity is easily challenged. Policies based on a deficit approach normalize segregation, foster impoverishment, and contribute to the social invisibility of people with these labels. As a result, dominant social norms remain unchallenged and make many of the forms of disability violence mentioned in this paper permissible.

At this point, it is clear to many labelled people and their allies that harmful assumptions about intellectual disabilities do not automatically disappear with the closure of major institutions, and that only continuous collective and conscious effort will destabilize the "unconscious terrain of habits" where deficit-based understandings of intellectual disability have deep roots. To combat these practices, we must continue to keep our focus on local and personal experiences and, as Zizek (2008: 143) suggests, "dare to disturb the underground of the unspoken underpinnings of our everyday lives." In the case of women labelled with an intellectual disability, this means examining our beliefs about competence, intelligence, vulnerability, and equality. As we fight for long-term structural change, we may want to pay attention to French philosopher Jacques Rancière's conceptualization of equality. Rancière proposes that equality is something like a principle and a practice (Mediapart 2013). It is a presupposition. In other words, we begin from a presupposition of equality. We begin from the idea that there is a power of thought that is equal. This method of equality is something that we can practice and negotiate on a moment-by-moment basis in our everyday interactions. As academics and activists, we realize that equality is not something we can sacrifice now in the hopes of achieving later.

References

ARCH Disability Law Centre. 2014. *Decisions, Decisions: Promoting and Protecting the Rights of Persons with Disabilities Who Are Subject to Guardianship*. Prepared for the Law Commission of Ontario's Project on Legal Capacity, Decision-Making and Guardianship. <lco-cdo.org/en/capacity-guardianship-commissioned-paper-arch>.

ARCH Disability Law Centre, Respecting Rights Committee. 2016. "It's Your Money." <https://youtu.be/GsfNmXSMzfk>.

____. 2016. "It's Your Life." <https://youtu.be/29CoAreZc2A>.

Arendt, H. 1970. *On Violence*. New York: Harcourt Brace.

Association for Community Living-Manitoba. 2010. "When Bad Things Happen to Women with Disabilities." In Diane Driedger (ed.), *Living the Edges: A Disabled Women's Reader*. Toronto: Inanna Publications & Education.

Barken, R. 2013. "A Place to Call Home: Intellectual Disabilities and Residential Services in Nova Scotia." *Canadian Journal of Disability Studies*, 2, 1.

Canada Mortgage and Housing Corporation. 2006. *Research Highlights: Housing for Adults with Intellectual Disabilities*. <cmhc-schl.gc.ca/en/inpr/rehi/rehi_018.cfm>.

Chouinard, V., and V. Crooks. 2005. "'Because They Have All the Power and I Have None': State Restructuring of Income and Employment Supports and Disabled Women's Lives in Ontario, Canada." *Disability & Society*, 20, 1.

Dyck, E. 2013. *Facing Eugenics: Reproduction, Sterilization, and the Politics of Choice*. Toronto: University of Toronto Press.

Fanon, F. 1963. *The Wretched of the Earth: The Handbook for the Black Revolution That Is Changing the Shape of the World*. New York: Grove Press.

Farmer, P., B. Nizeye, S. Stulac, and S. Keshavjee. 2006. "Structural Violence and Clinical Medicine." PLOS *Medicine*, 3,10.

Ghosh, N. 2015. "Sites of Oppression: Dominant Ideologies and Women with Disabilities in India." In T. Shakespeare (ed.), *Disability Research Today: International Perspectives*. Abingdon, Oxon: Routledge Press

Gould, S.J. 1981. *The Mismeasure of Man*. New York: Norton and Company.

Hansen, C.A., A.G. Barnett and G. Pritchard. 2008. "The Effect of Ambient Air Pollution during Early Pregnancy on Fetal Ultrasonic Measurements during Mid-Pregnancy." *Environ Health Perspect*, 1, 16.

Joffe, K. 2010. *Enforcing the Rights of People with Disabilities in Ontario's Developmental Services System*. Toronto: Law Commission of Ontario.

Lunsky, Y., J.E. Klein-Geltink, and E.A. Yates. 2013. *Atlas on the Primary Care of Adults with Developmental Disabilities in Ontario*. Toronto: Institute for Clinical Evaluative Sciences.

Mackenzie, C. 2014. "The Importance of Relational Autonomy and the Capabilities for an Ethics of Vulnerability." In C. Mackenzie, W. Rogers, and S. Dodds (eds.), *Vulnerability: New Essays in Ethics and Feminist Philosophy*. New York: Oxford University Press.

Malacrida, C. 2015. *A Special Hell: Institutional Life in Alberta's Eugenic Years*. Toronto: University of Toronto Press.

McLaren, A. 1990. *Our Own Master Race: Eugenics in Canada, 1885–1945*. Toronto: McClelland and Stewart.

Mitra, S. 2006. "The Capability Approach and Disability." *Journal of Disability Policy Studies*, 16, 4.

People First Nova Scotia. 2014. *People First King County Report*.

Petner-Arrey, J. and S. Copeland. 2014. "You Have to Care: Perceptions of Promoting Autonomy in Support Settings for Adults with Intellectual Disabilities." *British Journal of Learning Disabilities*, 43, 1.

Report of the Office of the U.N. High Commissioner for Human Rights. 2012. *Thematic Study on the Issue of Violence against Women and Girls with Disabilities*. <2.ohchr.org/english/issues/women/docs/A.HRC.20.5.pdf>.

Rose, N. 2007. *The Politics of Life Itself: Biomedicine, Power, and Subjectivity in the Twenty-First Century*. Princeton, NJ: Princeton University Press.

Russell, M. 1998. *Beyond Ramps: Disability at the End of the Social Contract*. Monroe, ME: Common Courage Press.

Select Committee on Developmental Services. 2014. "Interim Report." <ontla.on.ca/committee-proceedings/committee reports/files_html/INTERIMREPORTENG-Final.htm>.

Series, L. 2015. "Mental Capacity and the Control of Sexuality of People with Intellectual Disabilities in England and Wales." In T. Shakespeare (ed.), *Disability Research Today: International Perspectives*. Abingdon, Oxon: Routledge Press.

Statistics Canada. 2012. *Canadian Survey on Disability 2012*. <statcan.gc.ca/pub/89-654-x/89-654-x2015001-eng.htm>.

Stephen, J. 2007. *Pick One Intelligent Girl: Employability, Domesticity, and the Gendering of Canada's Welfare State*. Toronto: University of Toronto Press.

Stone-Mediatore, S. 2003. *Reading across Borders: Storytelling and Knowledges of Resistance*. New York: Paul Grave-MacMillan.

Walmsley, J., and K. Johnson. 2003. *Inclusive Research with People with Learning Disabilities: Past, Present and Futures*. London: Jessica Kingsley Publishers.

Wolfensberger, W. 1972. *The Principle of Normalization in Human Services*. Toronto: National Institute on Mental Retardation.

Worth, P. n.d. *People First of Canada.* <http://www.peoplefirstofcanada.ca/>.

Zizek, S. 2008. *Violence: Six Sideways Reflections.* New York: Picador.

Videos

Alberta Union. 2013. *Michener Centre: Evicting Our Most Vulnerable.* <youtube.com/watch?v=xbzeiQjbhYk>.

Mediapart. 2013. *Jacques Rancière invité de "En direct de Mediapart."* <youtube.com/watch?v=oBE_8yTQuLE>.

National Film Board of Canada. 2008a. *Diane Nabess.* <youtube.com/watch?v=TfyLkFOyj0A>.

___. 2008b. *Patricia Endall.* <youtube.com/watch?v=yKKUWCIqW4Y>.

___. 2008c. *Roberta Ann Silverson.* <youtube.com/watch?v=3pLfBb7bYas>.

___. 2008d. *Valerie Wolbert.* <youtube.com/watch?v=F4beGapo6zM>.

People First of Canada. 2008. *The Freedom Tour.* DVD.

Self-Advocacy Federation. 2017. *Death by Numbers.* <youtube.com/watch?v=X30wUGM7CLs>.

___. 2015a. *House of Horrors.* <youtube.com/watch?v=6FNR2RYgaBw>.

___. 2015b. *Mother Dearest.* <youtube.com/watch?v=K7jQRJTnaR4>.

Chapter 6

A Crisis of Poverty
Economic Disparities,
Disabled Women, and Abuse

Linda DeRiviere

Intimate partner violence (IPV) is a critical social and public health problem with many facets. Among the least explored of these is how it contributes to women's vulnerability to living in poverty. The Healing Journey study sought to address a gap in Canadian research on this topic. This seven-wave longitudinal study, coordinated by RESOLVE, a family violence research centre, was a collaboration of university and community partners in Manitoba, Saskatchewan, and Alberta. This study reveals certain individual and institutional characteristics that cause the incomes and employment prospects of abused women to be lower and more restricted. It also examines a less obvious obstacle to economic equality: the effect that IPV has on women's chronic health conditions and/or disabilities and particularly on how they interact with employment challenges.

Drawing upon some key themes in the study's results, I identify and analyze some of the main factors contributing to the economic disadvantage faced by women who participated in the workforce and to high instances of poverty, particularly among women with health issues and disabilities who have left an abusive relationship. Abused women often attribute their absence in the workforce to chronic health conditions and/or disabilities. In addition, there is a crisis in the relationship between younger abused women and the labour market. Within this context, the probability is that these women — especially those who reported chronic health conditions and/or disabilities — will experience a lifetime of poverty.

The role of IPV in women's health issues and disabilities has important policy implications, as this group of women has a high likelihood of being most affected by provincial labour market and welfare policies. A significant number of women in the Healing Journey study reported long absences from the workforce due to their health problems, and some experienced circumstances so severe that they will never be able to participate in employment again. For these women, the inability to be employed will likely result in a fragile economic position and increased reliance on government income supports, such as income assistance and social housing. Although this chapter will focus on the study's findings, they are corroborated by previous research (see DeRiviere 2014 for a comprehensive review of earlier studies).

The Healing Journey Study

A tri-provincial Canadian study titled *The Healing Journey: A Longitudinal Study of Women Who Have Been Abused by Intimate Partners* examined the participants' experiences of abuse, physical and mental health issues, and parenting issues, as well as support and service utilization. Trained interviewers administered questionnaires on a bi-annual schedule over 3.5 years from 2006 to 2009. The baseline interviews in Wave 1 included 665 women who were affected by IPV. Following a 37 percent attrition rate over the first five waves, 419 women remained in the study by Wave 6, of which 414 agreed to participate in a labour market study. The participants were recruited from Manitoba, Saskatchewan, and Alberta, with approximately 45.7 percent self-identifying as Indigenous Canadians. In addition, 4.6 percent of respondents were visible minorities, while another 3.9 percent were immigrants; three participants fell into both categories.

The longitudinal study had a prospective component in that women were recruited and then followed forward in time throughout the course of their healing journey. The labour market questionnaire supplemented the study with retrospective elements, in the sense that information was gathered on issues of interest that had occurred prior to the interviews. Labour market variables, such as employment and training, covered a period of at least five years from 2005 to 2009. The purpose of the labour market research was to learn about the trajectories of employment, earnings, and training outcomes throughout the healing journey of abused women, including women who had health problems and disabilities.

While there are numerous correlations between two or more variables (for example, employment rate and health/disability status), this does not necessarily imply a cause-and-effect relationship — that is, that one variable caused a change in the other. As with most social problems, the causal pathways are complex and circular. The advantage of the quantitative analysis is that comparatively larger samples and statistical procedures can be used to help better describe some of the patterns between and among the key factors that affect women's lives. The strength of a qualitative analysis is its ability to clarify these causal pathways. Nevertheless, any conclusions drawn from the empirical analyses in this chapter are generally corroborated by other studies and research on IPV and women's labour market outcomes.

The data used for the analyses were based on participants' perceptions of their physical and mental health status. The participants were asked for information about any physical or mental health conditions that affected their ability to function on a day-to-day basis, including the ability to hold down a job. These self-rated conditions included physical restrictions, sensory impairments, intellectual or mental health issues, and emotional disabilities. Whether their health conditions were permanent or transitory in nature, it was evident that the majority of women experienced chronic physical and mental health conditions, as well as permanent disabilities.

A detailed list of the participants' physical and mental health issues and disabilities is provided as Tables 6-A1 and 6-A2 at the end of the chapter. Some reported conditions may be misclassified, as the various categories of health afflictions may overlap. For instance, mental health issues may manifest themselves physically in the form of chronic back pain, headaches, sleeping disturbances, obesity, and eating disorders. In addition, the symptoms of post-traumatic stress disorder may overlap with depressive symptoms, and substance abuse may be a side effect of post-traumatic stress disorder.

All study participants had experienced physical violence in one or more intimate relationships over their adult lives, and 78 percent had experienced one or more types of childhood abuse. There was considerable overlap in the various forms of abuse reported by women (physical, sexual, financial, psychological, verbal, and so forth), and thus it was impossible to break down some of their health histories by types of abuse prior to the baseline interview. Even though the majority of women were physically separated from their abusers, the longitudinal study gathered data on current abuse, such as emotional or verbal abuse (40.1 percent) or physical violence (20.8 percent) by a new or former partner. Physical abuse after Wave 1 was frequently the result of the revolving door pattern of a woman separating from her partner and returning, often multiple times.

Health Status and Abused Women's Vulnerability for Poverty

In the Healing Journey's labour market study, we found that 52.2 percent of participants' household incomes were below Statistics Canada's low income cut-offs (LICOS), an income threshold below which a family will spend a higher-than-average share of its income on the basic necessities of life such as food and shelter (Statistics Canada 2010). To understand abused women's poverty is also to recognize that chronic health issues and disabilities are a mediating factor in the relationship between abuse and women's employment. In the labour market study, 78.7 percent of participants (326 of 414) reported a disability, long-term illness, or chronic health condition in at least one of the seven waves (Indigenous, 79.9 percent; visible minority, 84.2 percent; immigrant, 68.8 percent).

Approximately 39 percent of these participants (127 of 326) disclosed that a health condition affected their employment situation. For example, health conditions prevented some women from working more hours (29.9 percent of 127 women), while others were able to work only rarely or not at all (70.1 percent of 127 women). Chronic pain, post-traumatic stress, and depressive symptoms are well known to limit full workforce participation whether or not the abusive relationship remains intact (Dutton 2009; Kimerling et al. 2009; Smith, Schnurr and Rosenheck 2005; Chandler et al. 2005; Riger and Staggs 2004). It should be noted that, in the baseline interview, 56.3 percent of participants (Indigenous, 64.7 percent) attributed their health condition to past or current IPV. Since many women had left their abusive partner, the results suggest that chronic health conditions persisted even after the abuse ended.

Contrary to our expectations, 170 of 326 participants (52.1 percent) who reported a disability, long-term illness, or chronic health condition were employed, the majority on a full-time basis (128 of 170, 75.3 percent), even though they identified physical or psychological health problems such as mobility issues and chronic pain, severe depression, and post-traumatic stress symptoms. The data raise the issue as to whether economic necessity forced women into employment even though they were troubled with the serious after-effects of IPV, including trauma-related mental health conditions. In addition, we found no evidence that the length of time a woman had been in a current or previous abusive relationship had a bearing on her employment or health outcomes.

For women who had some connection to the workforce and experienced chronic health issues and/or disabilities, employment was frequently a temporary or intermittent experience irrespective of age (26.9 percent of the non-retired sample, n=402). One possible explanation for this is that the labour market has certain characteristics that do not favour individuals with multiple obstacles to employment or those who do not establish their vocational choices in a traditional way (for example, they experienced long absences from education/training programs or the workforce). This was the plight of many women in the Healing Journey study.

As shown in Table 6-1, a combination of certain characteristics helped to explain some women's low incomes and the reasons for their restricted employment opportunities. This, combined with stressors such as the fast-paced and competitive nature of the contemporary workplace, is likely to cause some physical and mental health conditions to flare up (such as depression, anxiety, and arthritis). One woman expressed concerns about her difficulties in finding an employer that would accommodate her disabilities, which suggests that employers are not always supportive.

In fact, a disconnection from the workforce could lead to more "dangerous dependencies" (Scott, London, and Myers 2002: 892), as some women, because of their limited finances, will return to an abuser or begin another abusive relationship with a new partner. Other women may join the sex trade and/or other informal labour market activities (such as selling goods or services for under-the-table cash) in order to obtain money to feed themselves and their families. The threat of dire poverty is a strong inducement to enter and remain in the workforce, but ongoing health problems may contribute to a pattern of discontinuous participation.

Table 6-1: Participant Characteristics (or Lack Thereof) that Caused Vulnerabilities for Poverty

	(1)	(2)	(3)	(4)
	No disabilities and/ or chronic health conditions		At least one physical/ mental health issue or disability	
Labour market characteristics, as of Wave 6	Works full or part time n=63	Not in the workforce n=25	Not in the workforce n=156	Works full or part time n=170
Years of full-time equivalent experience	14.0	5.3$^\alpha$	9.7$^\alpha$	14.1
Employed full or part time from 2005–09	41 (65.1%)	0	0	78 (45.9%)
Intermittent employment from 2005–09 (a)	22 (34.9%)	6 (24.0%)	76 (48.5%)	92 (54.1%)
Not in the workforce from 2005–09	-	19 (76.0%) (b)	80 (51.5%)	-
Multiple obstacles to employment (c)	2 (3.2%)	5 (20.0%)*	45 (28.8%)$^\alpha$	22 (12.9%)*
Training after Wave 1:				
College or trade school	24 (38.1%)	6 (24.0%)	33 (23.4%)	57 (35.2%)
University training	25 (39.7%)	4 (16.0%)$^\alpha$	16 (11.4%)$^\alpha$	58 (35.8%)
Education, as of Wave 6:				
Grade 11 or lower	5 (7.9%)	12 (48.0%)$^\alpha$	84 (53.8%)$^\alpha$	21 (12.4%)
Grade 12 or GED	9 (14.3%)	5 (20.0%)	25 (16.0%)	31 (18.2%)
College or trade school	22 (34.9%)	4 (16.0%)$^\alpha$	29 (18.6%)$^\alpha$	60 (35.3%)
University	27 (42.9%)	4 (16.0%)$^\alpha$	18 (11.5%)$^\alpha$	58 (34.1%)
Social assistance in Wave 6	2 (3.2%)	17 (68.0%)$^\alpha$	113 (72.4%)$^\alpha$	34 (20.0%)*
Social assistance in Waves 1 and 6	2 (3.2%)	16 (64.0%)$^\alpha$	101 (64.7%)$^\alpha$	24 (14.1%)*

* Statistically different from the estimate in Column 1.

α Statistically different from the estimates in Column 1 and 4.

(a) Employed full or part time or casually some years and not in the labour force other years.

(b) 68 percent of these women were young (average age 28.2) and lone parents, and all but one woman accessed social assistance in both Waves 1 and 6. Forty percent were Indigenous women.

(c) The participant disclosed at least two obstacles that prevented employment, such as disabilities, no jobs in their community, or ongoing abuse. Indigenous estimates for the multiple obstacles variable were not statistically different at 4.5 percent, 25.0 percent, 33.3 percent, and 15.3 percent, respectively.

Thus, a common theme in women's experience of poverty was the high rate of intermittent employment and/or non-participation for participants who confronted the double challenge of dealing with health issues and past or current IPV. As shown in Table 6-1, irrespective of health or disability considerations, the women who worked full time or part time (Columns 1 and 4) had more years of full-time experience and a higher level of formal education, including university and college, than women who were not participating in the workforce. Experience and education are, of course, highly valued attributes in the workplace. However, these same two groups of employed women were not necessarily similar in their patterns of continuous participation. As indicated by the intermittent employment variable, a higher proportion of employed women with disabilities or chronic health conditions (Column 4) experienced discontinuities in their paid work (54.1 percent) and faced multiple obstacles to employment (12.9 percent) compared to employed women with no reported health issues (Column 1, 34.9 percent and 3.2 percent, respectively). Employed women with disabilities (Column 4) were also more likely to supplement their earnings with social assistance than were employed women with no reported health issues (Column 1).

A significant proportion of women who were not in the workforce in Wave 6 (Columns 2 and 3) had experienced intermittent employment from 2005–09, irrespective of health or disability issues. However, the majority of these women were not engaged in the labour force over this five-year period. Likewise, fewer of these women had attended college or university, and approximately half had not completed a high school diploma. The women without disabilities or health conditions (Column 2) were likely to be young and lone parents, and approximately two-thirds accessed social assistance in both Waves 1 and 6. Their main obstacles to employment were highly related to parenting responsibilities, low levels of education, and lack of skills training. A minority of women in this group were full-time students, and a few other women reported no income sources but were being financially supported by an intimate partner or relatives.

Moreover, compared to an individual's personal or human capital attributes, workplace characteristics are at least as important a determinant of pay and benefits. Just over one-third of employed study participants with disabilities and/or chronic health conditions (Column 4) were covered under a collective agreement. Unionized employment is important because unions are more inclined to be attentive to women's issues, as well as to promote workplace accommodations for people with disabilities. Approximately 42 percent of employed women with a chronic health condition or disability had no medical benefits at work. This was partly explained by the fact that 38.6 percent of participants were employed in smaller organizations (twenty or fewer employees) that did not offer medical benefits. Moreover, many women were not employed by a large enough organization to qualify for an employer-sponsored medical benefits plan, including sick leave. This may partly explain the circular nature of their intermittent work patterns, since women who must leave work for health reasons are more likely to find subsequent employment in the peripheral workforce, which tends to offer few employee benefits. Some participants worked for larger organizations (more than one hundred workers), but these were frequently call centres or private companies in highly competitive industries (such as retail services) and jobs in the voluntary sector (such as community services). In these types of organizations, employee benefits and unionization would be a relatively rare occurrence.

Health Issues and Disabilities and the Workforce

When asked for the main reason why they were not in a paid job and not looking for work, ninety-seven women indicated that they were not engaged in the workforce due to a physical or mental health illness or a disability. Figures 6-1 and 6-2 show an age breakdown into two categories for ninety-two out of ninety-seven women who provided some information about their health and disability issues in the first six waves of the longitudinal study. The women in Table 6-1, Column 3 could be classified as women with disabilities or chronic health conditions and in the labour force. In the combined age groups, just over half of participants (52.2 percent) attributed their health issues to IPV or childhood abuse or a combination of both. Though sample sizes were small, all visible minority and immigrant women included in Figures 6-1 and 6-2 disclosed that they had depression as a health issue, and they also reported an average of 4.2 physical and mental health issues, which may help to explain their absence in the workforce.

As shown in Figure 6-1, a higher percentage of women over age 35 in most categories of mental health issues provided evidence that mental health issues may become exacerbated as women age. A higher proportion of women aged 35 and under confronted addictions over their healing journey (60.9 percent). These figures, while hinting at the role that substance abuse problems play in contributing to their poverty, must also be seen in light of the fact that the vast majority were young women in their prime years, when they would normally be forming an attachment to the workforce, and thus improving their chances for economic independence.

Though not shown in Figure 6-1, we also found that approximately half the younger women who were dealing with addictions experienced physical abuse over the course of the study, compared to fewer than 30 percent of the younger group of women with no reported addiction issues (and similar results for emotional abuse after Wave 1). Their harmful behaviours may be a response to the stress of ongoing abuse.

Although the above is primarily quantitative, there is an advantage to qualitative data, in that it captures the participants' stories about their experiences of abuse; that is, the stories give some depth to the actual experiences. For instance, life for many women was difficult, and some expressed disappointment in not having achieved their occupational and educational goals due to addictions, chronic exhaustion, and other severe disabilities. Older women were at a point of particularly low resilience in

Figure 6-1 Mental Health Issues as a Reason for Non-Participation in the Workforce, n (%)

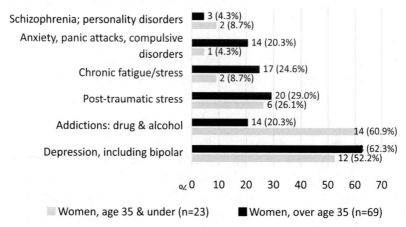

Women, age 35 & under (n=23)   Women, over age 35 (n=69)

which their coping skills were so poor that the slightest changes in their lives became major sources of stress. For example, with regards to her employment and educational aspirations, one participant reflected, "[I am] too burnt out from the violence and memories and stress — could not deal with it all." Their sense of chronic fatigue and stress was not surprising given the overwhelmingly high proportion of low-income and lone-parent women. Moreover, 31.6 percent of women over age 35 who were physically abused over the study period reported chronic fatigue, compared to 17.7 percent of women not physically abused during this time. Though not statistically different, the comparable rates for emotional abuse were 25.6 percent and 16.5 percent respectively.

In addition to their health challenges, many women were also dealing with multiple barriers to participating fully in economic life (see Table 6-1). One participant reflected on these issues: "[I have] problems, many small and big ones [such as] transportation, housing, a safe and stable living environment, my health — I have diabetes and schizophrenia."

These barriers should also be viewed within the context of the modern-day workforce where workers with a high degree of competitive skills and a strong attachment to their employment have a distinct advantage. It takes extensive investments to acquire the skills, work experience, and on-the-job training required to secure employment that pays a living wage. Furthermore, one must be able to incur high personal costs (such as substantive time and financial commitments), which is simply not possible for many women, especially those who are dealing with abuse and health challenges such as chronic pain, cancer, hepatitis, HIV, and other illnesses. Predictably, attaining adequate education or vocational training was a relatively rare event for study participants with chronic health conditions and/or disabilities. For many of these women, there were few options apart from dead-end jobs, which led to a discontinuous pattern in workforce participation. Furthermore, when women attempted to pursue vocational or educational training in the past, they frequently dealt with the multiple disadvantages of having their efforts sabotaged by a controlling abuser (60.9 percent of participants), juggling the dual demands of work and child rearing, and tending to personal health issues, which all played a role in interrupting these investments. The effects of such difficulties may have also been exacerbated by institutional factors: for example, a lack of safe and secure housing, transportation, and affordable childcare.

Other women revealed that they had low self-esteem and frequently experienced self-doubt. For instance, Indigenous women are often mistreated in the domestic and public spheres. With a history of cultural loss and cumulative trauma, family breakdown, and violence, many Indigenous women said they lacked the confidence to pursue their goals. Consequently, few of these women moved from income assistance to paid work between Waves 1 and 6.

In most categories of physical health issues in Figure 6-2, older women had physical health problems associated with aging, such as high blood pressure and cholesterol, heart conditions, arthritis, and diseases of the lungs. As women with health difficulties aged, their employment numbers dropped off substantially compared to women without health conditions or disabilities (age group 45–64: a drop from 94 percent to 51 percent). Older women typically gave accounts of chronic pain from physical injuries and/or unhealed broken bones. When asked about achieving her

Figure 6-2 Physical Health Issues Given as a Reason for Non-Participation in the Workforce, n (%)

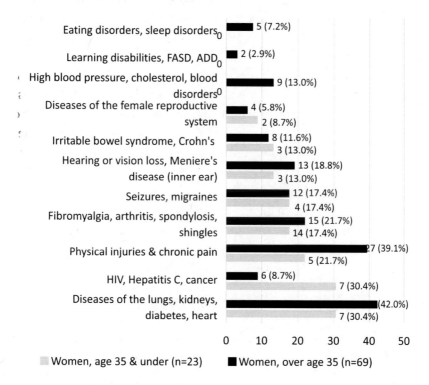

educational and occupational goals, one woman reflected on the physical health challenges that kept her out of the workforce: "So many broken bones ... collar bone never healed properly."

Abuse-related physical disabilities prevented another woman from realizing her dream of becoming a police officer. For yet another participant, who had aspired to become a nurse, experiences of physical abuse resulted in chronic back pain that limited her capacity to perform the tasks that the job required. Several other women stated that years of both physical and mental abuse had taken their toll and that they were simply not capable of working in a paid job. Some younger women were afflicted with serious illnesses, such as hepatitis C, HIV, or cervical cancer, that reduced their capacity to make personal investments in vocational skills training and in other poverty-alleviating attributes (such as the attributes listed in Table 6-1).

One woman had simply lost her passion and ability to allow herself to dream big because, as she remarked, "it's too dangerous to hope too much — dreams get taken away from you." The participants' narratives in the qualitative aspects of the study highlighted the fact that health issues and disabilities eventually erode an abused woman's coping processes. Whatever the exact reasons for these findings, the result was an intensification of poverty.

Finally, in examining the types of health issues and disabilities (listed in Tables 6-A1 and 6-A2) in women who disclosed physical and emotional abuse after Wave 1, there were no significant differences in the nature of health issues between abused and non-abused women, with the exception of a higher rate of addictions in women aged 35 and under, and similarly with chronic fatigue in women over age 35. It should also be noted that, in Wave 6, 82.6 percent of younger women and 60.9 percent of women over age 35 represented in Figures 6-1 and 6-2 accessed income assistance. When not engaged in the workforce, the study participants likely had no choice but to rely on income assistance. This is the topic of the next section.

Intimate Partner Violence, Disabilities, and the Depth of Poverty

Participating in the workforce is the primary method through which the majority of the working-age population in Canada obtains income and improves their potential for individual economic independence, though these outcomes are not necessarily guaranteed. For instance, employed women in the Healing Journey study were, on the whole, poorly paid workers, while those who lacked employment were virtually assured a life of poverty. In estimating the depth of poverty, Table 6-2 tells an important story of the desperate economic situation of women who have experienced IPV. Women who cited disabilities and chronic health conditions as the main reasons for their absence in the workforce were among the poorest of all study participants.

The poverty index is a more meaningful calculation than absolute wage levels or earnings and income sources, because the calculation considers household composition (size of the family unit) and community size (urban/rural area). The index is estimated by dividing total income sources by the poverty line for a similarly composed household. The calculation was based on Statistics Canada's LICO estimates (Statistics Canada 2010). A poverty index of 1.0 means that the individual's income sources situate their household at the poverty line. An index below 1.0 places the household below the poverty line, and an index above 1.0 means that household income is above the poverty line.

Irrespective of employment status, we found no significant differences in the depth of poverty between the ninety-two women with one or more of the conditions listed in Figures 6-1 and 6-2, and women without reported health issues. A similar result was found for women who disclosed multiple health issues. However, a deeper analysis showed that the depth of poverty was frequently related to the severity of the physical or mental health condition or disability. For instance, though sample sizes were frequently small, women with heart or lung diseases (chronic obstructive pulmonary disease, emphysema), advanced diabetes, or severe back or joint problems, or who were HIV positive, had contracted hepatitis C, or had a personality disorder or schizophrenia, generally had household incomes that were at least 50 percent below the poverty line.

For the entire sample (n=414), once household composition was taken

Table 6-2: The Depth of Poverty of Abused Women, by Personal and Labour Market Characteristics, and by Status of Disability and/or Chronic Health Conditions, n (poverty index)

Categories	Total Sample	Poverty Index	
		Non-Indigenous	Indigenous
Total sample	414 (1.10)	225 (1.22)	189 (.95)*
Personal characteristics:			
Immigrant	16 (1.02)		
Visible minority	19 (.98)		
Lone parents	178 (1.19)	97 (1.32)	81 (1.02)*
Women with multiple health issues	231 (1.02)	122 (1.16)	109 (.86)*
Labour market characteristics:			
Women with an intermittent employment history	108 (1.02)	54 (1.0)	54 (1.04)
Women who gave health issues and disabilities as the *main* reason for their non-participation in the workforce (participants in Figures 6-1 and 6-2):			
Age 35 and under	24 (.68)	11 (.93)	13 (.46)
Over age 35	73 (.74)	37 (.77)	36 (.71)
Women with no health conditions or disabilities:			
In the workforce on a full- or-part-time basis	63 (1.55)	41 (1.56)	22 (1.53)
Not in the workforce (a)	25 (.69)	9 (.68)	16 (.70)
Women with health conditions or disabilities:			
In the workforce on a full- or-part-time basis	170 (1.37)	106 (1.42)	64 (1.30)
Not in the workforce	156 (.66)	69 (.76)	87 (.57)
Women with multiple obstacles to employment	74 (1.12)	30 (1.23)	44 (.97)*
Accessed social assistance in Waves 1 and 6	143 (.68)	65 (.82)	78 (.56)*

*Statistically significant difference between Indigenous and non-Indigenous women.

(a) 68 percent of these women were young (average age, 28.2), lone parents, and all but one woman accessed social assistance in both Waves 1 and 6. Forty percent were Indigenous women.

into account, the poverty index was 10 percent above the poverty line on average, but half of the women (52.2 percent) had household incomes that were below the poverty line. The average poverty index for Indigenous women was approximately 5 percent below the poverty line, compared to 22 percent above the poverty line for non-Indigenous women; these were statistically different, which suggests that there is reasonable certainty that the difference is reliable and is probably a true one. Most poverty index estimates were not statistically different between Indigenous and non-Indigenous women. This simply means that the difference between the two has a higher chance of not being a true difference due to the estimates being relatively similar. This may also occur with small sample sizes or if there is variability in the data. Moreover, although sample sizes were too small for more detailed statistical analysis, the estimates indicated that women who were immigrants and/or visible minorities had income levels that hovered around the poverty line.

The depth of poverty calculation tells an important story about Indigenous women, who generally fared worse in many categories compared to non-Indigenous women (Table 6-2). The results showed that staying physically and psychologically healthy while maintaining a strong attachment to the workforce through continuous employment was key to avoiding poverty. This finding was particularly important for young Indigenous women, as employed Indigenous women with no health conditions and/or disabilities had household incomes that were 53 percent above the poverty line, which was comparable to 56 percent for non-Indigenous women. Furthermore, the sub-sample of women who reported an intermittent employment history from 2005–09 had an average household income that bordered around the poverty line. Although not shown in Table 6-2, the index was 48 percent above the poverty line for women who were continuously employed full-time or part-time from 2005–09.

Also striking was the difference between the ninety-seven women who gave health issues as the main reason for their non-participation in the workforce (26–32 percent below the poverty line) and 233 employed participants with no particular health conditions or disabilities (37–55 percent above the poverty line). On the whole, the depth of poverty of women with and without particular health issues or disabilities was highly dependent on whether or not they were engaged in the workforce.

Ideally, it would have been useful to include a live-in partner's income in the calculation, but most participants had little information about their partner's income sources, which limited the analysis. Since many participants were lone parents (44.4 percent), our main interest was to calculate the depth of the family's poverty in the absence of a partner who contributed to household expenditures. Similarly, debt load and assets would have benefited the analysis, but this information was also not requested due to the fact that the questionnaires were already lengthy.

Types of Abuse and Chronic Health Issues or Disabilities

Seventy-eight percent of women in the labour market study had experienced one or more types of childhood abuse (323 of 414 participants). It is particularly important to consider the role of childhood abuse in perpetuating unhealthy intimate relationships and, ultimately, contributing to detrimental health outcomes and other complications from disabilities. Children born with cognitive disabilities (such as learning disabilities or fetal alcohol spectrum disorder) are particularly vulnerable to childhood abuse. Some studies have reported high rates of traumatic stress symptoms in children who have witnessed parental violence. For instance, Graham-Bermann et al. (2006) found that a number of variables, such as the level of violence that children were exposed to, a mother's low self-esteem, and a low level of family income, predicted traumatic stress symptoms in the ethnic minority children under study.

Table 6-3 reveals differences in abuse outcomes among the four groups of women. Employed women with no reported health conditions or disabilities (Column 1) were less likely to have experienced childhood abuse in all categories. Irrespective of health conditions and disabilities, fewer employed women experienced emotional or physical abuse over the course of the longitudinal study (Columns 1 and 4) compared to women who were not engaged in the workforce. This underscores the significance of abuse prevention as contributing to more economically independent women in society. The non-employed participants who reported at least one physical/mental health issue or disability (Column 3) had the highest rates of childhood abuse of all groups. Furthermore, women who were not engaged in the workforce (Columns 2 and 3) also had higher rates of emotional and physical abuse after Wave 1 compared to employed women (Columns 1 and 4).

Although not shown in Table 6-3, Indigenous women who experienced physical abuse found themselves in a situation of dire poverty, with an average household income that was 35 percent below the poverty line (poverty index of Indigenous women, .65; non-Indigenous women, 1.04). Similarly, Indigenous participants who reported emotional abuse after the baseline interview had average household incomes that were 14 percent below the poverty line compared to 28 percent above the poverty line for their non-Indigenous counterparts.

The vocational development of women who experienced childhood trauma and/or IPV may have been harmed during the critical early years when they might otherwise have been acquiring an education and pursuing a vocation. The effects of trauma sometimes impede an individual's

Table 6-3: The Relationship of Types of Abuse and Chronic Health Conditions or Disabilities

Types of Abuse Experienced After Wave 1	(1)	(2)	(3)	(4)
	No disabilities or chronic health conditions		At least one physical/mental health issue or disability	
	Works full-or-part time n=63	Not in the labour force n=25	Not in the labour force n=156	Works full-or-part time n=170
Emotional abuse	19 (30.2%)	10 (40.0%)	80 (51.3%)a	57 (33.5%)
Physical abuse	9 (14.3%)	8 (32.0%)a	49 (31.4%)a	20 (11.8%)
Childhood abuse (including multiple types of abuse)	35 (55.6%)	19 (76.0%)	134 (85.9%)*	135 (79.4%)*
Physical	24 (38.1%)	14 (56.0%)	99 (63.5%)*	92 (54.1%)
Sexual	20 (31.7%)	14 (56.0%)	93 (59.6%)*	98 (57.6%)*
Psychological, emotional	28 (44.4%)	16 (64.0%)	110 (70.5%)*	114 (67.1%)*
Witnessed in the home	18 (28.6%)	15 (60.0%)	99 (63.5%)*	96 (56.5%)*
Neglect	12 (19.0%)	10 (40.0%)	78 (50.0%)a	63 (37.1%)*
No childhood abuse	28 (44.4%)	6 (24.0%)	22 (14.1%)*	35 (20.6%)*

* Statistically different from the estimate in Column 1.

a Statistically different from the estimates in Column 1 and 4.

learning capacity, particularly in the case of post-traumatic stress survivors. Moreover, chronic health conditions may contribute to problems with memory retention, concentration, and coping skills (Goodman et al. 2009; Kimerling et al. 2009).

Policy Implications

Although the Healing Journey study was specific to three provinces, the policy implications are generalizable to the rest of Canada. For instance, progress must be made towards changing counterproductive social attitudes (such as criticizing women who return to their abusers) and institutions (such as welfare agencies) in favour of promoting all aspects of the health and safety of women who have left an abusive relationship. Given that over half of the women in the Healing Journey study attributed their detrimental health issues to IPV, a need for public investments in abuse prevention initiatives is the most obvious policy implication, particularly for younger women in unhealthy relationships who may not always be able to recognize abusive behaviours. The poverty estimates show that healthy and employed Indigenous women have the potential to be as economically independent as non-Indigenous women.

In the study, not only did women sustain many physical injuries, but, equally important, they were forced to grapple with the psychological legacy of violence, which was manifested in high rates of depression, anxiety, chronic fatigue, and post-traumatic stress disorder. This has left many of them in a life of poverty, as women with work-limiting health issues had a long-term dependence on income assistance, housing supports, and other public services. Their economic dependence often creates a power differential with either the state (for example, welfare authorities imposing job-seeking and vocational training policies) or former abusive partners (for example, over child maintenance payments). Consequently, this is an important population to understand in terms of services and other public policies. The study also raises the question of whether domestic violence screening and other services should be integrated into health care settings.

Although employment and education are generally beneficial for women who have the capacity to pursue their aspirations, economic independence is not always possible. It is important to be mindful of the fact that the levels of inequality among and the experiences of abused women vary considerably. Workforce participation, or any expectation that a woman pursues a vocation under current welfare policies, cannot always be the end objective, as women with health conditions and disabilities are a disadvantaged group in the workforce for many reasons. Some women with more severe disabilities and/or illnesses will never be equipped to engage in the workforce, and they may consequently return to an abusive partner or start a relationship with a new partner because their own finances cannot cover their living expenses, and/or their functional limitations make them dependent on their abuser. This dangerous dependency has the potential for leaving women vulnerable to re-victimization (Scott, London, and Myers 2002).

In the Healing Journey study, we found that one-fifth of participants continued to experience physical abuse by an intimate partner during the study period, which suggests a revolving door pattern. Some of these participants were young women who had substance abuse issues, were accessing income assistance, and needed to be supported in their efforts at sobriety in order to leave their abusive situations. Another critical finding was that the depth of women's poverty intensified with the severity of illnesses and disabilities. These are important policy variables, and only a guaranteed annual income that provides a reasonable standard of living, as opposed to transitional or subsistence benefits, may moderate the relationship between abuse and physical or mental health challenges.

In situations where women are interested in vocational training or engaging more actively in the workforce, programming needs to be flexible (and wide ranging) to account for the fact that some women will have difficulty learning new skills in a training program due to the effects of past trauma. Thus, their integration into vocational training and the workforce needs to be slow and steady, but extensive enough to yield living wage employment. The current one-size-fits-all and short-term upgrading approaches tend to perpetuate women's employment intermittencies.

Furthermore, abused woman are frequently stigmatized in the workplace and blamed for their difficulties (Bornstein 2006). Many workplaces, particularly in smaller organizations, are not always accommodating to employees with limitations to normal functioning. Therefore, women may need to be matched to employment situations that are receptive to their circumstances and health issues (Kimerling et al. 2009). As indicated earlier, these employment situations are frequently unionized public sector occupations that afford reasonable employment protections and medical benefits/paid sick leave. In fact, this area of job creation has been given much less policy and programming attention. Career development and vocational training services could be added to programming in women's shelters or in other social service agencies that abused women access regularly. Finally, other measures include living wage legislation and strengthening employment protections in the private sector, as well as other appropriate legislation to ensure that all employee assistance programs, in both the public and private sectors, adopt policies that support and address the needs of battered women.

References

Bonomi, Amy E., Robert S. Thompson, Melissa Anderson, Robert J. Reid, David Carrell, Jane A. Dimer and Frederick P. Rivara. 2006. "Intimate Partner Violence and Women's Physical, Mental, and Social Functioning." *American Journal of Preventive Medicine,* 30, 6.

Bornstein Robert F. 2006. "The Complex Relationship between Dependency and Domestic Violence: Converging Psychological Factors and Social Forces." *American Psychologist,* 61, 6.

Chandler, Daniel, Joan Meisel, Pat Jordan, Beth M. Rienzi and Sandra N. Goodwin. 2005. "Mental Health, Employment, and Welfare Tenure." *Journal of Community Psychology,* 33, 5.

Coker, Ann L., Paige H. Smith, Martie P. Thompson, Robert E. McKeown, Lesa Bethea and Keith E. Davis. 2002. "Social Support Protects against the Negative Effects of Partner Violence on Mental Health." *Journal of Women's Health & Gender-Based Medicine,* 11, 5.

DeRiviere, L. 2014. *The Healing Journey: Intimate Partner Abuse and Its Implications in the Labour Market.* Halifax and Winnipeg: Fernwood Publishing; Co-published by RESOLVE Manitoba.

Dutton, Mary Ann. 2009. "Pathways Linking Intimate Partner Violence and Posttraumatic Disorder." *Trauma, Violence, and Abuse,* 10, 3.

Goodman, Lisa A., Katya Fels Smyth, Angela M. Borges and Rachel Singer. 2009. "When Crises Collide: How Intimate Partner Violence and Poverty Intersect to Shape Women's Mental Health and Coping." *Trauma, Violence, and Abuse,* 10, 4.

Graham-Bermann, Sandra A., Ellen R. DeVoe, Jacqueline S. Mattis, Shannon Lynch and Shirley A. Thomas. 2006. "Ecological Predictors of Traumatic Stress Symptoms in Caucasian and Ethnic Minority Children Exposed to Intimate Partner Violence." *Violence Against Women,* 12, 7.

Kernic Mary A., Victoria L. Holt, Julie A. Stoner, Marsha E. Wolf and Frederick P. Rivara. 2003. "Resolution of Depression Among Victims of Intimate Partner Violence: Is Cessation of Violence Enough?" *Violence and Victims,* 18, 2.

Kimerling, Rachel, Jennifer Alvarez, Joanne Pavao, Katelyn P. Mack, Mark W.

Smith and Nikki Baumrind. 2009. "Unemployment among Women: Examining the Relationship of Physical and Psychological Intimate Partner Violence and Posttraumatic Stress Disorder." *Journal of Interpersonal Violence,* 24, 3.

Kocot, Thomas, and Lisa Goodman. 2003. "The Roles of Coping and Social Support in Battered Women's Mental Health." *Violence Against Women,* 9, 3.

Lloyd, Susan. 1997. "The Effects of Violence on Women's Employment." *Law and Policy,* 9, 2.

Mechanic, Mindy B., Terri L. Weaver and Patricia A. Resick. 2008. "Mental Health Consequences of Intimate Partner Abuse: A Multidimensional Assessment of Four Different Forms of Abuse." *Violence Against Women,* 14, 6.

Nicolaidis, Christina, MaryAnn Curry, Bentson McFarland and Martha Gerrity. 2004. "Violence, Mental Health, and Physical Symptoms in an Academic Internal Medicine Practice." *Journal of General Internal Medicine,* 19, 8.

Riger, Stephanie, and Susan Staggs. 2004. "Welfare Reform, Domestic Violence and Employment: What Do We Know and What Do We Need to Know?" *Violence against Women,* 10, 9.

Scott, Ellen K., Andrew S. London and Nancy A. Myers. 2002. "Dangerous Dependencies: The Intersection of Welfare Reform and Domestic Violence." *Gender and Society,* 16, 6.

Smith, Mark W., Paula P. Schnurr and Robert A. Rosenheck. 2005. "Employment Outcomes and PTSD Symptom Severity." *Mental Health Services Research,* 7, 2.

Statistics Canada. 2010. "Low-Income Lines, 2008–2009." Ottawa: Minister of Industry and Income Statistics Division. Catalogue no. 75F0002M, no. 005.

Table 6-A1: Prevalence of Mental Health Conditions Compared to Other Studies (n=414 participants)

Mental Health Category	n (% of Study Participants)	Comparable Prevalence Rates in the Literature %
Depression (manic; bipolar), suicidal, post-partum stress	173 (41.8)	Depression, unless otherwise specified Chandler et al. (2005): 27.7; Kernic et al. (2003): 34.3; Bonomi et al. (2006): minor symptoms 39.8; severe 24.3; Nicolaidis et al. (2004): 68.0; Mechanic, Weaver, and Resick (2008): Severe 31.0, Moderate to severe 45.0; Coker et al. (2002): 31.5; suicide ideation 25.9; Kocot & Goodman (2003): 26.6; Lloyd (1997): 32.2-37.3
Addictions	76 (18.4)	Chandler et al. (2005): 13.1; Kernic et al. (2003): 26.3 (alcohol)
Post-traumatic stress	71 (17.1)	Mechanic, Weaver, and Resick (2008): severe 39.6; moderate to severe 31.8; Coker et al. (2002): 30.6; Kimerling et al. (2009): 11.6 among unemployed women; Kocot and Goodman (2003): 44.7
Chronic fatigue/stress	56 (13.5)	No studies emphasized these conditions
Anxiety, panic attacks, agoraphobia, obsessive compulsive disorder (OCD)	48 (11.6)	Chandler et al. (2005): social phobias 9.8, anxiety 9.5, panic attacks 10.3; Coker et al. (2002): anxiety 28.9; Lloyd (1997): anxiety 50.3-55.1
Schizophrenia, personality disorders (borderline, paranoid, dissociative), gender dysphoria	5 (1.2)	No studies emphasized these conditions

Table 6-A2: Physical Health Conditions (n=414 Study Participants)

Physical Health Category	Total Sample n	Not in Workforce n (%)
Conditions that cause chronic pain and/or mobility problems: degenerative disk condition; hips, legs, back, neck, and foot pain; after-effects of broken bones from abuse or accidents (such as motor vehicle); Pilonidal cyst; sciatic nerve condition; nerve damage (hands and/or feet); scoliosis; spinal stenosis; osteoporosis; osteoarthritis; nerve entrapment; hip replacement; fasciitis; polymyalgia (muscle pain).	82	41 (50.0)
Neurological/central nervous system disorders: multiple sclerosis; myelitis (inflammation of the spinal cord); restless leg syndrome; seizures; epilepsy; head and brain injuries; Bell's Palsy; pituitary tumors; memory issues; concussion affects memory/brain function; West Nile Virus.	23	14 (60.9)
Headaches; migraines.	14	3 (21.4)
Blood disorders; anemia; bleeding disorders; blood enzyme disorder.	9	3 (33.3)
Cancer: skin; bladder; leukemia.	9	6 (66.7)
Heart conditions; circulation issues; stroke; heart attack.	13	10 (76.9)
Hepatitis C; HIV.	18	12 (66.7)
Stomach, liver, kidney, spleen conditions; gall bladder; acid reflux; ulcers; kidney stones; pancreatitis; hernia.	20	8 (40.0)
Ears, nose, throat, mouth conditions; tumors, chronic laryngitis; hearing or vision loss; cataracts; inner ear conditions (Meniere's disease); sinus conditions; allergies; thyroid issues (hypo, hyper).	47	19 (40.4)
Lung conditions; asthma; tuberculosis; emphysema; nodules in lungs; chronic chest infections; chronic cough; chronic obstructive pulmonary disease (COPD); pulmonary embolism.	39	22 (56.4)
Diabetes; hypoglycemia.	25	14 (56.0)
Joint conditions: arthritis; tendonitis; carpal tunnel; fibromyalgia; temporomandibular joint disorder (TMJD); spondylitis.	45	22 (48.9)
Bowel diseases: Crohn's; irritable bowel syndrome (IBS); celiac; diverticulosis.	30	13 (43.3)
High blood pressure; hypertension; cholesterol.	32	12 (37.5)

Physical Health Category	Total Sample n	Not in Workforce n (%)
Female reproductive system: endometriosis; cervical cancer/abnormal cells; sexually-transmitted infections; breast abscess; ovarian cysts; uterine fibroid tumors/cysts; chronic vaginal yeast infections.	18	7 (38.9)
Learning disabilities: dyslexia; speech impediment; attention deficit (hyperactivity) disorder (ADD or ADHD); fetal alcohol syndrome, fetal alcohol effects, fetal alcohol spectrum disorder (FAS/FAE/FASD).	20	10 (50.0)
Obesity; eating disorders; bulimia; anorexia; self-mutilation.	7	4 (57.1)
Sleep disorders: insomnia; sleep apnea.	12	8 (66.7)
Skin conditions: psoriasis; shingles.	4	2 (50.0)

Chapter 7

Making Homelessness Harder
Possibilities for Radical Re-Orientation

Liza Kim Jackson and nancy viva davis halifax

Prologue: How to Read

We begin this chapter with advice: read slowly; read without an expectation of a straightforward narrative; read without the expectation of immediate comprehension; read as if you were reading a poem or a musical score; read knowing that the radical tendencies of the authors, the bodies through which we write, and the voices and gestures of those with whom we have shared time and space in community are present.

Our writing relies upon a feminist post-structuralist philosophy that introduces the reader to uncertainty, the contestation of master narratives, reflexivity, and considered attention to language. Ambiguity within language, as a potential of post-structuralism, introduces a doubling of signification and a loss of coherence, in this instance effecting comprehension of this text. As readers, writers, and thinkers we are re-oriented from the normative task of assuming a consensual interpretation toward relations of difference as we form meanings within spaces of uncertainty (Butler 1997; Derrida 1988). Thus, the act of reading begins to imagine and welcome forms of knowledge other than the rational, linear, normative, new, and objective (Code 1995).

Feminist post-structuralism disrupts the certainty of the rational subject that arrives from the Enlightenment: male, rational, white, able-bodied, cisgendered, economically secure. This taken-for-granted, normal, or normative subject is contested by the subject we discuss in this chapter — racialized, disabled, gendered, and classed otherwise. Our goal, to surface and revive knowledges that have previously only subtended what can be known and what can be told about (Lather 1996), relies upon "situated and embodied knowledges" (Haraway 1991: 191). Through our writing we welcome the ordinary, abjected, and tired and old knowings of the violences of poverty, homelessness, and disability. Embodied and old knowledges are included through the use of fragmented and poetic forms that signify not only a post-structural alliance, but also a crip one.

"Crip," a colloquial abbreviation of cripple, arrives stuttering, limping, rolling, stigmatized, disabled, crooked. Disability scholars (Chandler 2013; Fritsch 2013; Johnson and McRuer 2014; Kafer 2013; McRuer 2006; Sandahl 2003) analyze how crip and cripping challenge Western normative assumptions about bodies as normal, and about thought and thinking as straightforward and rational. Cripping our assumptions involves a turn toward an embodiment, an aesthetic, and a politics, as well as an analytic. We employ crip for its ornery nature; its inquisitive reach; its capacity to resist, oppose, and surprise; its amenability to our artist praxis.

Our crip artist praxis takes seriously the potential for violence inherent in the generally valorized Euro-Western linear and objectifying formal techniques and structures of knowledge representation. The creative work done in community anticipates our crooked writing — our writing mirrors persistence, endurance, chronicity. We are alert to the potential of violences as well as of failure. Our crip artist praxis may move from sensation to gesture, to sound, to word; crip writing arises from bodies that are different, uncertain, excessive, leaky. These bodies, which we conceptualize as "embodieds," lean into each other, intertwine, combine, entangle, separate. To write crip is to recognize and unleash the unboundedness of forms disallowed by the hegemony of normative writing practices. Crip writing re-situates disciplinary knowledge practices as fragmented, gestural, incomplete, unpredictable, and embodied. Calls for authority and the safety of rationality are re-situated as *under consideration*.

Considerations of crip embodiment demand relational knowing; we must be present to difference in order to recognize the bounds of the normative. As such, know as you read that our writing fails. We fail to adequately bring to you all of the "embodieds," their affective nuances, the tentative openings, the moments of fear or suspicion. Failure to meet the readers' expectations of coherence and a linear narrative introduces a risk that some bodies/knowings may remain incomprehensible and therefore vulnerable to further abandonment. The frustration of a wish for comprehension can unintentionally draw failure and violence together. Remember, our writing does not deliberately obfuscate, but is empathic to the reader who may, in a parallel fashion, wrestle with situating their knowledge practice/s within their own embodied positionality, language, and voice.

 Writers, thinkers, and readers in critical disability studies are diverse; non-normative embodiments have the capacity to articulate, perform, and invent form that contests normative rhetorical spaces (Ferris 2004). And so, in the company of violence, failure, persistence, and potentiality, we risk admitting the knowings and words of these/our diverse, unstable embodieds that demand re/form.

Tearing Bodies

> And the thing of it is, it's getting worse. It's not getting better, it's getting worse, because some of the stories I hear from ladies, I can't believe, you know, that they're in the system and the system is tearing them apart. (Red Wagon Collective and Women from the Junction 2013: excerpt from *R*)

It is getting worse: we can't tell it better. This quote from a co-researcher/artist with experiential knowledge of homelessness and disability offers sensory witness to the *tearing* that is systemic violence. Homelessness and poverty are two such violences experienced by women living with disability in contemporary global society, violences that are worsening and that draw a sociocultural response of indifference. Here we recuperate accounts of violence — economic, institutional, and more — that have been gathered by the Red Wagon Collective alongside women who live or have lived as homeless[1] in the Junction[2] neighbourhood of Toronto. The conditions of homelessness and disability[3] are laced through and threaded with a history of capitalism, in which some bodies thrive through the impoverishment of others. This *tearing* of bodies from one another constitutes an anti-relationality and an indispensable material perspective as a basis for our critique of violence and poverty. We note that the spaces where disability, homelessness, and poverty intersect are spaces in which bodies are subject to a diversity of micro- and macro-violences that lead to an acceleration of death (necro-capitalism). In our work, we collaborate on the development of a counter-movement: a social space that is amenable to and supports the creation of antidotes to those violences and a collective imagining that supports life. We recognize that when writing about violence, we have an ethical responsibility to acknowledge embodied endurance, agency, and resistant capacity.

Red Wagon Collective and the Monday Art Group

The Red Wagon Collective (RWC) originated in 2007 with its main project, *the Gathering Space*, located in a neighbourhood storefront as a base from which to create art.[4] Since 2007 *the Gathering Space* has worked with residents of the neighbourhood who would venture in, including women who were living at an adjacent shelter. Upon completion of the first phase of *the Gathering Space*, funding was secured (from the Toronto Arts Council and the Ontario Arts Council) to continue the project, specifically with the women residents of the shelter. The Monday Art Group (MAG) was established in order to complete a series of banners that hang inside and on the exterior wall of the shelter. When the project was done, the women expressed a strong desire to have MAG continue, so nancy and Kim have remained as long-term core members of RWC and continue to run the weekly art group. We recognize our symbolic privilege as white settler academics. But this privilege is also complicated by past histories of insecure housing/homelessness, addiction and poverty, queerness, and persisting histories of both physical and/or mental health difference and/or economic precarity. While our experiences overlap with those of the women with whom we work, we are also positioned relationally as employed and housed individuals, working through structures that both bind and separate us as women.

The MAG most often takes the form of a drop-in, open studio space where women who live or have lived at the shelter meet with women from the neighbourhood to drink tea, create, and endure. At the MAG we work on collective and multi-disciplinary practice. Our work includes installation projects that intervene in the public space of the neighbour-hood but also send tentacles out through Toronto and the province of Ontario through artistic intervention and through the forced mobility of the women with whom we work. Yet, our efforts remain partial: in each present moment, RWC is witness to multiple enactments of the progress of violences that we cannot halt and upon which we do not yet know how to intervene.

Since their beginnings, the practices of the RWC and the MAG have been to include difference and deviation in bodies and expressions. We experi-ence the disciplinary and exploitative nature of capitalism that squeezes profit from bodies as labourers, as consumers, and as material for the institutional complex. Othered[5] bodies that flow through and around, exceeding and disrupting capitalist discipline, normative standards, and expectations, accumulate in the shelter. This is evident in the high propor-tion of women who are at the shelter and identify as queer/transgender, of colour, and Indigenous, and those who live with disabilities and have endured economic impoverishment. While statistics help to describe in a certain way, the understanding they provide does not necessarily represent nor reflect the specific and lived knowledge of the women with whom we work: identities cannot be defined solely by their oppression; they require and demand an account of the complexity of experience and expression. In Canada, women make up 26 percent of the homeless population. However, women are at increased risk of hidden homelessness — overcrowded living and not having enough money for other necessities. Demographic statistics for women and homelessness are not available, but it is understood within the homelessness research community that those who experience poverty are at greater risk for homelessness. According to the Homeless Hub, Canadian Research on Homelessness website, while 9 percent of Canadians are poor (with around a quarter of Torontonians living below the poverty line), the poverty level rises to 36 percent of Indigenous women, 35 percent of visible minority women, 26 percent of women with disabilities, 21 percent of single parent mothers, and 51.6 percent of single mothers in lone-parent families. Within the youth homeless population, 25–40 percent identify as LGBTQ2 (<homelesshub. ca/about-homelessness/topics/population-specific>). According to Khosla (n.d.), in 2000, 45.6 percent of women over 65 who were single, divorced, or widowed lived in poverty. According to the Government of Canada (2013) website, 41 percent of the Canadian racialized population living in poverty live in Toronto.

In MAG, outsider bodies do not remain outside. MAG's praxis is both ameliorative and contestational; it means recognizing the unique, specific, and diverse expressions of women. MAG refuses the tangled logics of violences that attend upon disability, poverty, and homelessness through a focus upon the expressions of these women — even as we never forget their exclusion, the ways in which they are obscured, ignored, pathologized, and cut through by the trauma and re-traumatizing conditions of poverty and exclusion. Our response is materialized within an aesthetic practice of art-making that recognizes the complex agencies of those who gather to create their/our slow and persistent political call toward non-indifference.

What might be exemplary of our non-indifference, and grounded in RWC's reflexivity, is our attention to a primary form of violence that exists within writing: here, the framing of women according to a set of categorizations. Categorizations — cisgendered, straight, queer, Black, francophonie, disabled, poor — even as they slip across bodies (Butler 1997) are necessary for the purposes of certain forms of justice work, including that done textually, such as this chapter. The discursive constructions of the identities — women, homelessness, and the shelter — work within contemporary neoliberal Canada to maintain a confluence of oppressions. Thus, when questioned about our form of address to those with whom we do this work ("the women" as a category that can group, flatten, essentialize, and evoke assumptions, for instance, of biology), we struggled with the symbolic violence of our authority to use language to construct identity. How do we refer to someone whose individual personhood is made absent through language and whose name remains unknown? In response, we looked to the proximity of our inhabitation of the neighbourhood in which we live and work. As RWC and MAG we call and re-call as neighbours in a back-and-forth address. This address among neighbours troubles the cultural categorization through which the women, as *homeless,* are disqualified from recognition and belonging. The multiple differences that converge to categorize a body as homeless are quickly eclipsed into another category: not normal. Non-normative embodieds, (un)constructed as outsider, as othered and re/formed as objects of institutionalization and further victimization, abandonment, and erasure, are neighbours. Neighbours laced through and threaded with multiple intersections of race, indigeneity, class, queerness/sexuality, gender, and ability, working through and together weighing powerfully upon their exclusion.

Here we take up nancy's poetic practice, which introduces us as neighbours using the French feminine: *nos voisines*. In Toronto, where the English language is dominant, the use of French allows for the gendering of our neighbours; even so, *nos voisines* exists as a term of contingency, of intersections, that opens the potential of a gendered geography of relationship and recognition. The unfamiliarity of the term *nos voisines*, in this context (no longer *the women*), operating as an act of renaming within a text, may perform a disruption where the colonial dominance of English is opened for question.[6] Within this space of questioning, we encourage the reader to linger with the uncertainty of language, the optimisms of translation, slippages of meaning, and knowing, as well as to garner an altered acquaintance with the power of language and the potential violences of reified categories.

And so *nos voisines* — our neighbours — arrive as a provisional articulation, an unexpected and disruptive languaging of relationship that intersects across numerous lines of multiple differences (Mohanty 1988, 2003; Savage 2003; Shildrick 2005). *Nos voisines*, as a crip and neighbourly address, imagines the ground on which our creative co-habitation is occasioned. Our writing, through its desires for the presence of *nos voisines*, through our refusal of indifference, engages the reader as an audience with the thoughts of *nos voisines*, and intercedes in the typical exclusions of their/our knowledges.

> Who is she?
> She is young, she is old, she is an artist, she is a teacher, she is a lawyer, she is a daughter, she is a housewife, she is a poet, she is kind, she is pretty, she is a mother, she is a grandmother, she is an invalid, she is sick, she is a sinner, she is helpless, she is lonely, she is defenseless, she is homeless. (RWC and Women from the Junction 2013: excerpt from *J*)

Nos voisines provide us with embodied evidence of poverty, disability, and more as we chat over cups of tea and handwork at MAG. We do not force discussion topics according to a research agenda — we follow, we listen, and we participate — we are present. Our conversations are both oblique and direct, addressing the wretched impoverishment that endures beyond policy shifts and statistical analyses, including the decades-long lists for subsidized housing, the lack of accessible units, the pain of it all. Sometimes, *nos voisines* do not want to talk about their oppressions. These are tender and sometimes risky subjects within a shelter; MAG becomes a momentary escape from contending with the exhaustion of the violences, and the continued lack of response, the political and social indifference.

Our writing, attuned to the possibility of failure and of error and the inadequacy of any symbolic system (Rosler 2006), responds with the creation of a reflexive and crip text. The text brings forward fragmented and incomplete perspectives to create a *pentimento*, choral knowledge/s that are untidy, excessive, full of difference, and always "imagining otherwise" (McRuer 2006: 32). Here the words of *nos voisines* present to us their homelessness and disability. Praxis knits across "theory/research divide[s]" and is indicative "of a shared feminist commitment to a political position in which 'knowledge' is not simply defined as 'knowledge *what*' but also as 'knowledge *for*'" (Stanley 2013: 15; emphasis in original). Knowledge *for* and *with* and *alongside* is another reflexive attribute of our non-indifference. Their/our words embrace in poems, where fragments of language create a different space of reading, allowing for the necessary pauses, the space of breath in crip activist praxis. *Our writing meanders.* Our inclusions aim to consciously crip the expected knowledge forms that the reader might anticipate within academic practice (McRuer 2006). *Trips, halts, repeats, stammers.* Our writing is angled with contradictions.

> Have problems, that why we're here for help
>> Help is helping the problems *we have*
>> Have to have a good heart to work at the shelter
>> Group in church that's helping should be of nice mind to care
> for homeless and "saving people" from starvation and a provid-
> ing a place to live,
>> not a place to make fun of people and step on homeless humans
>> making homelessness harder (RWC and Women from the
> Junction 2013: excerpt from *MH*)

The Disabling Normative Body, aka Bourgeoise

In part, disability is materialized within an economic and physical environment that is reproduced and built for a normative body. Within the capitalist geography and social structure, those whose embodiments are deemed non-productive are unsupported, null, invisible, unvalued, or unengaged are rendered, by degrees, disabled. Disability theorists Erevelles and Minear (2010) note that disability is a primary intersectional category in that it analyzes the social construction of non-normative, othered bodies as not only deficient but also monstrous. They describe how notions of a deficient monstrous body are then socially enacted through racism, where racialized bodies are deemed *incapable* of a civilized normativity and thus subject to institutional controls. McLintock (1995) further analyzes how working-class bodies are, in some historical moments, also racially coded as coarse, backwards, without intelligence, inarticulate, and prone to violence and immorality.

The valorization of the normative body can be linked to the system of bourgeois dominance that originated in Europe and is globalized through colonization and transnational capitalism. The bourgeois system privileges both economically and socially the performance of white, cisgendered male, ableist embodiment. Importantly, the bourgeois body that all bodies are conditioned to aspire to within capitalism is defined by its rights to acquire private property. At the same time, the white cisgendered male bourgeois body is supported by and defined against othered bodies that form the ground and the resource for the vampiric meanness of his figure. Bodies deemed monstrous and lumpen[7] are frightening to the white bourgeois normative body, which depends on their disciplining and distancing to maintain their social, political, and economic power and their identity as moral, hard-working, able, and rational.

These othered bodies are rendered landless and then denigrated in public space, their labour is unvalorized and thus they are forced into marginalized and precarious economic spaces in order to subsist. There are many forms of denigrated life: women's unpaid and affective work; informal forms of labour; migrant labour; sex work; drug trade; and bartering, gifting, panhandling, dumpster-diving, trading, and whatever means of subsistence people can find to support their endurance (Blaney and Inayatullah 2009; Bourke, Dafnos, and Kip 2011; Braidotti 2013;

Gleeson 1999; McIntyre and Nast 2011; Povinelli 2011; Puar 2009). These bodies can be construed as monstrous, lumpen, outside — drawn as exploitable and expendable. Disability geographer Gleeson (1999) notes that the lumpen class is historically populated by those with impaired embodiments. Disability, suggests Erevelles, can be a container for multiple forms of othering — of racialization, of class, of gender, of queerness, and of indigeneity. Disability is thus a leaky term, inclusive of bodies born with impairments, those who become impaired, those whose bodies are disabled through social structures of power. The unifying moment for all these bodies is their construction as monstrous and thus their exclusion from value.

> lifestyle of people unknown
> family; world; anxiety; apart; unknown; sick.
> die once and twice became (?)
> who knows who am I?
> cried; cried and cried
> shelter and shelter changing
> here … here, there and there
> sick exhausted and pass out.
> Hospitalization and who care?
> Doctor and nurse are wall
> gave food and go home
> away
> where is home?
> Shelters or park can I go
> God help me out for the day.
> Tomorrow who am I?
> No family, stay in the park
> what happen in my future?
> Stay alone or dying?
> (RWC and Women from the Junction 2013: excerpt from *MH*)

Making Homelessness Harder

There are multiple factors that affect homelessness. RWC primarily understands homelessness to be caused by the socio-economic processes that create hierarchies of embodiment (homophobia, ageism, transphobia, racism, abandonment, social death), and not by individual disposition or circumstance (Cho, Crenshaw, and McCall 2013; Crenshaw 1989, 1991; Hulchanski 2009b; Lyon-Callo 2002; MacKinnon 2013). In the Canadian context, modern hierarchization of bodies occurs through colonial dispossession and the normalizing forces of capitalist private property. Kawash (1998: 320) understands homelessness as "an increasingly violent form of exclusion ... from public spaces" in order to protect the propertied against the propertyless. The civic violences of spatial exclusion practised on homeless embodiments include: the appropriation of Indigenous lands and resources through Canadian policy and legislation; Canada's lack of a national housing plan; Ontario's Safe Streets Act of 1999; the criminalization of poverty, racial profiling, and criminalization of the homeless via ticketing in numerous jurisdictions in Canada; police brutality, including murder; the lack of safe, secure, affordable housing; institutional abuse within shelters, hospitals, prisons, group homes, nursing homes, and foster care; and the increased absence of essential services. All these forces compound to make the social spaces of homelessness spaces of violence. For women, this also means increased vulnerability to sexual assault and other forms of gender-based violence (Khandor and Mason 2007).

Bodies subject to intersections of oppressions are more vulnerable to violence and exclusion from urban spaces. For example, being Indigenous is complicated by the trauma of colonial dispossession in its complex forms, by gender and disability, and thus the risk of homelessness and violent death multiplies exponentially. Further complicating this violence is the fact that, at the legislative level, Indigenous peoples who are living in "substandard on-reserve housing" are considered housed (Patrick 2014: 16). This precariousness extends to urban Indigenous populations where "one in fifteen urban Aboriginal people are homeless, compared to one out of 128 non-Native Canadians" (Belanger, Awosoga, and Head 2013: 14) on what is stolen native land.

The onset of neoliberal economics means that "our affordable housing supply has been reduced and our system of income and social supports has been undermined" (Gaetz 2010: 25). Emergency shelters re-inscribe a charitable model of homelessness, and although needed, they are not equipped for or accessible to physically disabled embodieds, those with chronic illness, or people with sensory or learning differences and/or madness. A focus on increasing the number of emergency shelters can make us forget that other housing solutions exist (such as co-op and co-housing) and are sporadically in use (Waegemakers and Turner 2014). Shelters in Toronto run at full capacity, and in winter, homelessness activists must advocate for additional crisis relief beds at Metro Hall, where a roof is provided but indifference is enacted through a lack of actual comfort or care. Shelters originated as part of an emergency response to Canada's reduced housing supply and do not replace what is needed: the development of a strong and coordinated national housing plan (Gaetz 2010). In order to better address homelessness one must move toward long-term solutions based on strategies to redistribute wealth, such as a living wage for all that ensures that no one exists in "poverty so deep that even poor-quality housing is not affordable" (Hulchanski 2009a).

> My hours, of course, at work started to be cut off. I started another job, but the money that I was seeing and hours I was getting was so little. With all the money that I saved I had to eat and pay my bills. Everything was becoming expensive, my paycheck was becoming smaller ... it's our money. Absolutely. The lowest of the low. Those big guys they have big money, they have an account in the islands somewhere. We don't even know in a Swiss bank and they're hidden. They don't even want to mention. They run away from paying. (RWC and Women from the Junction 2013: excerpt from J)

What RWC witnesses are how the embodiments of *nos voisines* are informed and pressed upon by multiple networks of social and structural relations — politicians, physicians, health care workers, legislators, administrators, police, and (if we continue) emergency shelter staff, jailers, rapists, neighbours, local business owners, families. We orient toward the reality of how precariousness is produced — the weary material existence formed through the deliberate poverty strategies of the Canadian government at all levels that especially impact disabled bodies and disable poor bodies, bodies we can also read as raced, gendered, and queer.

Here is being trapped.
You can't have what you need.
It's like there is no freedom.
Like there are borders where you are
stuck, you can't cross and get what
you need. And we appreciate what
is given, but there is like a place where
you are not allowed to have choices.
At heart it's about what we need.
(RWC and Women from the Junction 2013: excerpt from *MH*)

The social relations of disability, homelessness, and poverty have been naturalized. They are the taken-for-granted social ideologies that present disability, homelessness, and poverty as individual problems, paid labour as a necessary contribution from each person that will result in being housed, and health as produced through exercise and healthy eating and not by solving poverty. These are only some of the ordinary violences that are obscured as the larger crises that capitalism orchestrates claim attention. Homelessness is an actively disabling structural violence that attacks and re-attacks bodies. Shelters across Canada are overwhelming spaces of (in)difference wherein the evidence of lives lived along multiple and public dimensions are reduced to a single category: homeless (Cho, Crenshaw, and McCall 2013; Crenshaw 1989, 1991; MacKinnon 2013). To exclude homelessness from the category of violence would be to ignore the suffering and the death-accelerating impact of poverty and homelessness on bodies. It would be to misunderstand these root causes: the historical violences of colonialism and capitalism that have produced modern and endemic forms of homelessness and disability.

"Anyone Can Become Homeless"

And when I am awake I'm always hungry. (RWC and Women from the Junction 2013: excerpt from *J*)

The shelter in which the RWC's practice is located is one of many providing emergency shelter in the City of Toronto. The shelter sits in uneasy relation with the gentrification of the Junction and remains a site of marginality where women are not included in the neighbourhood's self-definition or vision of what it could become (Kawash 1998). *Nos voisines* say, "Don't they know they're building their condo across from a women's shelter?" Imagining that a lack of knowledge was the problem and that if the condo builders did know maybe there would be an opportunity to do something about the lack of affordable housing. Or alternately, fear of the intensification of their impoverishment within a gentrified landscape, and in response a plea for acceptance of their presence: "Do they know we're here?" Experiences of diminishment stand in stark contrast to the healthy gentrified body, which is supported and nourished and is entitled to extend itself through space (Kawash 1998; McIntyre and Nast 2011; Povinelli 2011; Yates 2011). These realities exist on top of each other, as parallel but segregated universes only tenuously connected. *Nos voisines* tell us, "Anyone can become homeless":

> I did collapse … I want to sleep but you're not allowed to in the shelter. There are rules and regulations. You have to wake up by nine. It doesn't matter how exhausted you are, you know, and then you take your umbrella, you take your clothes and you end up whatever corner is available to you and I don't want to complain about the shelter, I appreciate what they did for me however … I don't know … I mean I like to stand by this and try to come back to my feet but I found it very, very hard and it's only been ten days, not even ten days. I don't know why … I'm just going to keep my fingers crossed that I will not quit. I will not quit. (RWC and Women from the Junction 2013: excerpt from J)

Our conversations with *nos voisines* and shelter staff, as well as our own observations, tell of the disabling conditions of life in this particular shelter. As an institution, the shelter exists as a building, a literal shelter, but it is also a discipline, a rigid set of rules that must be adhered to and that are inscribed onto the bodies of women (Foucault 1995). "Can't go upstairs to your bedroom before 4 p.m. Can't have food in your room. Can't have your own medication — it must be dispensed by staff…" (*nos voisines*). The autonomy of the woman deemed homeless is undermined. She is infantilized and blamed, viewed as disabled and incapable simply because she is homeless (Erevelles 1996; Kawash 1998; Lyon-Callo 2002). "It's like the military up there" (*nos voisines*). Women from across a spectrum of embodiments are housed together, some more willing and able to conform to the house rules than others. Those who cannot conform experience service restrictions, which are policies developed by shelters: "She had a drink in her room when she wasn't supposed to ... they wouldn't even let me have an empty bottle" (*nos voisines*). In shelters, a parsimonious and anti-relational neoliberal approach of social austerity enforces behavioural conformity through threats of, and expulsion from, the shelter.

> And then I'm there sitting out on the street
> because even the shelter, the last possible
> places to be safe, isn't safe for me.
> (RWC and Women from the Junction 2013: excerpt from *R*)

Nos voisines often lack access to health care and space for recuperation following medical procedures. Accommodations are not made for disability or difference, which are essentialized as problems, as other, less than, inferior (Shildrick 2005; Stiker 1999; Titchkosky 2000). The lethality of difference essentialized as non-normative is not forgetful (Braidotti 2013; Shildrick 2005). *Nos voisines* tell us that disabled women are more prone to being moved to another shelter if they are perceived as having difficulties adhering to rules, or if they fail in their ability to enact normative embodiment while navigating inaccessible building structures. "They told me this morning they are moving me to another shelter, I don't know why, I don't know where I don't know when" (*nos voisines*). The constant daily travel that marks long-term homelessness is an added stress for women who are already living with embodied differences of street ageing, fatigue, pain, chronic illness, and disability:

> I'm sorry I died. I was going up and down those stairs with a blood clot ... I was taking medication for blood clots and because the elevator was broken all the time and I had to go down and up the stairs when I shouldn't be, the blood clot got loose, I went to the hospital and I died in the hospital with a blood clot because I didn't have the use of a fucking elevator. Okay. I've seen a lot of deaths in my building ... in ten years, over disability stuff and that's what I have seen ... over disabilities. (RWC and Women from the Junction 2013: excerpt from *L*)

The marginality of the shelter as a social site is reflected in the building itself, which contains parallel universes: renovations of staff spaces and fresh paint take care of the aesthetic comforts of the workers while the living conditions of the women are not attended to. Beset by maintenance issues, the building itself can seem abandoned: sewage flooding, broken elevator, lack of hot water, broken toilet, lack of heat, removal of electrical outlets for charging cell phones or other electronics. Women report that the blankets provided do not keep them warm and, conversely, that there is no air conditioning when it is hot. Control over bodies repeats in endless cycles, which includes the application of toxins that are metabolized by human, insect, and rodent bodies. Attacks on bodies include the provisioning of food that is industrial, highly processed, and often beyond its best-before date, including charitable donations of spoiled vegetables. The absence of fresh fruit and vegetables and the overall lack of nutrition in meals served leave *nos voisines* craving:

> I dream for some … definitely different food. Something I used to have but I can't afford it because it's like fifteen dollars for a salad or whatever I want with raspberries with whatever they serve it on King St. somewhere. (RWC and Women from the Junction 2013: excerpt from *J*)

There is no room for difference within the social space of the shelter, only privation. Prescriptions for special diets, health-related nutritional requirements, cultural and ethical expressions, or desires for food from home are denied.

The lack of engagement in a greater social world, the sense of being trapped in a parallel reality, exacerbates hopelessness, alienation, boredom, memory loss, and pain. When sharing a room with someone you do not know it may be hard to sleep, and *nos voisines* report that lack of rest contributes to stress and depression. In accord with the medicalization of homelessness, women are rendered deviant through the distribution of diagnoses (Lyon-Callo 2002). Isolation is exacerbated through symbolic violence where pity and stereotyped portrayals in the media naturalize an infantilized image of homeless women as dependant, disabled, and monstrous (Lyon-Callo 2002). Symbolic violence occurs when people are made to feel that their exclusion is due to their own inadequacy, while the historical, social, political, and economic causes and human rights abuses remain invalidated and uncontested (Wacquant 1993; Weininger 2005).

Rather than functioning as a space of safety and security — as home — the women's shelter works in tandem with a network of institutions that control and contain the poor through surveillance, control, and study: welfare, the prison system, public housing, and the policing of public space (Wacquant 2009).

Capitalism is a system that is ethically untenable within a democratic society that claims liberty as a foundational value (Eagleton 1990; Braidotti 2013). RWC agrees that all inequality is produced ideologically and materially against a philosophically open field of being in which inequality cannot make sense (Braidotti 2013; Code 1995; Shildrick 2005). We cannot justify our own oppression:

> Even if I do find a place on my own [or] if they find housing for me, I'm afraid. Like, can I survive out there? (RWC and Women from the Junction 2013: excerpt from *H*)

We feel that any understanding of homelessness and disability must include a careful consideration of the impacts of capitalism, as an anti-relationality, on the social fabric, on the psyches and bodies and communities of *nos voisines*.

> I don't know why I kept wrote these 2 words: mind and heart
> Heart, god made every human with a good heart
> Heart good; good heart have to be [part] of it.
> It's heart and mind that always combines to each other
> Otherwise it's come apart
> If apart then becomes good and bad
> nice and evil
> Evil mind worse than evil heart
> Heart can change
> Change mind is hard
> (RWC and Women from the Junction 2013: excerpt from *MH*)

In summary, within the space of the MAG, accounts of multiple levels of violence arise — economic, institutional, social, and symbolic — as experienced by women who are insecurely housed and who experience forms of embodied difference/s. Theory, even if conceptualized as social action, is not enough. We propose, therefore, a praxis in which knowledge about capitalism is co-produced and takes a form that extends from and circulates back to the bodies whose lived experiences are the basis of the work.

Praxis as Antidote

The homeless/disabled body is subject to dissection, it is a body to be analyzed as a problem to be fixed, it is a body that is culturally constructed and spectacularized. Historian Joseph Fracchia astutely notes the operation of a symbolic violence in the gap between those who research and write and those subject to oppression who are written about. While the researcher observes the "horror" of impoverishment, those subject to it experience "the writing on the body, painfully decipher[ing] the meaning of the words through [their] wounds" (Fracchia 2008: 37).

> When things start to go down I would walk. That was my way of medication, of medicating, of fixing my brain or fixing my life or figuring out what next do I do. And the exhaustion and

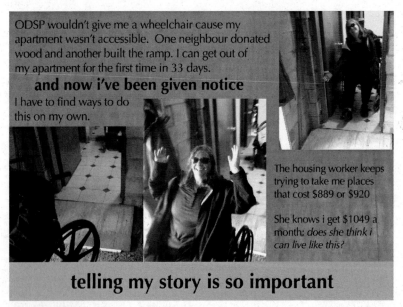

Banner by S. Red Wagon Collective and Women from the Junction. 2013. We Have a Message: Women's Stories of Aging, Disability and Homelessness, un-paginated.

the tiredness or whatever we are feeling, it's because there is no program for us. There is no stimulation to push the buttons inside and say, hey, today is this, you have to do something. All you do, you have time for medication, for lunch, for breakfast, you feel like you are in a camp or in the army somewhere. So, no stimulation. That's why we feel exhausted. That's why. (RWC and Women from the Junction 2013: excerpt from J)

We critique an academic form of knowledge that veers towards the violent. To contend with some of the problems encountered in conventional evidence, proof, and argument-based academic forms, we suggest instead a social praxis art. A crip social praxis (SPA) does not dissect or abstract our embodiment, but recognizes diverse and unruly forms of knowledge as integral, ameliorative, and possibly liberatory. In other words, we do not see academic literature on the subject of disability, homelessness, and art methodology as sufficient in itself. We do not take praxis to mean just doing fieldwork within an academic context. Nor do we take the ultimate goal of praxis as being the development of knowledge, even when co-produced, whose ultimate form is disembodied theory on paper, as demanded by Canadian funding bodies and the academy. We call for cripping the division between embodied and intellectual knowledge forms, understanding them as indivisible and necessarily performed together. To work alongside and towards a shared inclusive language and the correlation of knowledge across difference as a liberatory praxis requires a crip compass orienting us toward insecurity, wincing, and joy — toward a future of nonviolent relations.

Cripping, Tripping Praxis

Contemporary art theory has introduced social practice arts as a form which regards the social, or relationality, as the artists' material/medium (Gablik 1991; Jackson 2011; Jackson 2009; Kester 2004; Lacy 1995; Rosler 2006; Taylor 2006). The crip lens also troubles the purely symbolic, allowing for the materiality of body within the medium of the social. Crip social praxis arts unfold from the specificity of disabled embodiments, which bear critical and sometimes rebellious expressive knowledge on the part of those who are not supposed to express anything at all worth considering. Crip knowledge/s can be rebellious in their non-conformity and non-performativity (McRuer 2006), in their refusal to pass as — or to perform momentary conformity within — the social relations of a disabling society.

Patti Lather's contributions as a feminist, post-structuralist educational theorist are amenable to art historian Grant Kester's writings on community and dialogical arts. In Lather's (1986) discussion of praxis, her emphasis on reciprocity and open-ended discourse extends Kester's (2004: 90) dialogical practice, which proposes that "An alternative approach would require us to locate the moment of indeterminateness, of open-ended and liberatory possibility ... in the very process of communication that the artwork catalyzes;" one that is not "insensitive to the specific identities of speaking subjects" but is a "dialogical exchange based on reciprocal openness." The basis for establishing such a communicative exchange lies phenomenologically in the co-presence of our/all bodies as *nos voisines*. The relationships are present between the artists, the women, the shelter, and the gentrifying neighbourhood. A phenomenology of enactment includes total support for doing and making. Opening to the world through reconceptualizing arts practice, we enter a back-and-forthing across world, ideas, and making (Abram 1996; Bolt 2010; Gablik 1991). This is an iterative and performative (Butler 1997; Taylor 2006) phenomenological (Ahmed 2006; van Manen 2014) praxis from which we return radically reoriented. We do not want to reproduce the violence of our contemporary sociocultural realms with their cries for productivity, progress, certainty ... being present is key. We say: *Yes, if you can.* There are moments of silence in MAG where each is deeply present with their work: breathing alongside others, noting subtle changes, sitting close or at a distance with the intent of listening, being fully present. The research is performed as a deep embodied presencing towards changing the world we now live in. For RWC, capitalism becomes the monstrous other, to which the homeless/disabled body speaks back.

Knowledge Production: Is Our Knowledge Power?

For RWC, crip SPA is not just an aesthetic and material self-expression, but is a form of knowledge production — it is evidence — about the embodied lives lived within and beyond the social space of the women's shelter. An enacted, lived, produced, and shared knowledge that registers and finds recognition among bodies and across the senses (Abram 1996; Code 1995;

Hennessy 1993; Lather 1986; Marx 1988; McRuer 2006; Wacquant 1993). Challenging relational patterns in order to make possible multiple forms of knowledge exchange is inclusive of a decolonial perspective. Mignolo (2000: 81) writes that "an other thinking" would lead to the openness of the "unforeseeable diversity of the world" and of "unheard and unexpected" forms of knowledge. Our work is to stitch and colour within spaces of endurance, opening new spaces for altered economies of knowing, being, making, and exchanging.

> Do you have another needle? I just need a bit more thread. Can I take these with me? Do you have a minute? There is less than an inch left I just need some help in sewing up this heart. Can you hang on, just a sec? I feel too old for this, I'm sixty-seven now. These pants don't fit. Do we have any elastic just a bit would do? I am so hungry. Can anyone spare a token? I didn't sleep last night. There is nothing wrong with her heart. I read in the guardian that his body weight was incompatible with life. I can show you how to make a poodle and if you run out you can make a clown. They cut his benefits. I finished that one, it's really good. Gillie is still waiting. (davis halifax, *nos voisines*, 2015)

Art language *can* cope with contradictory knowledge forms (desires/impulses/needs to transgress and conform), and does not need to reach for a completed form of truth (facts, numerics, rhetorics, unified frameworks, knowledge that replaces older, less valid forms – that is, knowledge as competition). Instead, it works as texture, colour, affect between official forms and upsets and transgresses them; co-knowledge creation can be a map of sociality within the larger unknown (Gablik 1991; Clover 2011). A critique of elitist forms of knowledge puts forward the position that knowledge produced by excluded bodies is valuable and has critical weight. This work is about recognizing the expression of homeless disabled bodies also gendered/queered as dialectically important in a tense conversation towards an open future.

> I want to be treated as a real artist ... which I am ... and not a burning sensation. (RWC and Women from the Junction 2013: excerpt from *A*)

But what is this embodied knowledge generated from a site of homelessness and disability? It is knowledge of being impoverished that does not get heard. It is knowledge about an oppression that has been ongoing within capitalism since its inception, and even before, and it is therefore not the *new* knowledge demanded by academia. It is tiring old knowledge, especially for those living it, and the repetition of it nags. Yet there is nothing that can contain this repressed knowledge, which builds up pressure, causing anguish, and which is met by disbelief (Scarry 1985). Embodied knowledge makes an ethical demand. This is the knowledge that is invested in the knitting of a pair of baby booties or a wash cloth, or the activity of *nos voisines* on a street corner, sitting, stitching together a public art work: *the art of conversation* (RWC and MAG 2012).

> It might sound off the wall … is there any way that we can get those higher ups to come and live in the shelter system for a month with only the clothes on their back? 'cause then they would really know. (RWC and Women from the Junction 2013: excerpt from *A*)

Cultural Economy: Mending the Social Fabric

We do not draw a number of conclusions from our work, but in line with our crip and artistic temperament, we look for the unknowable, inconclusive specificity, the unnameable, and the self-named (Gablik 1991; davis halifax 2009). We find at the heart of the work a movement between bodies, a complex of tenuously fluxing exchanges based in the materiality of life. Performance theorist Shannon Jackson (2011) orients our gaze towards the material relations of support that subtend art production but often remain invisible in artworks. RWC understands that the economic web (political economy) of our work is an important part of the work. For us a redefinition of economy is synonymous with culture and cannot be separated from the mutuality of our survival (Blaney and Inayatullah 2009; Gibson-Graham 2008). Thus, all the exchange relations that build towards our coming together to create, contribute to how we understand what we are doing and becoming.

Our work, then, circulates within the realm of lumpen and diverse economies, of social reproduction as the feminized economic spaces of maintaining the social fabric (Gibson-Graham 2008; Gleeson 1999;

McLennan 2011). Social reproduction often takes the form of unpaid work, associated historically with women and the oppressed, often explained as child-rearing and other forms of caring-based or affective work that makes capitalist accumulation (profit) possible (Fraser 2014). Craft practices are also an important herstorical dimension of social reproduction. "My mother taught me to knit; I don't follow patterns — I just have to look at something" (*nos voisines*). The making of material objects is simultaneously the mending of a rift in the social fabric.

> We want a brick house full of rooms … you know and lots of things for women. (RWC and Women from the Junction 2013: excerpt from *X*)

Our critique observes RWC's designated poverty within a neoliberal society of over-consumption. And yet exchange *does* happen. In a space of scarcity, we manifest endurance into an ethics of abundance. "I don't need much" (*nos voisines*). We are only sporadically funded, and we work within material contingency: the materials come from Goodwill, are recycled, or, when we do have a bit of a budget, purchased. If we buy beads they are expensive and are quickly used up. We shop weekly for materials sometimes from Walmart, the Dollar Store, or art stores. Shopping is part of the performance. But we also think about the violence that subtends mass production; Walmart and the Dollar Stores, supported by exploited racialized labour there, intersect problematically with impoverished and poor bodies here, connected and competing at the bottom end of the system of capitalist production.

There is a whole complex ritual of working without. Some of *nos voisines* want to take as much as they can, some to squirrel away, some to take only what they need and give back what they don't use, some to make stuff to give back to the group to sell. Some women want rules like sign-up sheets. We negotiate distribution. We develop work on an ethics of sharing. Sometimes women don't come back.

The work creates useful objects, objects for warmth or contemplation. These often circulate as gifts, binding together family and friends into communities of mutual survival. They circulate also in recognition of how *nos voisines* are most often each other's first responders in a crisis, sharing knowledges that allow for survival. "I love her. She brought me vegan food while I was in the hospital." A pair of culottes knitted in a week are passed on to another; busy hands have calmed the spirit. Pleasure is found in the receiving and pleasure also in the warmth this pair of culottes provides. A card made for a child who's far away — for the moment. And we, RWC, are within this gifting and affective economy. We receive hats, paintings, homemade vegan cakes and dips, apples and cosmetics; whatever is circulating in this scant economic space — among these bodies — becomes an object for recognizing the social dimension in gratitude and love.

> One day I felt a great energy and I was going downtown to see the gay parade or Canada Day or whatever, and then I just rolled back again into my different energy. I struggle, I walk to the beaches and write the poems, because you know, you want to express yourself. (RWC and Women from the Junction 2013: excerpt from J)

The aesthetics of our work is determined both by the conditions of lack that we work with and by the exuberance of creative bodies. There is a different kind of vision/appreciation that we as RWC contribute: it's allowed to be what it is. Error, failure, mistakes, absences are part of the ontology (the core being) of crip art work: you don't have to rip out the row of crochet, missed stitches belong, learning is tacit and embodied, hand over hand and through observation (Shotwell 2011). RWC advises: imagine differently — do not plan to knit an item in one colour but work with small supplies, make small things. That *nos voisines* might imagine the work as another lack of resources intertwines with RWC's imagining dialogue. The dialogue weaves with the materials and the conditions in which we create. RWC wants to open up the material world, but we don't have the access either. The neoliberal real constricts distribution, stresses our bodies, constrains relations. If the arts/theory world looks from the outside at what we are doing as artists within the larger community, they critique it from within already prescribed conventions. Our response is that those conventions do not apply to this work: we are thinking and doing differently (Gablik 1991). Our work addressses the totality of the processes of material aesthetic practices and the relationalities that subtend them.

Back and Forth

The work of RWC supports the development of alternate perceptions; as such, our praxis advances knowledge of the lived experiences, and orients toward the needs, interests, and capacities of *nos voisines*, of homelessness, and of the ethics of a proposed social responsibility. *Our desire is to redistribute indifference.* Without praxis-based work, political engagement and theoretical analysis remain abstracted from the communities and bodies from within which the knowledge arises.

RWC's praxis has implications across scales from the embodied to the national. In the MAG, we create an inclusive space where everyone's presence, skills, and knowledge are validated; we work against state restrictions (the Safe Streets Act and state-enforced poverty through acts including Ontario Works and Ontario Disability Support Program) to create spaces of crip belonging that challenge received understandings of democracy and its processes. On the scale of art and academia, RWC argues for the political recognition of aesthetic knowledge forms and the agency of their producers that have often been disqualified through disempowering biomedical and social work frames. Our work thinks unlike dominant Euro-Western epistemologies. We suggest that the difference is of use; that incomplete, excessive, inadequate knowledge/s and knowing/s are helpful as we advance important public questions about violence, poverty, and disability. The production and inclusion of the critical knowledges of *nos voisines* challenge dominant and narrow notions of Canadian society and its normative citizen insofar as they complicate the "typical" subject of homeless or disabled research. This knowledge, produced with ethical considerations, reveals a further contradiction between the violence experienced by *nos voisines* and the values of our liberal democracy: equal opportunity and the right to difference within Canada's multicultural paradigm. This work reaches through the fog of bland and limited Canadian nationalist self-perceptions toward a disruptive and revolutionary inclusivity.

We started this chapter with a call for non-indifference against the repetitive refrains of the homelessness/disability "problem." RWC hopes to interrupt the proposals for homelessness and housing policy that have been deemed failed by *nos voisines* and others. Orienting the work around a deep praxis demands the sharing of space and the co-production of knowledge in community. This co-production can act slowly, with kindness, toward the construction of a world that listens and responds, and that is not indifferent to those who are left outside its care.

The inclusion of *nos voisines* as participants in knowledge and social transformation asks for a long-term commitment, recognition, and a place within academic discourse. It is difficult to sustain indifference when sharing space and co-producing knowledge with homeless, disabled, poor bodies. Inclusion necessitates redefining the communities in which we live and circulate, no matter what kind of negative differences and segregations society lays upon their/our bodies. Continued research on the role of art as a basis of democratized inclusion and expression of knowledge is vital. As inclusion expands into other disciplinary, social, and political fields, possibilities become available, for movement on reforms to a national housing plan in the short term, and more radical transformation of capitalist and colonial relationalities in the long term.

Trying to Undo the Violences

RWC recognizes and problematizes the vulnerability to violence experienced by women with disabilities. We have outlined how multiple forms of disablement and class (constituted through disability, gender, sexuality, and race) are intersectionally knotted within a neoliberal Canadian context and its relentless roll-back of services and supports. Neoliberal, and more recently, far-right political and economic strategies serve to increase the violence and violent conditions that women with disabilities endure. Our discussion of the representation of othered bodies demonstrates another form of violence, which further disables women from participation. Our work with *nos voisines* and our experience of disability and homelessness, our engagement with crip forms of knowledge production, and crip social praxis art, are offered as ameliorative and resistive practices. We are all implicated in the violences of capitalism; disentangling ourselves through decolonizing, feminist, and reflexive tactics furthers egalitarianism and democratic relationalities. Our critique of capitalism as an inherently violent sociality is integral to a fuller awareness of its devastating effects and its subtle and extreme accumulated harms. The engagement with material, emotional, intellectual conditions of daily life across multiple intersectional positionalities in a social space marked by crushing poverty, disability, and homelessness is MAG, is the art.

> I don't know what to do. I feel so strong about doing something, anything. I mean, sincerely, if I have to go on a hunger strike I would, because everybody needs a life, everybody ... especially when they are so honest and they work so hard and they lost everything. How do you make it right? We feel like losers but I'm not. That's me. That's how I feel. That's who I am. (RWC and Women from the Junction 2013: excerpt from J)

Acknowledgements

The project Women's Stories of Aging, Disability and Homelessness was supported by our community partner, with funding from the Canadian Centre on Disability Studies and the Faculty of Health, York University. Women of the Red Wagon Collective and the Monday Art Group gave many hours of their time to make the project happen. Our group includes women with a spectrum of complex lived experiences and incredible stories to tell of precarious housing, disability, and aging, women who live/d in and around the Junction. They want an audience that listens; they want a response.

Notes

1. Living as homeless includes living in precarious, unsafe housing and shelters, and couch surfing. In addition to the empirical work of RWC, we rely on the work done by the Canadian Homelessness Research Network and the Homeless Hub research unit at York University for an understanding of its complexities: homelesshub.ca/CHRNhomelessdefinition.
2. The Junction is a rapidly gentrifying neighbourhood, a neighbourhood constructed as sketchy where poor and working-class people are being displaced through the influx of middle-class, wealthy people, property speculation, and condo development seen as revitalization.
3. Our intent is not to collapse conceptions of homelessness and disability; rather, we acknowledge that these categories encompass diverse, unstable, fluid, intersecting, embodied differences and inequities.
4. The original artists in the collective were Loree Lawrence, Amy Kazymerchuk, and Noah Kenneally. Liz Forsberg, nancy viva davis halifax, and Liza Kim Jackson joined the collective in 2008 and 2009 during its second phase to complete the banner project.

5. The other refers to "one part in a totality of which two components are necessary to one another" (Simone de Beauvoir quoted in Waterston 1993: 27). More specifically, the normative bourgeois body is wholly dependent upon the non-normative body for its empowerment: the bourgeois body literally lives off the multiple forms of labour of oppressed bodies, as well as deriving its sense of moral superiority from the charitable relations that it establishes to keep the oppressed in their place.

6. In Indigenous resistance movements we hear also that we are all in a relation of treaty people on First Nations territory, with those of us non-Indigenous folks positioned as guests.

7. The monstrous can be understood through a white bourgeois lens as a "lumpen" or street criminal, unruly, disorderly, amoral, and abject mass — as difference — effeminate, childlike, undeserving, poor, a vector of contagion, tainted, mutated, mad, crip, racially impure, and always a threat to the dominant social order and the normative bourgeois body (Davis 1995; Garland-Thomson 2002; Hadley 2008; Malchow 1993; Moretti 1982; Shildrick 2002; Stiker 1999).

References

Abram, David. 1996. *The Spell of the Sensuous: Perception and Language in a More-Than-Human World*. New York: Pantheon.

Ahmed, Sara. 2006. *Queer Phenomenology: Orientations, Objects, Others*. Durham and London: Duke University Press.

Belanger, Yale D., Olu Awosoga, and Gabrielle Weasel Head. 2013. "Homelessness, Urban Aboriginal People, and the Need for a National Enumeration." *Aboriginal Policy Studies*, 2, 2.

Blaney David L., and Naeem Inayatullah. 2009. *Savage Economics: Wealth, Poverty, and the Temporal Walls of Capitalism*. New York and London: Routledge.

Bolt, Barbara. 2010. *Heidegger Reframed: Interpreting Key Thinkers for the Arts*. London and New York: IB Tauris.

Bourke, Alan, Tia Dafnos and Markus Kip (eds.). 2011. *Lumpencity: Discourses of Marginality*. Ottawa, ON: Red Quill Books.

Braidotti, Rosi. 2013. *The Posthuman*. Cambridge, UK: Polity Press.

Butler, Judith. 1997. *Excitable Speech: A Politics of the Performative*. New York and London: Routledge.

Chandler, Eliza. 2013. "Cripping Community: New Meanings of Disability and Community." <nomorepotlucks.org/site/cripping-community-new-meanings-of-disability-and-community>.

Cho, Sumi, Kimberlé Williams Crenshaw and Leslie McCall. 2013. "Toward a Field of Intersectionality Studies: Theory, Applications, and Praxis." *Signs: Journal of Women in Culture and Society*, 38, 4.

Clover, Darlene. 2011. "Success and Challenges of Feminist Arts-Based Participatory Methodologies with Homeless/Street Involved Women in Victoria." *Action Research*, 9, 1.

Code, Lorraine. 1995. *Rhetorical Spaces: Essays on Gendered Locations*. New York and London: Routledge.

Crenshaw, Kimberlé Williams. 1989. "Demarginalizing the Intersection of Race and Sex: A Black Feminist Critique of Antidiscrimination Doctrine, Feminist Theory and Antiracist Politics." *University of Chicago Legal Forum*, 1989, 1, Article 8.

___. 1991. "Mapping the Margins: Intersectionality, Identity Politics, and Violence against Women of Color." *Stanford Law Review*, 43, 6.

Davis, Lennard. J. 1995. *Enforcing Normalcy: Disability, Deafness, and the Body*. New York and London: Verso.

davis halifax, nancy viva. 2009. *Disability and Arts-Informed Research: Moving toward Postconventional Representations*. Amherst and London: Cambria Press.

___. 2015. "nos voisines" in *hook*. Hugh Maclennan Poetry Series. Montreal and Kingston: McGill Queen's University Press.

Derrida, Jacques. 1988. *Limited Inc*. Evanston: Northwestern University.

Eagleton, Terry. 1990. *The Ideology of the Aesthetic*. Oxford: Basil Blackwell.

Erevelles, Nirmala. 1996. "Disability and the Dialectics of Difference." *Disability & Society*, 11, 4

Erevelles, Nirmala, and Andrea Minear. 2010. "Unspeakable Offenses: Untangling Race and Disability in Discourses of Intersectionality." *Journal of Literary & Cultural Disability Studies*, 4, 2.

Ferris, Jim. 2004. "The Enjambed Body: A Step toward a Crippled Poetics." *The Georgia Review*, 58, 2.

Foucault, Michel. 1995. *Discipline and Punish*. New York: Vintage and Random House.

Fracchia, Joseph. 2008. "The Capitalist Labour Process and the Body in Pain: The Corporeal Depths of Marx's Concept of Immiseration." *Historical Materialism*, 16, 4.

Fraser, Nancy. 2014. "Behind Marx's Hidden Abode: For an Expanded Conception of Capitalism." *New Left Review*, 86.

Fritsch, Kelly. 2013. "On the Negative Possibility of Suffering: Adorno, Feminist Philosophy, and the Transfigured Crip to Come." *Disability Studies Quarterly*, 33, 4.

Gablik, Suzi. 1991. *The Reenchantment of Art*. New York: Thames and Hudson.

Gaetz, S. 2010. "The Struggle to End Homelessness in Canada: How We Created the Crisis, and How We Can End It." *The Open Health Services and Policy Journal*, 3.

Garland-Thomson, Rosemarie. 2002. "Integrating Disability, Transforming Feminist Theory." *NWSA Journal*, 14, 3.

Gibson-Graham, Julie Katherine. 2008. "Diverse Economies: Performative Practices for 'Other Worlds.'" Manuscript based on the Progress in Human Geography Lecture, March 2006, Chicago AAG.

Gleeson, Brendan. 1999. *Geographies of Disability*. New York and London: Routledge.

Government of Canada. 2013. "Snapshot of Racialized Poverty in Canada." <esdc.gc.ca/eng/communities/reports/poverty_profile/snapshot.shtml>.

Hadley, Bree. 2008. "Mobilising the Monster: Modern Disabled Performers' Manipulation of the Freakshow." *M/C Journal*, 11, 3.

Haraway, Donna. 1991. *Simians, Cyborgs, and Women: The Reinvention of Women*. London and New York: Routledge.

Hennessy, Rosemary. 1993. "Women's Lives/Feminist Knowledge: Feminist

Standpoint as Ideology Critique." *Hypatia,* 8, 1.

homelessness. Canadian Homelessness Research Unit. <homelesshub.ca/CHRNhomelessdefinition>.

Hulchanski, J.D. 2009a. "Homelessness in Canada: Past, Present, Future." Keynote speech presented at Growing Home: Housing and Homelessness in Canada. Calgary, Alberta.

____. 2009b. *Finding Home: Policy Options for Addressing Homelessness in Canada.* The Homeless Hub.

Jackson, Kim. 2009. "The Reproduction of Capitalism and Culture in the Junction." Unpublished masters thesis, Interdisciplinary Studies, York University.

Jackson, Shannon. 2011. *Social Works: Performing Art, Supporting Publics.* New York and London: Routledge.

Johnson, Merri Lisa, and Robert McRuer. 2014. "Cripistemologies." *Journal of Literary & Cultural Disability Studies,* 8, 2.

Kafer, Alison. 2013. *Feminist, Queer, Crip.* Indiana University Press.

Kawash, Samira. 1998. "The Homeless Body." *Public Culture,* 10, 2.

Kester, Grant. 2004. *Conversation Pieces: Community and Communication in Modern Art.* Berkeley, L.A. and London: University of California Press.

Khandor, Erika, and Kate Mason. 2007. "The Street Health Report 2007." Research Bulletin #2, Women and Homelessness. Toronto, ON: Street Health.

Khosla, Prabha. n.d. "Women's Poverty in Cities." Women in Urban Environments. <twca.ca/wp-content/uploads/2013/02/Women_Poverty_in_Cities.pdf>.

Lacy, Suzanne (ed.). 1995. *Mapping the Terrain: New Genre Public Art.* San Francisco: CA: Bay Press.

Lather, Patti. 1986. "Research as Praxis." *Harvard Educational Review,* 56, 3.

____. 1996. "Troubling Clarity: The Politics of Accessible Language." *Harvard Educational Review,* 66, 3.

Levi, Ron, and Mariana Valverde. 2006. "Freedom of the City: Canadian Cities and the Quest for Governmental Status." *Osgoode Hall Law Journal,* 44, 3.

Lyon-Callo, Vincent. 2002. "Medicalizing Homelessness: The Production of Self-Blame and Self-Governing within Homeless Shelters." *Medical Anthropology Quarterly, New Series,* 14, 3.

MacKinnon, Catherine A. 2013. "Intersectionality as Method: A Note." *Signs,* 38, 4.

Malchow, H.L. 1993. "Frankenstein's Monster and Images of Race in Nineteenth-Century Britain." *Past and Present,* 139, 1.

Marx, Karl. 1988. "Private Property and Communism." *Economic and Philosophic Manuscripts of 1844.* New York: Prometheus Books.

McClintock, Anne. 1995. *Imperial Leather: Race, Gender, and Sexuality in the Colonial Contest.* Routledge.

McIntyre, M., and H.J. Nast. 2011. "Bio Necro Polis: Marx, Surplus Populations, and the Spatial Dialectics of Reproduction and 'Race'." *Antipode,* 43, 5.

McLennan, M. 2011. "Our Streets! Practice and Theory of the Ottawa Panhandlers' Union." In A. Bourke, T. Dafnos and M. Kip (eds.), *Lumpencity: Discourses of Marginality.* Ottawa, ON: Red Quill Books.

McRuer, Robert. 2006. *Crip Theory: Cultural Signs of Queerness and Disability.* New

York: New York University Press.

Mignolo, W. D. (2000). *Local histories/global designs: Coloniality, subaltern knowledges, and border thinking.* Princeton University Press.

Mignolo, Walter D. 2009. "Coloniality: The Darker Side of Modernity." In Sabine Breitwisser (ed.), *Modernologies; Contemporary Artists Researching Modernity and Modernism.* Catalog of the Exhibit. Barcelona, Spain: Modernologia/Modernologies/Modernology at the Museum of Modern Art.

Mohanty, Chandra Talpade. 1988. "Under Western Eyes: Feminist Scholarship and Colonial Discourses." *Feminist Review,* 30, 1.

___. 2003. "Under Western Eyes Revisited: Feminist Solidarity through Anticapitalist Struggles." *Signs,* 28, 2.

Moretti, Franco. 1982. "The Dialectic of Fear." *New Left Review,* 136, 10.

Ontario Disability Support Program Act, 1997, S.O. 1997, c. 25, Sched. B.

Ontario Works Act, 1997, S.O. 1997, c. 25, Sched. A.

Patrick, Caryl. 2014. *Aboriginal Homelessness in Canada: A Literature Review.* Toronto: Canadian Homelessness Research Network Press.

Povinelli, Elizabeth. 2011. *Economies of Abandonment: Social Belonging and Endurance in Late Liberalism.* Durham and London: Duke University Press.

Puar, Jasbir. 2009. "Prognosis Time: Towards a Geopolitics of Affect, Debility and Capacity." *Women & Performance: A Journal of Feminist Theory,* 19, 2.

RWC (Red Wagon Collective) and MAG. 2012. Installation. "The art of conversation. Tel.talk. Curators Paola Poletto, Liis Toliao, and Yvonne Koscielak. Toronto.

RWC (Red Wagon Collective) and Women from the Junction. 2013. *We Have a Message: Women's Stories of Aging, Disability and Homelessness.* Toronto: anagraphia.

Rosler, Martha. 2006. *3 works.* Halifax: The Press of the Nova Scotia College of Art and Design.

Safe Streets Act, 1999, S.O. 1999, c. 8.

Sandahl, Carrie. 2003. "Queering the Crip or Cripping the Queer? Intersections of Queer and Crip Identities in Solo Autobiographical Performance." *GLQ: A Journal of Lesbian and Gay Studies,* 9, 1.

Savage, Mary C. 2003. "Can Ethnographic Narrative Be a Neighbourly Act?" In Yvonna S. Lincoln and Norman K. Denzin (eds.), *Turning Points in Qualitative Research: Tying Knots in a Handkerchief.* Walnut Creek, CA: Altimira Press.

Scarry, Elaine. 1985. *The Body In Pain: The Making and Unmaking of the World.* New York and Oxford: Oxford University Press.

Shildrick, Margrit. 2002. *Embodying the Monster: Encounters with the Vulnerable Self.* London: Sage.

___. 2005. "The Disabled Body, Genealogy and Undecidability." *Cultural Studies,* 19, 6.

Shotwell, Alexis. 2011. *Knowing Otherwise: Race, Gender, and Implicit Understanding.* University Park: Pennsylvania State Press.

Stanley, Liz (ed.). 2013 [1990]. *Feminist Praxis: Research, Theory and Epistemology in Feminist Sociology.* New York/Oxon: Routledge.

Stiker, Henri J. 1999. *A History of Disability.* Ann Arbor, MI: University of Michigan Press.

Street Health Report. 2007. "Research Bulletin #2." Women and Homelessness.

Taylor, Diana. 2006. "Performance and/as History." *TDR*, 50, 1.

Titchkosky, Tanya. 2000. "Disability Studies: The Old and the New." *Canadian Journal of Sociology/Cahiers Canadiens de Sociologie*, 25, 2.

Van Manen, Max. 2014. *Phenomenology of Practice: Meaning-Giving Methods in Phenomenological Research and Writing*. Walnut Creek, CA: Left Coast Press.

Wacquant, Loic. 1993. "On the Tracks of Symbolic Power: Prefatory Notes to Bourdieu's 'State Nobility.'" *Theory, Culture & Society*, 10.

___. 2009. *Punishing the Poor*. Durham and London: Duke University Press.

Waegemakers, Jeanette, and Alina Turner. 2014. *Housing First in Rural Canada: Rural Homelessness and Housing First Feasibility Across 22 Rural Canadian Communities*. Alberta: University of Calgary.

Waterston, Alisse. 1993. *Street Addicts in the Political Economy*. Philadelphia: Temple University Press.

Weininger, Elliot B. 2005. "Pierre Bourdieu on Social Class and Symbolic Violence." In Elliot O. Wright (ed.), *Approaches to Class Analysis*. Cambridge, UK: Cambridge University Press.

Yates, Michelle. 2011. "The Human-As-Waste, the Labor Theory of Value and Disposability in Contemporary Capitalism." *Antipode*, 43, 5.

Section III

Violence and
Social Services

Chapter 8

Home Care
Gendered Violence in Independent Living Attendant Services

Christine Kelly

D isability activists and scholars have long demonstrated how care operates as a complex form of oppression. This oppression ranges from subtle to overt, and encompasses individual experiences of coercion, physical and emotional abuse at the hands of "caregivers," and denial of agency, as well as systemic forms of oppressive care such as forced institutionalization and sterilization of disabled bodies. The oppressive potentials and histories of care also include the coercion of gendered, racialized, and/ or globalized bodies into caring servitude with tangible financial and social consequences (Nakano Glenn 2010), abuse of caregivers (Armstrong et al. 2011), and the social devaluation and erasure of the labour of care (Kittay 1999). However, care is not always oppressive. Care is potentially transformative and can form the foundation of fulfilling relationships and careers (Kittay 1999). The adequate and meaningful provision of care can "mediate citizenship" for people with disabilities and others who require support to participate in daily life (Krogh 2004). Unquestionably, care is a tension both in and beyond the context of disability (Kelly 2013).

Attendant services informed by Independent Living represent a practical policy response that confronts care as a multi-faceted form of oppression while simultaneously holding potential as an emancipatory form of service delivery (Kelly 2014). A qualitative study of the Ontario

Direct Funding program points to three themes related to abuse and violence: the expanded sense of violence and feelings of risk experienced under direct funding; lived experiences of gender-based violence from the perspectives of people with disabilities and attendants; and racialized and gendered hiring practices. Discourses of empowerment and choice falter, and gender, race, and impairment become salient in light of potential and actual abuse of service users and attendants. These abuses take place within a social and cultural background where both disability and gendered forms of labour, including attendant work, are devalued.

Independent Living and Direct Funding

Independent Living movements in North America aim to promote models of attendant services that emphasize choice, control, and empowerment for disabled people who require assistance with daily needs. This shift extends beyond notions of "cheaper" or "more efficient" service delivery to speak back to a history and ongoing reality of the mass institutionalization of disabled bodies. Institutionalization conveys social messages that devalue disability; it enacts daily violences through denial of choice and the routinization of daily life and can lead to abuse, injury, and even murder of disabled people (see Ben-Moshe, Chapman. and Carey 2014). There are a range of mechanisms to implement Independent Living, from shared supported living arrangements, outreach services arranged by an agency, to the most contentious and potentially liberating approach, direct funding. Under direct funding, individuals with disabilities are given funds to hire and manage attendants, thus providing flexibility and control over the services. In contrast to other models of attendant services, even those with Independent Living orientations, direct funding enables disabled people to choose who will assist them and when and where these services will be delivered. Many other attendant service options are tied to specific locations (such as the apartment), whereas direct funding attendants can "follow" the person with a disability to different locations. Because of these benefits, direct funding models of support are advocated by Independent Living movements in the United States, Canada, and the United Kingdom (Barnes 2007; Keigher 2007; Yoshida et al. 2004). The Ontario Direct Funding program in this study is administered by an Independent Living centre.

Independent Living does not exist without criticism, as some activists and scholars find the model perpetuates the myth of independence and does not include a radical re-visioning of the social order or of disability (Mingus 2011). The success of Independent Living has also led to a phenomenon where the phrase "Independent Living" is deployed in a variety of contexts that may not necessarily have any connection with or awareness of the historical movement and philosophy. Further, the phrase can even be utilized in settings that are quite oppositional to the ideals behind Independent Living. It is essential, then, to critically evaluate the use of this phrase in care settings.

Direct funding typically includes increased responsibility and administrative duties for disabled service recipients. In a broader landscape, direct funding programs, including the one in this study, are part of neoliberal and austerity trends that individualize, "down-shift" (that is, shift responsibility from governments to the non-profit sector or to individuals), and cut services. These changes take place under the guise of "choice" and represent examples of how neoliberalism is not just a top-down policy framework, but is enacted by individual citizens (Larner 2000). Disability activists strongly promote direct funding for its tangible benefits in daily life, and part of this activism highlights the cost-effectiveness of this style of service delivery. Simultaneously, the same (or parallel) groups of disabled people protest other cuts to social spending that disproportionately affect disabled and chronically ill people (Goodley, Lawthom and Runswick-Cole 2014). Direct funding policy mechanisms represent conflicting trends in policy and social justice spheres that, like care, can be empowering, flexible, destructive, and systematically oppressive all in the same instance.

These themes are, in part, the result of a qualitative study exploring conceptualizations of and resistance to a concept of "care" within the Ontario Direct Funding program. "Self-manager" is the term used by the Ontario program to refer to people with disabilities who receive funding for attendant services. The study included fifty-four in-depth, semi-structured interviews with nineteen people who were key to the formation or administration of the program (six of whom were also self-managers), fourteen self-managers receiving funding, fifteen attendants, and six informal supports, as well as an analysis of relevant material in the public domain. The interviews were conducted in 2011 and transcribed "intelligent verbatim" style, and the thematic analysis was informed by feminist and disability scholarship around care. A limitation of the study was the limited number of people of colour among self-managers (there was only one) and attendant participants. This is especially problematic in light of a pilot survey on the demographics of care workers in Ontario that estimates approximately 40 percent are visible minority women (Lum, Sladek, and Ying 2010).[1] On three occasions, despite attempts to encourage them to participate, attendants declined because English was not their first language. Thus, commentary on the racialized and globalized nature of care work is preliminary and based on surrounding literature and second-hand accounts from the study participants. All participants are given pseudonyms.

Expanded Sense of Violence and Feelings of Risk

Independent Living attendant services attempt to create different spaces and understandings of care and support. While incredibly liberating as an opportunity to control who, when, and how support is managed, direct funding also brings a new set of vulnerabilities, as the administrative structures are significantly diminished or absent, leaving little recourse for arranging back-up support or filing complaints about attendants.

The concept of abuse incorporates conventional understandings of physical and emotional abuse, which unfortunately take place within these contexts. However, our understandings of abuse must also incorporate the risk of leaving a person stranded (Saxton et al. 2001). In this study, the risk of being stranded, whether it is because an attendant is late or does not show up, or because something happens between available hours, results in significant anxiety among the self-managers. For example, one self-manager shared, "you have to rely on attendants. There's been a couple times where I've been really stuck. I've been in the bed and have had to go to the washroom really bad. And my attendant came late." This story did not end well as the self-manager was forced to soil the bed while he waited for the attendant to come.

Jason, a self-manager, shares:

> Two weeks ago, there was a night where one of my attendants was sick and I don't want them coming in when they're sick. And

there was only one other person who could do that shift, the night shift … He had been up all night the night before playing video games, so he wasn't really feeling much like doing an overnight … I said, "You know I have no one else, so if you don't come in tonight I'm not sleeping. I'm sleeping in my chair. I gotta work tomorrow. I'll be in the same clothes. There's not much I can do here. I don't know what you want from me, I'm sorry but I, I have nothing else. Do me a favour here, you know?" So, he was like, "Well I'm gonna be honest with you, it's a real pain in my ass. It pisses me off but I'll come in." So, he came in and we had a little bit of a discussion and I thought everything was smoothed out, but apparently not because he gave his two weeks' notice a couple days later.

Jason had to plead with the attendant to come in and do him "a favour," a favour that amounts to the basic human dignities of being able to go to the bathroom, sleep in a bed, eat, and get ready for work in the morning. The risks of being stranded are far beyond inconvenience; they move into the world of abuse. Even in this example, while the attendant ultimately relents and comes to help Jason, he manipulates him and tries to make him feel guilty about his "unreasonable" request. The attendant seems oblivious to the power dynamics of this interaction, as what he characterizes as a "pain in the ass" will prevent fairly serious physical and emotional distress for Jason. This is not to say that attendants should remain on call at all times, but points to the need for formalized systems of back-up that can be deployed without moralizing, guilt-ridden interactions that themselves may be considered on a spectrum of cultural or emotional abuse related to disability, vulnerability, and care.

Other self-managers talked about being stranded in minor ways:

Isabelle: The one anxiety I had going into direct funding is once an attendant's gone I can't just call them to come back. I have to wait until the next person, whenever that might be. So that was a bit anxiety-provoking in the beginning. But that didn't last long. That anxiety didn't last long.

Jason: It's exciting to have new attendants, I like that, new people in my life, but it's nerve-wracking as well. You know you bring on these new people and what if they're terrible? What if they're not great? What if they don't show up? What if they don't do the job? Maybe I misread them entirely in the interview, and if that's the case, then what do I do?

These examples demonstrate how being stranded can have emotional and physical repercussions. Isabelle says that her anxieties "didn't last long," although there were other points in the interviews where she expressed similar concerns. The sense of vulnerability is not exclusively linked to direct funding, but is based on individual and collective histories of abuse and coercion at the hands of caregivers in a variety of settings.

Some of the attendants understand how important their jobs are, since they often come in during extreme weather or when sick. One female attendant comments, "[if I was sick] I think I'd probably be like, 'Hey I feel like shit, do you have anyone else?' And then if they didn't have anyone I would just go." Another male attendant shared a story of being quite ill but continuing to assist the self-manager rather than leave in the middle of a shift. Unlike Jason's attendant, who ended up quitting, most of the attendants interviewed took their roles and positions very seriously.

Experiences of Gendered Violence

Beyond being stranded, self-managers and attendants both experience gendered violence within attendant service settings. Some self-managers shared stories of physical and/or financial abuse as well as sexual harassment and assault, while many of the female attendants reported having to deal with unwanted sexualized attention. Almost all the self-managers had lived in other attendant service arrangements prior to direct funding, and the stories of abuse and coercion came from across their life experiences, aligning with how endemic caregiver, intimate partner, and other forms of violence are against disabled people, especially women (Brownridge 2006; Nosek et al. 2001; Mays 2006; Odell 2011; Rajan 2004). Even in a program that seeks to reverse power dynamics and create a respectful delivery of services, abuse and coercion are lurking possibilities and realities for many disabled people.

One self-manager reluctantly shared her experience of abuse, although she was understandably uncomfortable about providing specific details.

When asked if she had ever hired a man as an attendant, Hélène shared that she did once, but had to fire him because he was abusing her. She further clarified that having female attendants does not necessarily protect a person from abuse. After the abuse, she went for help to the local Independent Living centre. She shares:

> Hélène: At the beginning they try to prove it to you that they are good people. So he was really good with me and then slowly…
> CK: It started happening.
> Hélène: Yeah. But he was an abuser a long time. He's been in prison for abusing. But you don't know that.
> CK: Did you report him to the police?
> Hélène: What happened was I went to Independent Living for, to help for that, to make him go. But I didn't have any attendant [as a back-up]. But my thinking was not all there. I was so tired, emotionally and physically and all that. Like I didn't think of anything. [They] were going to bring me to a shelter for a while. But there was no shelter for disabled people available at that time.

Without a back-up system in place, Hélène is faced with a very difficult decision. She could fire her attendant and report the abuse, but then she would have no one to help with the essential activities of daily life and could not access the emergency shelters. More generally, when self-managers recognized abuse in various forms they were not always able to dismiss the attendants immediately, because they first needed to find another person. Finding reliable, relationally suitable attendants is very difficult for all of the self-managers, especially since many people only work as attendants on a temporary basis. Hélène continues:

> I would say about most people don't report any abuse like that. So, nothing really [changes]. You can meet a lot of people who are in that situation. Disabled or not. It's very scary sometimes.

Hélène further shared that prior to working with her, this person had been in prison four times for abusing disabled clients. She resolved this situation by relying on an informal emergency attendant system operating through the local Independent Living centre while she searched for a new attendant. This support was available only because a specific employee volunteered to serve in this role beyond her job description and the mandate of the centre.

The problem of not being able to report abuse because back-up support is lacking is further compounded by the feelings of vulnerability. In a situation of fairly serious financial abuse, one self-manager had won a $4000 prize in a lottery game and an attendant bullied him into splitting the winnings. It took the self-manager weeks before he summoned the nerve to fire the person. He said, "I didn't know what he would have done ... We are pretty vulnerable population. And I think about that all the time." The self-manager is acutely aware of his vulnerable position in relation to the attendants, to the point that he was coerced out of fear into giving the attendant money and was unable to address the situation for a couple of weeks.

Moore and Breeze (2012) explore questions of gender, fear, and violence in the context of public toilets. The men in their study were fearful of violence in the public washrooms, whereas the women felt relatively safe. They argue that situations in which the "familiar gender hierarchy no longer applies" lend themselves to increased feelings of fear among men (Moore and Breeze 2012). This gender role disruption also takes place when men with disabilities require daily physical assistance, at times exacerbating feelings of vulnerability.

The potential for abuse of disabled people is well documented. And, people involved in the administration, development, or oversight of attendant services do comment on techniques used to address it. For example, Reg, a community researcher, comments:

> The thing is there are elements of abuse. For example, I remember dealing with an 82- year-old former OPP officer who was sexually assaulted by a male PSW worker from a reputable agency ... You have to ask questions such as where's the oversight for potential abuse? And how do you protect the client?

Reg went on to speak about the role of monitoring technology that would enable warning systems and police record checks. He also spoke about an attitudinal change required of home care agencies, in which many of the staff were dismissive of this widespread problem.

George, a policy maker when the Ontario Direct Funding program was established, commented on the need for formal mechanisms for addressing abuse and exploitation of attendants:

> In some cases you have to have a mechanism to avoid exploitation. We see that in home care all the time. It's serious! We've got some weird stuff going on! … How do you put in staff? How do you allow them to hire staff if you know they're going to exploit them, or worse, abuse them? In some cases physically, or sexually abuse [them].

George's comment was supported by the attendants. These experiences are often gendered and racialized in that women are more likely to report harassment and unwanted sexual violence. As Armstrong et al. (2011) found in other long-term care settings, care workers face a high risk of abuse. In this study, attendants reported instances of mainly verbal abuse; for example, one attendant, Mathieu, spoke about how attendants are "talked down to and there's disparaging remarks made." Some attendants also talked about feelings of being taken advantage of (such as staying longer to help even if they were not paid) or becoming too emotionally involved. The attendants most frequently mentioned or alluded to unwanted sexual advances, especially from male self-managers towards female attendants. Attendants spoke about "inappropriate comments to the female staff" and "incidents of attendants being put into positions where they felt uncomfortable or being propositioned."

Indeed, gendered violence is a reality within "caring" arrangements, and this violence flows both towards and from disabled people. This reality applies to arrangements that strive towards empowerment and social participation, such as direct funding. It is not direct funding specifically that leads to abuse and mistreatment between disabled people and their attendants, a concern often raised by opponents to this model; rather, it is a problem endemic to the provision of support and likely linked to the social devaluation of gendered labour, such as care work, as well as disability as a social category. In some ways, Independent Living attendant services, including direct funding, attempt to address and prevent the violences of care. Independent Living philosophy, however, is only one tool that cannot fully account for the risks and deeply embedded social messages at play.

A final example of violence highlights the fact that male self-managers also experience abuse. This example is from a health crisis where Jim had a prolonged hospital stay:

> Jim: You have no idea what I went through. I was abused twice.
> I: While you were at the hospital recently?
> Jim: "I need to be turned. Please turn me. I'm going to develop a sore." "Ok, here we go." The one woman grabbed me by the neck and pulled me back by the neck of my t-shirt. I said "No not like that! You've gotta reach under my shoulder." She dug her claws in and tried to get her purchase on my shoulder. Then they turned me. I said "Now can you pull my --" and out the door they go out. So I was in the position of having to yell "Help!" I'm not the kind of person that's neurotic. And they just wouldn't answer me, they wouldn't answer my bell. They wouldn't come to me. They wouldn't do what I wanted. They wouldn't let me self-direct. They didn't know how to do it. I had a broken leg that time. I had a broken leg both times actually. It's a long story. It's a side story, but I was abused quite regularly and consistently. So I hired my own help. It cost me thousands.

Jim preferred his own attendants to the extent that he used a large amount of his personal funds to hire his "own help." In other parts of our conversation, Jim explained how he nearly died during his hospital stay, largely because of poor care. The health professionals refused to listen to his knowledge about his previous infections and positions that best support his breathing. Self-direction as promoted by Independent Living extends far beyond preferences or catering to the whims of a self-manager, but can mean life or death. The terrible hospital stay experienced by Jim suggests that the consumer-control model of Independent Living/direct funding mechanisms may decrease the potential for abuse. Other research has demonstrated that large-scale institutions constitute a "logic of incarceration" that acts as a form of social control. Thus, efforts for deinstitutionalization inherently reduce the risks of violence (Chapman, Carey, and Ben-Moshe 2014). Other research finds factors such as family ties, race or ethnicity, social supports, language compatibility, and provider turnover more relevant to the risk of abuse than funding mechanism (Matthias and Benjamin 2003).

Gendered and Racialized Hiring Practices

Direct funding enables people of colour and members of religious, linguistic, sexual, and other minorities to hire attendants with the same backgrounds, or at the very least accepting worldviews. On the other hand, it can also enable discrimination on the basis of these same factors. It is not possible to estimate the demographic profile of self-managers or attendants in the Ontario Direct Funding program based on this study. However, an evaluation of the pilot program (which served 102 people at the time) identified 16 percent of attendants as being "visible minorities" and 10 percent whose "first language [is] neither English nor French"; it did not provide information on country of birth (Roeher Institute 1997). Immigrants to Canada, whether racialized people or not, are often encouraged by employment agencies to consider working as care providers. It is estimated that approximately 40 percent of care workers are visible minorities, a much higher percentage than in the Direct Funding pilot evaluation (Lum, Sladek, and Ying 2010). Both home care and long-term care settings are known to have a potential for racialized violence (Bourgeault et al. 2010). From the perspective of self-managers, Fernández et al. (2007) found that the more expansive U.K. direct payments program has a low uptake of direct funding by ethnic minorities and/or immigrant populations. The profile of the participants in this study (which may not be representative due to the sample size) suggests a slight possibility that the Ontario Direct Funding program includes a bias towards white professional people to utilize *and* work as attendants as compared to other attendant services and long-term care arrangements. The ways in which racialization, success rates of application, and employment practices play out under Direct Funding in Ontario remain important areas of further inquiry.

All of the female self-managers in this study expressed some degree of discomfort about the idea of male attendants helping them with their most intimate personal care. Women are socially conditioned to feel a constant sense of risk in both public and private spaces (Stanko 1990). This conditioning is reproduced within discussions of sexual assault and rape, which commonly stress the need for women to "avoid" dangerous situations rather than placing the onus on re-constructing forms of masculinity that do not involve violence, control, and domination. Disabled women must make decisions amid a tense context where, like all women, we are conditioned to feel continually under threat and "at risk" *at the same time* as having an empirically higher chance of experiencing gendered violence. Unfortunately, the onus is thus on the individual women to change our behaviours (that is, in this case, not hiring male attendants) rather than finding mechanisms to change the behaviours of men and the social conditioning of masculinity. Given this context and the flexibility of direct funding, the female self-managers independently decided to avoid hiring male attendants, no matter what types of references they had.

The question of gender within a personal care relationship extended into discussions about formal gender policies in other attendant service arrangements that prevent male attendants from helping women with their personal care. For example, attendant Adam describes the policy at an Independent Living supportive living unit where he works in addition to being a direct funding attendant:

> The calls are gender specific most of the time, although they only have one person working the overnight shift because it's twenty-four-hour care and the overnight person is always female because the idea is that males who are clients aren't necessarily all that picky about the gender of the person who's helping them, whereas the female clients would be if a male came to help them to the washroom at night.

This particular attendant framed the policy as the "pickiness" of women with disabilities. He seemed unaware of the prevalence of abuse in these situations and was actually offended[2] by the gendered policy:

> I discussed this with one of the administrators there because I thought it was sort of assuming that male attendants are going to behave badly or sexually assault the people that they're helping. And I was kind of offended by that actually because why is it more likely for a male attendant to do that than it is for a female attendant?

Later, he added, "It seems like a double standard, like a reverse discrimination in a way." We discussed this matter further, and I mentioned the statistical reality that women with disabilities experience a rate of violence

22.5 times higher than men with disabilities (depending on the type of violence) and that in Canada, 83 percent of police-reported violence against women is committed by men (Sinha 2013). Still, the attendant remained skeptical:

> Adam: Are male attendants more likely to sexually assault?
> I: Yes.
> Adam: They are? Really?

This frustrating conversation strongly suggests a lack of awareness and the persistence of misconceptions even among those working directly in this line of work. It is uncomfortable for attendants to consider that they are in a position of power over their disabled clients, and that they themselves or their colleagues could (and do) abuse people with disabilities.

Other attendants were more aware of the potential for abuse and were not offended by these gender-specific policies (which, admittedly, are not a panacea). Ultimately they still downplayed the potential for abuse in attendant services. Mathieu, an attendant, expressed feeling relief at not having to help female clients with their personal care:

> I: Do you ever help women?
> Mathieu: Well not, obviously not with personal care.
> I: You're not comfortable or they're not comfortable?
> Mathieu: I think it would be a mutual thing I guess. I feel a little uncomfortable just because … most women who would need personal care are gender specific in that they would only want other women doing their personal care. But men tend to be, of course they don't really care, care one way or the other. Generally mostly male clients would be fine with them if it's a girl or guy and I guess this is how it is.

As we continued, Mathieu explicitly mentioned the risk of sexual abuse:

> It's just a risky situation. Especially since you're going to be doing this [inaudible] privately in a room somewhere and this involves you taking off someone's, vulnerable person's clothes and helping them. Anything could happen where you feel you're helping them and that person feels that you actually touched

them inappropriately but obviously if you're helping them in the washroom then [there] might be a chance that you might touch them somewhere they wouldn't want to be touched.

Again, even though Mathieu is more aware of the prevalence and potential for abuse, he talks about it almost being accidental and rare, or something that does not actually happen, but rather is misconstrued by the person with a disability. Perhaps this is how this specific attendant, who has been dedicated to this work for a long time, makes sense of this situation. He cannot imagine abusing the people he works with and wants to believe that other attendants are not abusive either. Yet another attendant talks about her experience working at a summer camp for children with disabilities:

[The camp administrators] didn't want to [have one] counsellor, one camper alone in a closed room together. I guess they were worried, not only could the counsellor potentially take advantage of the camper. Hopefully it would never happen, but also at that stage I guess their camp director had told us it's [the children's] word against yours. So even if you do nothing wrong, but something, if you're performing personal care or something like that, they might misconstrue something that you're doing.

Part of the reason the phrase "attendant services" instead of "care" is promoted in Independent Living is to professionalize the intimate experiences of support (Kelly 2011). Professionalizing also helps to remove the historically developed charitable and moral esteem bestowed upon those who do this line of work. The moral esteem can work to protect the helping professions from critique, as people are positioned as "good" and "helpful" (Chapman 2012). The negative effects of care that socially devalues disability include all types of abuse that leave power imbalances intact. The topic of abuse is challenging to talk about for attendants, who often see themselves as "caring" people (Christensen 2010). The job of an attendant is vital to the survival and ability of people with disabilities to thrive, but this important role does not mean attendants are incapable of abuse, especially in light of research that finds requiring personal assistance increases vulnerability for abuse (Nosek et al. 2001). This creates a challenging situation in which the prevalence of abuse of disabled people has been well documented, but attendants are often unaware, dismissive, or even trained in ways that assume all claims of abuse are suspect and that disabled people are likely to misinterpret well-meaning behaviours.

Scholars speculate that direct funding service users may discriminate against certain demographic groups when hiring; yet many more formalized attendant service settings implement policies that prohibit male attendants from assisting women in an effort to prevent violence against female service users. Through these policies gender is simplified to binary male versus female, and indeed, the approach does not address generalized and gendered harassment directed at male service users or attendants. Independent Living responses to the looming threat and lived experiences of gendered abuse demonstrate how the philosophy confronts oppression against people with disabilities but is not well equipped to incorporate gender as a category of analysis.

Concluding Thoughts

The intimacy of all attendant services sits at the confluence of disability and feminized and racialized labour. This is a difficult context that holds high potential for abuse. Parallel to beliefs about colonization in settler states like Canada, many people erroneously believe the era of institutionalization is over, that institutionalization represents a vanished historical response to disability. In fact, the last three government-funded regional centres in Ontario closed only in 2009. In 2012, former residents of the regional centres succeeded in securing class action settlements from the Ontario government, and the legal proceedings around the settlements revealed the extent of abuse and maltreatment that had taken place in the centres.

Even when institutions are closed, the transition to community care often means institutionalized practices on a smaller scale (see Ben-Moshe et al. 2014). The more abstract legacies of institutionalization include pervasive misconceptions about disability and disabled people. Independent Living and direct funding mechanisms push back against the overwhelming history and ongoing reality of institutionalization. Nevertheless, they are not immune to reproducing conditions of vulnerability, violence, and systemic, gendered oppression of disabled people and attendants. In work to promote Independent Living attendant services, applying a gendered lens sensitive to the risks and realities of violence could help evolve services in ways that continue to strive towards empowerment of all disabled people and support for attendants.

Notes

1. The cited study is very small, but tracking care workers in Ontario is very difficult because they are unregulated, work in multiple settings, under different pieces of legislation, and are sometimes hired privately. Demographic reports are rough estimates for this population.
2. The tendency for individual men to be offended in discussions of gender inequality, especially in the context of abuse and violence, has been mocked in a popular social media trend in 2013–2014. Demonstrated through memes, webcomics, and discussion board comments, the "not all men" trend refers to the tendency for individual men to intervene in even the most serious discussions, "But not all men are like that/would do that!" For example, see this 2014 webcomic created by Matt Lubchansky: <http://www.listen-tome.com/save-me/>.

References

Armstrong, Pat, Hugh Armstrong, Albert Bannerjee, Tamara Daly and Marta Szebehely. 2011. "Structural Violence in Long-term Residential Care." *Women's Health and Urban Life*, 10, 1.

Barnes, Colin. 2007. "Direct Payments and Their Future: An Ethical Concern?" *Ethics and Social Welfare*, 1, 3.

Ben-Moshe, Liat, Chris Chapman and Allison C. Carey (eds.). 2014. *Disability Incarcerated: Imprisonment and Disability in the United States and Canada*. New York: Palgrave Macmillan.

Bourgeault, Ivy Lynn, Jelena Atanackovic, Ahmed Rashid and Rishma Parpia. 2010. "Relations between Immigrant Care Workers and Older Persons in Home and Long-term Care." *Canadian Journal on Aging/La Revue canadienne du vieillissement*, 29, 1.

Brownridge, Douglas A. 2006. "Partner Violence against Women with Disabilities." *Violence against Women*, 12, 9.

Chapman, Chris. 2012. "Colonialism, Disability, and Possible Lives: The Residential Treatment of Children Whose Parents Survived Indian Residential Schools." *Journal of Progressive Human Services*, 23, 2.

Chapman, Chris, Allison C. Carey and Liat Ben-Moshe. 2014. "Reconsidering Confinement: Interlocking Locations and Logics of Incarceration." In Liat Ben-Moshe, Chris Chapman and Allison C. Carey (eds.), *Disability Incarcerated: Imprisonment and Disability in the United States and Canada*. New York: Palgrave Macmillan.

Christensen, Karen. 2010. "Caring about Independent Lives." *Disability & Society*, 25, 2.

Fernández, José-Luis, Jeremy Kendall, Vanessa Davey and Martin Knapp. 2007.

"Direct Payments in England: Factors Linked to Variations in Local Provision." *Journal of Social Policy*, 36.

Goodley, Dan, Rebecca Lawthom and Katherine Runswick-Cole. 2014. "Dis/ability and Austerity: Beyond Work and Slow Death." *Disability & Society*, 29, 6.

Keigher, S.M. 2007. "Consumer-Direction in an 'Ownership Society': An Emerging Paradigm for Home and Community Care in the United States." In Clare Ungerson and Sue Yeandle (eds.), *Cash for Care in Developed Welfare States*. New York: Palgrave Macmillan.

Kelly, Christine. 2011. "Making 'Care' Accessible: Personal Assistance for Disabled People and the Politics of Language." *Critical Social Policy*, 31, 4.

___. 2013. "Building Bridges with Accessible Care: Disability Studies, Feminist Care Scholarship and Beyond." *Hypatia*, 28, 4.

___. 2014. "Re/moving Care from the Ontario Direct Funding Program: Altering Conversations among Disability and Feminist Scholars." *Social Politics: International Studies in Gender, State & Society*, 21, 1.

Kittay, Eva Feder. 1999. *Love's Labour: Essays on Women, Equality, and Dependency*. New York: Routledge.

Krogh, Kari. 2004. "Redefining Homecare for Women with Disabilities: A Call for Citizenship." In Karen R. Grant, Carol Amaratunga, Pat Armstrong, Madeline Boscoe, Ann Pederson and Kay Willson (eds.), *Caring for/Caring about: Women, Home Care and Unpaid Caregiving*. Aurora, ON: Garamond Press.

Larner, Wendy. 2000. "Neo-Liberalism: Policy, Ideology, Governmentality." *Studies in Political Economy*, 63 (Autumn).

Lum, Janet, Jennifer Sladek and Alvin Ying. 2010. *Ontario Personal Support Workers in Home and Community Care: CRNCC/PSNO Survey Results*. Toronto: Canadian Research Network for Care in the Community.

Matthias, Ruth E., and A.E. Benjamin. 2003. "Abuse and Neglect of Clients in Agency-based and Consumer-directed Home Care." *Health Social Work*, 28, 3.

Mays, Jennifer M. 2006. "Feminist Disability Theory: Domestic Violence against Women with a Disability." *Disability & Society*, 21, 2.

Mingus, Mia. 2011. "Moving Toward the Ugly: A Politic Beyond Desirability." [Blog.] <leavingevidence.wordpress.com/2011/08/22/moving-toward-the-ugly-a-politic-beyond-desirability/>.

Moore, Sarah E.H., and Simon Breeze. 2012. "Spaces of Male Fear: The Sexual Politics of Being Watched." *British Journal of Criminology*, 52, 6. doi: 10.1093/bjc/azs033.

Nakano Glenn, Evelyn. 2010. *Forced to Care: Coercion and Caregiving in America*. Cambridge, MA: Harvard University Press.

Nosek, Margaret A., Catherine Clubb Foley, Rosemary B. Hughes and Carol A. Howland. 2001. "Vulnerabilities for Abuse among Women with Disabilities." *Sexuality and Disability*, 19, 3.

Odell, Tracy. 2011. "Not Your Average Childhood: Lived Experience of Children with Physical Disabilities Raised in Bloorview Hospital, Home and School from 1960 to 1989." *Disability & Society*, 26, 1.

Rajan, Doris. 2004. *Violence against Women with Disabilities*. Toronto: The Roeher Institute.

Roeher Institute. 1997. *Final Evaluation Report: Self-managed Attendant Services in Ontario: Direct Funding Pilot Project.* Toronto, ON: Centre for Independent Living Toronto (CITL).

Saxton, Marsha, Mary Ann Curry, Laurie E. Powers, Susan Maley, Karyl Eckels and Jacqueline Gross. 2001. "'Bring My Scooter So I Can Leave You': A Study of Disabled Women Handling Abuse by Personal Assistance Providers." *Violence against Women*, 7, 4.

Sinha, Maire. 2013. "Measuring Violence against Women: Statistical Trends." *Juristat.* <statcan.gc.ca/pub/85-002-x/2013001/article/11766-eng.pdf>.

Stanko, Elizabeth Ann. 1990. *Everyday Violence: How Women and Men Experience Sexual and Physical Danger.* London: Pandora.

Yoshida, Karen, Vic Willi, Ian Parker and David Locker. 2004. "The Emergence of Self-Managed Attendant Services in Ontario: Direct Funding Pilot Project — An Independent Living Model for Canadians Requiring Attendant Services." In Jennie Jacobs Kronenfeld (ed.), *Chronic Care, Health Care Systems and Services Integration.* Bingley, United Kingdom: Emerald Books.

Chapter 9

Taking Action
Gender-Based Violence, Disability, and the Social Determinants of Health

Karen K. Yoshida, Mary Bunch, Fran Odette,
Susan L. Hardie, and Heather Willis[1]

For disabled and non-disabled women alike, it is clearly healthier to live free of violence and abuse. Disabled women face unique needs, barriers, and concerns in dealing with health issues such as physical injury and psychological trauma and in accessing appropriate health services, from emergency first responders to therapy and rehabilitation. Moreover, traditional health approaches do little to address the social causes that leave disabled women more vulnerable to violence in the first place, that minimize the perceived significance of their experiences of abuse, and that limit their access to avenues to speak out, take action, or benefit from supports and services. Disabled women not only face higher risk of violence and abuse because of patriarchal and harmful views of women and the resulting gender discrimination, they also must contend with ableism, the "socially constructed characteristics of disAbility that positions people with disAbilities as an 'inferior' group to non-disAbled people" (Odette 2013: 3). They may also be dealing with racism, transphobia, homophobia, or other systemic forms of oppression. Disability scholars have been working for decades to separate disability from health, critiquing the idea that disability is a biomedical concern and arguing instead that disability is a form of social oppression. In this chapter we are looking at both health and disability as social and political concerns. We focus on the social rather than the biomedical aspects of health in the lives of disabled women who experience violence and abuse. Our analysis is based on the presumptions that violence in the lives of disabled women is not inevitable and that it is not caused simply by the random bad behaviour of some individual men. Rather, the violence has structural causes, such as ableism, poverty, racism, community design, lack of access to education, family structure, lack of economic opportunities, and involvement in the justice system (CMHA 2011: 8).

Three inter-related lenses inform our analysis. These are the social determinants of health (SDOH) model, the social model of disability, and a feminist intersectional approach to thinking about violence and abuse. The first of these is a broad view that examines how physical, social, and political environments create situations that positively or negatively impact people's health. The World Health Organization defines the social determinants of health as "the conditions in which people are born, grow, live, work and age" (WHO 2012: 2). These conditions are shaped by the distribution of money, power, and resources — that is, by economics, social policies, and politics (WHO 2013); they affect people's access to nutritious and adequate levels of food, the availability of potable water, the degree to which their environments are clean and safe, and their exposure to violence and trauma (both domestic and external, such as war and risky work). Such socio-economic factors further impact people's levels of stress, their access to social support, and their degree of choice and opportunities. Health is thus not only genetic and biological, but also socially determined.

This social determinants of health model fits with the view of disability as socially constructed. The social model of disability highlights the physical and social barriers, as well as exclusionary policies and practices in the environment that render people "disabled" (Public Health Agency of Canada 2007; Oliver 1990). People are considered disabled when they experience "long-term physical, mental, intellectual or sensory impairments which, in interaction with various attitudinal and environmental barriers, hinders [sic] their full and effective participation in society on an equal basis with others" (U.N. Enable 2010, cited in Vecova Centre for Disability Services and Research [Vecova] 2011: 6). The social model of disability emphasizes the negative attitudes and social and environmental barriers that disable persons, not the presence of impairment. For example, for wheelchair users, disablement is caused by the ubiquity of stairs and lack of ramps, not the biomedical cause and functional fact that a person does not walk. These models of health and disability emphasize the dynamic processes at play in "environments" that produce health and illness, disability and ability, and various states of being in between these categories.

A feminist intersectional approach (Mays 2006; May 2012) highlights the ways other structures of privilege and oppression intermingle in the lives of disabled women in Canadian society. Disabled women's social locations are marked by other factors such as race, age, economic class, sexual orientation, and geographical location. The experience of marginalization can be compounded when a person experiences multiple sites of marginalization; for example, disabled women who are older are often unemployed and thus more likely to live in poverty than younger women. But intersectionality does not merely suggest an additive or "pop bead" approach, in which disability-related marginalization occurs separately from racism or ageism (May 2012: 162). Rather, a person's multiple social locations combine in complex ways that cannot be easily disentangled. For example, for young, non-disabled women, sexism often manifests as sexual objectification. Disability does not necessarily intensify this experience and increase the level of objectification (although it might, in some cases). Indeed, disabled women find they are often desexualized, so that sexism can play out very differently when it interacts with ableism (Clare 2015).

Together, the social determinants of health approach, the social model of disability, and intersectionality allow us to examine the social conditions that produce greater risk of violence for disabled women and to work toward changing those circumstances.

This chapter is divided into two sections. In the first section, we review the health literature on violence against disabled women. In the second, we present an innovative community-academic research study conducted in 2005–2006 that used message boards and chat rooms to consult with disabled women across the country on important health issues. This study offers insight into disabled women's experiences of violence and abuse, the conditions that impact the actions they take to leave abusive situations, and disabled women's recommendations for more effective responses to issues of violence and disability. We analyze these message board and chat-room consultations by means of an intersectional feminist disability approach. From all this, we discuss the conditions that would foster violence-free and safer lives for disabled women, a process for intervention, guidelines for sensitive practice, and considerations for health practitioners and service providers working with disabled women.

Disability and Abuse

Negative and harmful views of women increase the risk of violence and abuse for all women. But not all women share the same level of risk, types of experiences, and access to support and services when they experience violence. Women are not a homogenous group. Their safety, health, and well-being, as well as their perceived credibility, value, and status in society, vary according to intersecting forms of privilege and oppression related to disability, as well as such factors as race, sexual orientation, Indigenous status, income level, ethnicity, gender identity and expression, and age. Compared to other Canadians, disabled people are more vulnerable to virtually every kind of abuse. They experience both physical and sexual assault twice as much as their non-disabled counterparts (Perreault 2009). Disabled women (those with cognitive impairments and those with activity limitations) are four times more likely than non-disabled women to experience sexual assault (Martin et al. 2006). The risk increases at the intersection of disability with other social conditions. Disabled women who are old or young, who are immigrants or unmarried, or who are racialized, socially isolated, or live in poverty face increased risk of experiencing intimate abuse or violence (Martin et al. 2006; Nosek et al. 2006; Yoshida, Du Mont, Odette and Lysy 2011). Particular elements of impairment also seem to affect vulnerability to violence and abuse. For instance, people live in greater risk of violence if they are less mobile or if they report experiencing severe impairment, higher levels of depression, serious or chronic mental illness, multiple health conditions, and pain (Nosek et al. 2006, Du Mont and Forte 2014; Perreault 2009; Yoshida, Du Mont, Odette and Lysy 2011). Certain environments pose greater risks as well. For instance, living in an institution increases vulnerability, because institutional living tends to be isolating, separates people from family and community life, and is restrictive in terms of developing supports (Vecova 2011; Perreault 2009). Disabled women also identify other forms of abuse: poor treatment in systems of service provision and social assistance, racism, denial of services and/or inappropriate treatment by caregivers, discrimination on the basis of their disability, and destruction of property (DAWN/RAFH 2011).

Violence against disabled persons might be perpetrated by spouses, family members, caregivers, neighbours, or friends. Canada's General Social Survey (2004) showed that both disabled men and women know the perpetrator of abuse in two out of three violent incidents (not including spousal violence), compared to about half of incidents involving non-disabled people (Perreault 2009). The survey also revealed that disabled persons were two to three times more likely to experience severe forms of violence by a spouse (such as being sexually assaulted, beaten, struck, or threatened with a weapon). In another Canadian study, Brownridge (2006) examined partner abuse against disabled heterosexual women who lived in intimate partnerships when compared with non-disabled women. He found that the likelihood of experiencing violence was 40 percent greater for disabled women. His analysis revealed that perpetrator behaviour traits of "patriarchal dominance" (where a partner prevents a woman from knowing about or accessing family income), "sexual posses-siveness" (where a partner demands to know who the woman was with and where she was at all times), and "sexual jealousy" were linked to the increased risk for partner violence.

The increased vulnerability of disabled women has numerous social causes, stemming from their devalued social position and the general insecurity produced by living in an ableist society. One significant factor is the power imbalances associated with support relationships. Women using attendant services such as assistance with activities of daily living (such as dressing, bathing, or eating) by paid employees or unpaid car-egivers (such as family members and partners) can be at increased risk of abuse at the hands of the persons providing these supports (Linton 1998; Chappell 2003; Young et al. 1997; Womendez and Schneiderman 1991; Roeher Institute 1994; Vecova 2011; DAWN/RAFH 2011). Their reliance on daily intimate care partially explains the circumstances in which disabled women might experience or be exposed to abuse for longer periods of time compared to non-disabled women (Nosek 2001; Young et al. 1997).

Health Consequences

We were not able to identify any research that looks specifically at the social determinants of health combining gender, disability, and violence. This is hardly surprising, considering the general paucity of research on the health consequences of abuse and violence for disabled women. A few studies, including other chapters in this book, examine the health consequences for disabled women with specific pain-related disorders who have experienced partner violence. These women were more likely to have chronic pelvic pain, fibromyalgia, and gastro-intestinal disorders (Campbell et al. 2002; McCauley et al. 1995; Alexander et al. 1998; Drossman et al. 1990). One study examined the frequency and types of disability among women experiencing intimate partner violence compared with women who never experience this form of violence (Coker, Smith, and Fadden 2005). It found that all types of intimate partner violence were associated with having an impairment (blindness or glaucoma, nervous/ neurological or muscular disorders) and in particular with having impairments resulting from chronic pain and mental illness.

It is generally accepted that there are three possible causal links between partner violence and disability: the presence of impairment may increase the risk of violence; the violence may directly cause the impairment through injury; or the violence might indirectly lead to impairment through the long-term effects of living in an abusive environment. Implicit in the first of these hypotheses is the understanding that an intimate partner's violence is not caused by the presence of an impairment per se ("her blindness made me do it"), but rather by the disabling social circumstances, the social devaluation of disabled women, the power imbalances in the care relationship, lack of supports, poverty, and the resulting frustration and stress this places on relationships.

Decisions to disclose and/or "leave" an abusive person are strongly affected by social determinants. Many disabled women live in poverty, a situation that leads to lack of control over aspects of personal life, such as who provides care and the ability to leave a bad situation (National Clearinghouse on Family Violence 2009). Indeed, a woman with disabilities might be dependent on her abuser for personal care (Vecova 2011). Disabled women may likewise be reluctant to leave a home that has been adapted. They may rely on specialized transportation, which requires planning and scheduling, and on attendant care that might be tied to their place of residence. In some cases, a woman may be reluctant to leave because she fears taking action that would result in being institutionalized (DAWN/RAFH 2009). More generally, the undervaluing of disabled women in society often leads these women to blame themselves for the abuse they experience or to feel that they deserve it, exacerbating the tendency for self-blame connected to low self-esteem that also exists for non-disabled women who are abused (Chappell 2003; Vecova 2011; National Clearinghouse of Family Violence 2009). Women who consider leaving an abusive person grapple with feelings of shame, the fear of losing their children, homemaker, or other support services, and the need to deal with the associated economic and physical consequences (Chappell 2003). Disabled women do not always recognize the violence they are experiencing as abuse; and they may not be aware of their rights or of available services for violence and abuse intervention, or they may not know to access them (Vecova 2011; DAWN/RAFH 2011).

Service Providers

There has been significant improvement in public awareness about violence against women in general and increased access to services for many women. However, disabled women who are abused remain invisible and marginalized. Inaccessible services and supports (disability related or non-disability related) have serious consequences for women living with disabilities. Ableism and other forms of marginalization exacerbate the trauma resulting from physical injuries and from associated mental health issues such as depression and stress, as well as increasing women's risk of homelessness and of engaging in responses to trauma such as alcohol and drug use. Providers of services and supports need to be aware of these consequences. This need is evident in a growing body of qualitative research that focuses on the responsibilities of health providers to develop and implement services and to work with disabled women in respectful and sensitive ways (Womendez and Schneiderman 1991; Chang et al. 2003). However, crucial gaps in research remain. For instance, although disabled women are among the most vulnerable to abuse, only 10 percent of women in shelters report having a disability (Statistics Canada 2011). This reported use of shelters by disabled women reflects only a small proportion of disabled women who have experienced violence. Clearly, this group is not able to access these services. Shelters still have a long way to go in becoming accessible. Only half have wheelchair access, only 75 percent have accessible entrances, and only 66 percent have accessible bedrooms and bathrooms, according to Statistics Canada's *Family Violence in Canada* report (2011). Disabled women say that accessibility is not reducible to ramps and wide doorways (DAWN/RAFH 2009). Far fewer shelters offer telecommunication devices for the deaf or TTY/TDD (22 percent), sign language interpretation, large print (17 percent), or materials in braille (5 percent) (Statistics Canada 2011).

Moreover, there has been little research that speaks to issues of universal screening, recognising abuse, and sensitive practice as these apply to disabled women. These practices are central to provider action.

Universal screening for intimate partner violence by health practitioners is an important area where social determinants of health intersect with medical practice. Intimate partner violence refers to "the experience or threat of physical or sexual violence or financial or psychological/emotional abuse by a current or ex-partner" (Mason 2006: 21). The screening process demands some awareness of the social and political context in which disabled women live. In other words, practitioners must be able to determine medical factors of impairment and signs of injury, and also to read the social cues, recognize warning indicators, and analyze the risk context in a way that is sensitive to disability. Research shows that health professionals may not believe that they are equipped to serve disabled women within this "pseudo-screening" context and that "screening" is increasingly problematic for disabled women (Curry and Navarro 2002). For example, screening about abuse within a medical context assumes that there is privacy for the practitioner and the woman, but some disabled women may require the presence of a spoken language interpreter, sign language interpreter, or personal attendant. Researchers are starting to acknowledge the complexities of the issues in determining the effectiveness of "screening" (Mason 2006). Service providers are beginning to develop best practices. As Mason argues, "responding appropriately to domestic violence includes normalising the issue and developing an atmosphere of trust in the office and with the patient" (2006: 23).[2] By "normalizing the issue," Mason presumably refers to normalizing the experience of speaking about violence and abuse so that women are more comfortable disclosing it and seeking support. Further best practices include developing a greater awareness of the kinds of behaviours that constitute subtle forms of abuse experienced by people who are reliant on partners or family to provide personal care; safety planning that accounts for disability-specific considerations; and asking questions in a "culturally competent manner" (Curry and Navarro 2002: 4). The Center for Research on Women with Disabilities (CROWD) has prepared resource materials for physicians responding to what could be/are abuse situations. These identify the issues affecting women around disclosures, explore reasons why physicians don't ask about abuse, propose taking cues from medical histories, and advise what physicians can do for patients who have been abused (Nosek 1995). The resource highlights the importance of awareness, training, and critical reflection about screening for abuse when working with disabled women.

There still remains little Canadian qualitative health research on disabled women's experiences with violence and abuse. There is even less research and discussion on what providers need to do to extend appropriate support and services. The DisAbled Women's Network Canada (DAWN) was highlighting the issues of violence and abuse facing disabled women as early as 1989, bringing these issues to the attention of violence against women services and federal and provincial governments. Today, studies like the ones conducted by Vecova Centre for Disability Services and Research (2011) and DAWN (DAWN/RAFH 2009; 2011) continue to bridge this gap. They show that disabled women, while highly vulnerable to all sorts of abuse, face many barriers to taking action and living safely. Among these are a lack of awareness of available services, a lack of accessibility of services responding to abuse, a need for disability-related sensitivity training among service providers, a need for funding to improve services, and a need for prevention, self-defence, and self-advocacy training for disabled women themselves. These critical matters demand significant investment on the part of government funders and policy makers.

Women with Disabilities "Chat" about Violence[3]

In our study on disabled women's access to health-related services with the National Networks on Environments and Women's Health, we focused on four areas that affect the health of disabled women: general health, mental health, reproductive health, and gender-based violence. Our study was guided by a working group of key stakeholders and conducted by a research team that included disabled women, health professionals, and academics with expertise about health, disability, and gender-based violence.

We used online chat rooms and message boards to broadly explore the social determinants of health in the lives of disabled women. The women who participated in these digital focus groups shared their multi-layered knowledge of and experiences of violence and abuse. They talked about where abuse takes place, the forms of abuse women experience, and the complexities associated with taking action to leave an abusive situation or seek help as a disabled woman. The participants also made recommendations for more effective responses to issues of violence and disability.

SDOH *Study Methodology*

This national consultation with urban disabled women used a qualitative online methodology intended to enhance inclusion and accessibility. Not only does the methodology reflect the principles of accessibility and health promotion by generating dialogue in an accessible forum where women could speak out about their experiences, it also positions participants as experts and knowledge producers rather than as objects of study. The qualitative approach facilitates an in-depth understanding of the experiences of violence, and it provides a forum for disabled women to share their knowledge and experience in their own words — both with one another and with others. Speaking for oneself is an extremely important aspect of disability politics, for this community has historically been treated as objects of study to the extent that disability research has itself sometimes been abusive. "Nothing about us without us" is a well-known slogan of the disability rights movement. It is a principle that is reflected at every level of our project, in the working and research teams (which include disabled women in leadership roles), in the conduct and analysis of the research itself, and in the creation of this chapter and other modes of dissemination.

Participants were identified by contacting disability organizations and Centres of Excellence for Women's Health across Canada. Women in the study were not asked to identify if they are cisgendered or transgender. Since distinctions between cis and trans have not been made in any of the national statistical tools or the studies cited in this chapter, the authors presume that although transgender persons are not visible, and the implications of multiple gender identities in relation to violence and abuse are not evident, all gender groups might be included in the data captured under the terms "women" and "men." The final group consisted of sixteen English-speaking research participants who lived with multiple, diverse embodied differences. Participants described their impairments as physical (11), hearing (2), visual (1), learning (2), and mental health (2). They lived with multiple health conditions: blood disorders (2), chronic pain (2), coronary disease (1), diabetes (1), hypothyroid (1), multiple chemical sensitivities (1), reflux (2), and multiple other long-term health conditions (2).

Participants were selected because they represented the broadest diversity with regard to geographic area, disability, and age. They came from Atlantic Canada (5), central Canada (7), and western Canada (4); and they represented a range of age groups: 18–29 years (3), 30–39 years (3), 40–49 years (4), 50–59 years (5), and 60–69 years (1). We did not collect participant information on ethnicity or race. Because of our small sample size, we kept these target areas narrow. However, we were anticipating qualitative data that additionally spoke to intersectional issues associated with such factors as race, class, and sexual orientation.

For the online workshops, the message board used *EnableLink*, a programming package that allowed people of various abilities to participate in the discussion; it lasted for three days so that people in different time zones could participate at their convenience. The main discussion topic was: "Discuss your experiences in accessing health services in Canadian cities, with respect to … services related to violence and abuse." The message board was monitored by a facilitator who engaged the participants and posted questions based on their responses. A summary document was circulated to the participants in preparation for the chat-room discussion, which took place in "real time."[4] Chat rooms were divided geographically, with one set in Ontario, Quebec, and the Atlantic provinces, and another in the western provinces. Within each region, one chat room focused on General Health Care and Violence and Abuse, and another focused on Mental Health and Reproductive Health Care. We developed major themes from the message board and chat-room data.[5]

Ableist Context and
Assumptions about Disability

Our research question was broad, allowing considerable room for participants to interpret what they considered "health," "health services," and "violence" in relation to disability. The participants created their own pseudonyms to use on the message board and in the chat rooms. The women were well informed and spoke about issues from their own individual experiences, and, in some cases, from expert perspectives. They implicitly reflected a social model perspective on disability and a social determinants of health approach in their discussions. They largely focused on the social context that impacted their safety and their access to services, and on the intersectional systems of oppression that disabled women navigate when they access formal and informal supports and services related to disability and to violence.

The participants identified ableism as a root cause of abuse, an obstacle to the identification of abuse, and a barrier to accessing violence-related services. Women contextualized their experiences of marginalization in the community and the assumptions held about disabled women as child-like and asexual. A number of the women spoke of the consequences associated with living in an urban Western culture predicated on ableist values, a culture that does not take into consideration the diverse lived experiences of women who may be living with violence. One result is the invisibility of intimate partner violence for this group, since disabled women are often presumed to be single and asexual and cast as recipients of care rather than actors in relationships. For example, Kupyd shared, "If violence is ever discussed in terms of people with disabilities, it is rarely acknowledged in terms of an intimate relationship. The institutional setting is acknowledged as is the caregiver situation, but rarely the intimate relationship setting." This narrow relational context for violence can contribute to difficulties experienced by disabled women fleeing violence, who may not be viewed as credible or as needing violence-related services. Kupyd continues, "Overall the issue of abuse of people with disabilities is downplayed in our society. This is due I think to a lot of old chestnuts about those of us with disabilities being viewed as childlike or asexual and many other stereotypes."

While ableism was identified as a significant problem that both increased risk of violence and decreased access to supports to end violence, the women contextualized disability as one thread in an intersecting web of social positions, forms of oppression, and privilege that impact health and well-being. They discussed the ways that social-structural circumstances related to race, class, and sexual orientation, among other factors, contribute to abuse and its invisibility in the lives of disabled women. For example, Hypathia wrote:

> The biggest problem is the way violence is defined by society and the women's movement. It doesn't take into account the diversity of daily living among different groups of women, the way in which structure forces some people to live. Nor do we evaluate the economic implications of violence against women.

Forms of Violence and Abuse

Like other women, those participating in our discussions identified their homes as a one of the main sites of abuse, which often takes place in intimate relationships. However, disabled women may be more vulnerable to abuse when they are recipients of care and personal assistance from either paid or unpaid caregivers. Thus the women identified the other main sites of abuse as health care settings and institutions. They experience the forms of harm that non-disabled women in abusive situations endure, as well as some that are specific to care relationships, the presence of impairment, and disability-related barriers. As Hypathia reported:

> I think that there is so much hidden violence in places like institutions that is not reported or understood, (believed or identified) to be an act of violence. Example, being tied really tight in the adapted transport, even when you say, "this is hurting me" and driver does nothing to reduce the pressure.

The types of harm reported by the women were varied. They identified forms of violence along a continuum, ranging from subtle to direct, from acts immersed in everyday experience to forms of abuse that increase in intensity and risk. MJ highlights the range of experiences considered to be abuse:

> Starting small — you're dumb etc. even carrying joking too far, to slowly building to full blown violence as well, abuse can be

anything from having someone push you to something you don't want to do, name calling, withholding finances, basic necessities, or even leaving a dependent person long periods of time by themselves.

Barriers to Leaving and Seeking Service

Leaving an abusive situation is difficult for many women, because of their feelings of low self-worth, their financial and emotional dependence on an abusive person, their ties to home and community (who may not find abuse claims credible), and the immense insecurity and disruption to routines of daily life that leaving might cause. Disabled women face even greater barriers to leaving abusive situations because of disability-related issues pertaining to physical and structural accessibility. Graceful points out, for example, that some disabled women who rely on their abuser for personal care may not be able to leave without personal assistance:

> All women ... may find it hard to leave abusive relationships because of economic dependence on their spouses/partners, or other family members, or because they have children, or to bring themselves to the hospital after being physically/sexually assaulted, but if you are somewhat reliant on the abuser for help getting activities of daily living done on a daily basis it can be harder, or if that person may be a personal care attendant, you've hired through an agency. What happens when you need help packing your bags and leaving the situation?

For some women, being able to actually leave may be more difficult because of the need to negotiate the many services and systems in their lives. As Participant 7 commented, "I didn't have it in me to navigate the system." She spoke directly about the difficulty disabled women experience when trying to leave:

> [Women] stay in unsafe relationships because they could not have easy access to the supports they required. For some the situation has to be really bad before they would seek assistance ... It is such a struggle to get through daily life, everywhere you go there are barriers for me, whether they are buildings and/or attitudes, financial etc.), this is brutal for my self-esteem. If my boyfriend

is verbally, emotionally and or physically abusive I don't have it in me to fight that too.

Grateful 76 wrote about seeking assistance in getting one's belongings together in order to leave and feeling worried for the safety of others providing assistance:

> Hypothetically, I know if I ever, (personally) were in that situation, I'd have to call on someone to help me pack and leave the home or get the police to come and remove the person, either way, depending on the situation, I could be endangering the safety of someone else, not to mention having someone else know details of my private life I may not want people to know. In terms of transportation to a shelter or hospital, I'd have to call a cab or accessibility transportation or a friend or family member.

The need for disability-related assistance when leaving an abusive situation can result in a lack of confidentiality and privacy for women who need assistance communicating with health professionals, police, and crisis counsellors. As Grateful 76 explains:

> Again, "confidentiality" is raised. If I'm lucky enough to get out of the situation and need medical treatment, and consent to an exam, I'd need someone to come with me to provide me with assistance, physically during the exam, again where's the confidentiality in that.

The women identified several key areas of concern with respect to responses of service providers, including health professionals. The first pertains to the need to have longer appointment times to talk to one's physician about the abuse or simply having the physician ask the right question to create an opening for her to disclose if she chose to. Mee wrote:

> Also there needs to be a focus within the medical system that women experiencing abuse need resources and the chance to express themselves using open ended questions … there needs to be an understanding that such an appointment would take more than your run-of-the-mill ten minutes. Actually that is [a] problem for women with physical disabilities. It may take longer

to communicate something or to change etc. Also women who do not have rapport with a doctor are less likely to disclose.

Other women spoke about the increased need for service providers to be able to make the links between disability and other aspects of their identity and social location in the complex power relations that make up both private and public spheres. This might indicate a need to be aware that a person is negotiating her location in multiple structures of oppression, such as ableism, racism, and poverty. It also speaks to the need for cultural sensitivity. Like other Canadian women, disabled women come from many different cultural and religious backgrounds, and these shape their options and choices as much as do disability-related concerns. Justica said:

> Professionals in the field have difficulty supporting women with disabilities particularly from ethno-cultural communities. They often times fail to understand the sometimes interweaving mechanisms of violence, culture and disability and how this affects a women's ability to reach out for support.

Service providers, including police, need training about disability in order to respond effectively when disabled women report violence. As Kupyd put it, "Professionals such as police receive no or limited training in working with people with disabilities." Likewise, the women in our study identified the need for the violence against women sector to address the inaccessibility of services, including making shelters physically accessible, providing information in accessible formats, providing attendant and American Sign Language (ASL) interpretation services, and training staff about disability. Kupyd makes this point very clearly:

> I know that many violence against women organizations do fine work but do not have an understanding of those of us with disabilities. Literature is not in accessible format, staff has not received training, shelters are not physically accessible. Shelters do not for the most part make provisions for attendants. [Violence against women services] are also hesitant to take women with developmental disabilities or mental health diagnosis requiring medications, or [there] is a lack of qualified ASL interpreters.

Ways Forward

In both the message board postings and chat-room discussions, women made recommendations regarding access to services for reporting, leaving, and healing from violence. They proposed that all involved services — from hospitals, to shelters, to police — be fully accessible. They recommended disability-related, rights-based training for service providers that would sensitize them to the structural issues of disablement. They proposed changes that would shift responses from individualized models to social ones, and that would invest resources in building more inclusive societies. These recommendations centred on three main themes:

1. Ensure full accessibility of violence against women services, including full communication and access to information. As BC deaflady put it:

   > Rape crisis centres, [shelters], etc. might be the best vs. police, but my experience tells me they are not accessible to deaf women … how many have TTYs [a text telephone used by deaf persons]? How many have access to qualified (not volunteer) interpreters? Or therapists? Or even have the basic safety equipment deaf women need (flashing lights, doorbells, fire alarms, clocks, etc.).

2. Establish training initiatives for medical students, service providers, and disabled women, including access to information within the parameters of rights-based education and responsibilities. For example, Justicia wrote: "Training medical students and women with disabilities as counsellors would create important change. Other service providers would also benefit from disability-specific training."

3. Shift from services and responses that focus solely on individuals to broad social change, with government investment in social inclusion and disability rights. BC deaflady recommended such a change to improve accountability and address some of the inequities in programs and services: "There should be a patient's bill of rights clearly in every doctor's/hospital examination or ward room." In addition, government was seen as key to implementing strategies to promote change and create opportunities for greater inclusion through the provision of core funding or start-up funds. According to Grateful 76:

   > Provincial/federal governments [should] encourage/legislate

organizations to be more inclusive to open their programs/services for those with disabilities ... but give little in terms of "extra" funding for them on an ongoing basis to make sure it continues outside of the initial start-up phase or pilot project.

Macro- and Micro-Structural Change

Freedom from violence and abuse is a key social determinant of good health. This is a high-risk area for disabled women, especially when faced with multiple modes of oppression, like poverty and racism. Our study highlighted this intersectional approach to disability and gender in situations of violence and abuse. The women paint a clear picture of the health of disabled women being compromised by their higher risk of violence and abuse. This risk is compounded by ableist culture that devalues disabled women, social exclusion, racialization, poverty, and other social conditions. That is, intimate violence has key structural causes. This points to the need for broad political and economic investments towards ending disablement, sexism, poverty, homophobia, racism, institutionalization, and other inequities that lead to poor health outcomes and vulnerability to violence. We need to change the macro-circumstances whereby some people are at greater risk of harm because they are poor, they are not valued socially, and/or they do not have what they need to be move freely in their community, to communicate publicly or privately, and to make choices in their lives. These circumstances, as the World Health Organization (2013) points out, indicate the need for long-term political and economic changes concerning the distribution of money, power, and resources in society. Both the social determinants of health perspective and the social model of disability perspective emphasize that resources need to be directed toward reducing poverty, creating accessible infrastructure, and bolstering social supports, in order for people across different social locations to enjoy health and well-being. Health is an issue not only of health policy, but also of a range of social policies. For disabled people, this includes access to income and services that would allow them control over their lives such that they could change their living situation, including their caregivers, if need be, and access a continuum of violence intervention services.

At the more immediate, micro-level of change, there are changes that can have immediate positive effects on the lives of disabled women who have been abused. What follows are some recommendations for policy and practice that responds to violence against disabled women include dedicated resources, access to information, and training initiatives.

Dedicated Resources

Currently, there is a lack of dedicated funds/resources for organisations to provide accommodations (such as ASL/LSQ interpretation or attendant services). It is expected that monies to increase physical access of a women's shelter (for example, ramps, accessible washrooms, a telecommunication device) could/should come out of existing program funds. Thus, there needs to be strong policy directives from government and private funders to increase funding lines to the violence against women sector services to ensure that accommodations are provided, but not at the expense of existing services. Additionally, providing true inclusion within the shelter goes beyond physical access such as ramps to also make sure that all of the shelter's services are accessible, including its programming and social spaces, so that disabled women don't become isolated within the shelter. Children who accompany women to shelters may also be disabled, so accessibility measures should also be implemented in any spaces and programs used by children staying in women's shelters.

Access to Information

We know that for many women, access to disability-relevant, as well as culturally and linguistically relevant, information related to abuse prevention is vital. However, resources dedicated to ensuring access to pertinent information are limited. There is a paucity of information regarding diverse experiences related to healthy relationships, sexuality, and abuse prevention as it speaks to the experiences of disablement and young women in the current education curriculum. It is vital that young disabled people, like their non-disabled peers, are exposed to information on healthy sexuality and relationships. As well, young disabled people experience barriers to inclusive sex education in part because of physically inaccessible sexual health classrooms. They need to be able to access relevant and current information in a format that is user friendly and accommodating to different access needs. For example, resources should be available in plain language, braille, and audio book. Videos should include closed captioning and visual description options. Sex education teacher training should also include attention to accessibility pedagogy and universal learning.

Training Initiatives

There is a need for frontline and management staff working in organizations that come into contact with disabled women to receive training about violence against disabled women, including violence against women services and disability organizations. Such training can facilitate greater partnership and collaboration between agencies and the disabled community, as well as sharing of resources. Collaborative training increases knowledge transfer about issues of violence and the impacts of intersecting systems of oppression on women's experience of abuse and trauma. This education should also aim to provide greater continuity of services not only for disabled women but for all women, as service providers in different agencies develop awareness of the possible gaps in service, as well as services that might be available to fill those gaps.

There is also a strong need to train health professionals specifically in the integration of universal screening and inclusive practice. For some disabled women, interacting with a provider is possible only if the woman is accompanied by someone who has assisted in bringing her to the agency or by a communication facilitator, a deaf-blind intervenor, or a sign language interpreter. Yet, while the provision of accommodations that involve third parties is essential, it also counters the assumption of privacy and confidentiality in screening. Additionally, having a third party present during such disclosures may increase the woman's sense of vulnerability and concern about being able to obtain services, especially when the pool of service providers is small. Protocols therefore need to be in place to ensure that disabled women (indeed, any women requiring translation/interpretation) can communicate privately with health professionals if they wish, with access to the appropriate communication technologies to be able to do so.

Key to all of the approaches is that health care providers build bridges with advocates and women themselves by negotiating partnerships with women that are respectful of their different social locations and skills/knowledge. These partnerships will create lines of communication for women to share their experiences, to be validated, and to begin moving towards opportunities for "healing." Given that Canada has signed on with the *United Nations Convention for the Rights of Persons with Disabilities*, we suggest active partnerships among disabled women, service providers, policy makers, and government in order to advance the actions for change recommended by disabled women.

Notes

1   The authors thank the women who participated in all facets of the study for sharing their stories, insights, and recommendations for improving violence against women services for disabled women. We use "disabled women" as a sociopolitical term. We use "women with disabilities" if other references use the term in their works.

2. Domestic violence and intimate partner violence are synonymous, and many of the authors we cite use the former term. We use the latter because it is neither gender specific nor heteronormative.

3. For a more detailed description of the methodology see Yoshida et al. 2009.

4. Phorum software was used for the online chat room, which allowed for real-time discussions between facilitators and participants. These services were delivered in partnership with Canadian Abilities Foundation and the Adaptive Technology Resource Centre, Faculty of Information Sciences, University of Toronto.

5. There are some limitations to our data. First, they are a combination of key informant responses and women's own lived experiences, even though women were not required to declare their own experiences or issues. Second, the diversity of the study group did not reflect the experiences of women with intellectual disabilities or with limited literacy; it did not reflect ethno-racial, linguistic, transgender, and sexual diversity. Third, while technical assistance before and during the online sessions was provided to help facilitate participation, there were still some technical problems that hampered a few participants from responding to parts of the message board discussion.

References

Alexander R.W., L.A. Bradley, G.S. Alarcon et al. 1998. "Sexual and Physical Abuse in Women with Fibromyalgia: Association with Outpatient Health Care Utilization and Pain Medication Usage." *Arthritis Care & Research,* 11.

Brownridge, Douglas A. 2006. "Partner Violence against Women with Disabilities." *Violence Against Women,* 12.

Campbell, J., A.S. Jones, J. Dienemann et al. 2002. "Intimate Partner Violence and Physical Health Consequences." *Archives of Internal Medicine,* 162.

Chang, J.C., S.L. Martin, K.E. Moracco, L. Dulli, D. Scandlin, M.B. Loucks-Sorrel, T. Turner, L. Starsoneck, P.N. Dorian and I. Bou-Saada. 2003. "Helping Women with Disabilities and Domestic Violence: Strategies, Limitations, and Challenges of Domestic Violence Programs and Services." *Journal of Women's Health,* 12.

Chappell, M. 2003. *Violence against Women with Disability.* British Columbia: Institute against Family Violence.

Clare, E. 2015. *Exile and Pride: Disability, Queerness, and Liberation*. Durham: Duke University Press.

CMHA (Canadian Mental Health Association). 2011. *Violence and Mental Health: Unpacking a Complex Issue*. A discussion Paper. Toronto: Canadian Mental Health Association.

Coker, A.L., P.H. Smith and M.K. Fadden. 2005. "Intimate Partner Violence and Disabilities among Women Attending Family Practice Clinics." *Journal of Women's Health*, 14.

Curry, Mary Anne, and Fran Navarro. 2002. "Responding to Abuse against Women with Disabilities: Broadening the Definition of Domestic Violence." *End Abuse Health*, Alert 8, 1.

DAWN/RAFH (DisAbled Women's Network). 2009. "Bridging the Gaps: Violence, Poverty and Women's Shelters: An Update in Non/Resources for Women with Disabilities." Montreal QC: DAWN/RAFH Canada.

___. 2011. "Women with Disabilities and Abuse: Access to Supports." Montreal, QC: DAWN/RAFH Canada.

Drossman, D.A., J. Leserman, G. Nachman et al. 1990. "Sexual and Physical Abuse in Women with Functional or Organic Gastrointestinal Disorders." *Annals of Internal Medicine*, 113.

Du Mont, Janice, and Tonia Forte. 2014. "Intimate Partner Violence among Women with Mental Health-Related Activity Limitations: A Canadian Population Based Study." *BMC Public Health*, 14, 1.

Linton, Simi. 1998. *Claiming Disability: Knowledge and Identity*. New York: New York University Press.

Martin, S.L., N. Ray, D. Sotres-Alvarez, L.L. Kupper, K.E. Moracco, P.A. Dickens, D. Scandlin and Z. Gizlice. 2006. "Physical and Sexual Assault on Women with Disabilities." *Violence Against Women*, 12, 9.

Mason, Robin. 2006. "Domestic Violence: Recognizing and Responding." *Women's Health: Research and Practice Issues for Canadian Physicians*. Ottawa, ON: Canadian Women's Health Network.

May, V. 2012. "Intersectionality." In Catherine Orr, Anne Braithwaite, and Diane Lichetenstein (eds). *Rethinking Women's and Gender Studies*. New York: Routledge, 155-172.

McCauley, J., D.E. Kern, K. Kolodner et al. 1995. "The Battering Syndrome: Prevalence and Clinical Characteristics of Domestic Violence in Primary Care Internal Medical Practices." *Annals of Internal Medicine*, 123.

National Clearinghouse on Family Violence. 2009. *Violence against Women with Disabilities*. Ottawa: National Clearinghouse on Family Violence.

Nosek, M.A., R.B. Hughes, H.B. Taylor and P. Taylor. 2006. "Disability, Psychosocial, and Demographic Characteristics of Abused Women with Physical Disabilities." *Violence Against Women*, 12.

Nosek, M.A., C. Clubb Foley, R.B. Hughes and C.A. Howland. 2001. Vulnerabilities for Abuse Among Women with Disabilities. *Sexuality and Disability*, 19(3): 177–189.

Nosek, Margaret A. 1995. "The Physician's Guide to Domestic Violence." *Center for Research on Women with Disabilities*. Volcano, CA: Volcano Press.

Odette, Fran. 2013. *Ableism — A Form of Violence Against Women. Critical Reflections by Fran Odette.* Learning Network Brief (11). November. London, ON: Learning Network, Centre for Research and Education on Violence Against Women and Children. <vawlearningnetwork.ca/violence-agasint-women-disabilities-deaf-women>.

Oliver, Mike.1990. *The Politics of Disablement.* London: Macmillan.

Perreault, Samuel. 2009. "Criminal Victimization and Health: A Profile of Victimization among Persons with Activity Limitations or Other Health Problems." *Canadian Centre for Justice Statistics Profile Series.* Ottawa: Canadian Centre for Justice Statistics. Catalogue no. 85F0033M - No. 21.

Public Health Agency of Canada. 2007. "What Determines Health? What Makes Canadians Healthy or Unhealthy?" <phac-aspc.gc.ca/ph-sp/determinants/determinants-eng.php>.

Roeher Institute for National Clearinghouse on Family Violence. 1994. *Violence and People with Disabilities: A Review of the Literature.* Ottawa: Family Violence Prevention Division.

Statistics Canada, Canadian Centre for Justice Statistics. 2011. *Family Violence in Canada Report.* Ottawa: Statistics Canada.

Vecova Centre for Disability Services and Research. 2011. "Violence against Women with Disabilities: Violence Prevention Review." Calgary: Vecova Centre for Disability Services and Research.

Womendez, C., and K. Schneiderman. 1991. "Escaping from Abuse: Unique Issue for Women with Disabilities." *Sexuality and Disability,* 9.

WHO (World Health Association). 2012. "Social Determinants of Health Fact Sheet." March 9. <http://www.wpro.who.int/mediacentre/factsheets>.

___. 2013. The Economics of Social Determinants of Health and Health Inequalities: A Resource Book. Geneva: World Health Organization.

Yoshida, K.K., J. Dumont, F. Odette, and D. Lysy. 2011. "Factors Associated with Violence and Abuse among Canadian Women Living with Physical Disabilities." *Health Care for Women International,* 32, 8 (June-July): 762–775

Yoshida, Karen, Fran Odette, Susan Hardie, Heather Willis and Mary Bunch. 2009. "Women Living with Disabilities and Their Experiences and Issues Related to the Context and Complexities of Leaving Abusive Situation." *Disability and Rehabilitation,* April: 1–10.

Young, M.E., M.A. Nosek, C. Howland, G. Chanpong and D.H. Rintala. 1997. "Prevalence of Abuse of Women with Physical Disabilities." *Archives of Physical Medicine and Rehabilitation,* 78.

Chapter 10

"What Women Want"
Pacific DAWN Talks to Women with DisAbilities about Escaping Violence

Pat Kelln and Stephanie Parent

> Women with disAbilities live at the intersection of gender and disAbility, as well as other social identities such as race, sexuality, and socioeconomic status. As a consequence, women with disAbilities experience higher rates of violence and lower rates of service access than their non-disabled peers. (Thiara and Gill 2012)

The Pacific DisAbled Women's Network (Pacific DAWN) is a cross-disability organization open to women with any type of disAbility living in British Columbia and the Yukon (2005). Pacific DAWN accepts a woman's self-identification of disAbility for membership. The capitalization of the "A" in disAbility is an idiosyncrasy of DAWN groups to emphasize that they focus on abilities rather than disabilities. In keeping with the *United Nation's Convention on the Rights of Persons with Disabilities* (United Nations 2006: 4), Pacific DAWN agrees that "disability is an evolving concept and that disability results from the interaction between persons with impairments and attitudinal and environmental barriers that hinders [sic] their full and effective participation in society on an equal basis with others."

Recognizing jurisdictional issues, the original group set up both a national and a provincial organization for women with disAbilities in Canada. The provincial organization was established to deal with provincial and local matters, such as police protocols for domestic violence and how they are implemented, and with issues such as government cutbacks and other problems faced by women with disAbilities. The federal organization is focused on issues that affect all women with disAbilities across Canada, such as the United Nations resolution on the rights of women with disAbilities.

Given the significant challenges and vulnerabilities encountered by women with disAbilities who experience violence, Pacific DAWN identified a need to ask women with disAbilities what they wanted. After hearing from many women with disAbilities that the services currently offered by anti-violence organizations and transition houses are inadequate, Pacific DAWN set out to better understand and document the lived experiences of women with disAbilities who have experienced (or continue to experience) violence. The intent was to better inform the design and delivery of anti-violence services by gathering feedback from women who have experienced both disAbility and abuse. This is in the spirit of the internationally adopted slogan, "Nothing about us without us" (Yeo and Moore 2003). Pacific DAWN designed a survey so that women with disAbilities could discuss their experiences with violence, often for the first time, as well as their experiences trying to access anti-violence support services.

This was a priority for Pacific DAWN because widespread structural and systemic discrimination against women with disAbilities, coupled with a lack of services, means that they are more likely than non-disabled women to remain in situations that expose them to various forms of violence (Ali, Mowry and Ho 2011). Further, studies of women with disAbilities who have experienced violence (see, for example, DAWN Canada 2007; Chang et al. 2003) tend to ask *service providers* whether or not they are able to meet the needs of women with disAbilities, rather than asking women with disAbilities themselves about their experiences.

The "What Women Want" Survey

According to a national survey of shelters and transition houses conducted by DAWN Canada in 2008, approximately 45 percent had turned away women with disAbilities at some point because they were unable to accommodate their specific accessibility needs (Smith 2009). Many "accessible" residence shelters do not go beyond mobility concerns (such as ramps to enter the premises) and many of these shelters fail to consider other issues such as the accessibility of washrooms (such as whether a user of a mobility device like a wheelchair can open and close doors), the height of light switches, or the presence of fire alarms designed to warn deaf people (Smith 2009). The questionnaire developed by DAWN Canada (2007) facilitates a thorough evaluation of the physical accessibility of shelters and transition houses for women. While a small number of surveys of shelters, transition houses, and victim services have been conducted to determine the physical accessibility of these buildings (Smith 2009), rarely have women with disAbilities been asked what type of anti-violence services they prefer to use and/or would like to have available.

Given the lack of research in this area, Pacific DAWN decided that it was essential to consult with their members in order to better understand the variety of experiences accessing anti-violence services. The group received positive feedback about the project; as one respondent commented, "It's about time that women with disabilities are being asked what they want." Unfortunately, as is the case with many non-profit organizations, there was no money available to pay members to prepare a funding proposal. This meant that Pacific DAWN had to rely on volunteer labour, in this case those who did not already have jobs or were not busy seeking employment. Despite these barriers, the group was committed to having women with disAbilities conduct the research.

An initial questionnaire was drafted and reviewed by members of Pacific DAWN to ensure that factors pertaining to a variety of disAbilities were taken into account. The final version was also commented on by members of the Feminist Research Education Development Action (FREDA) Centre, who also developed an electronic version. Unfortunately, Pacific DAWN was unable to secure funding for expansion of the "What Women Want" survey, but still felt that the research was sufficiently important to proceed without funding. The lack of funding, however, limited the scope of the research. The final questionnaire contained twenty questions and a number of sub-questions (see Appendix).

The main goals were to determine the following:

1) Whether women with disAbilities prefer to access anti-violence services in a home specific to women with disAbilities or to access anti-violence services in a home available to both disAbled and able-bodied women;
2) Whether the results are different for a woman who became disAbled as an adult than they are for a woman who was born with a disAbility;
3) What type or types of disAbilities the responder has;
4) Whether she has children;
5) What her income level is;
6) Whether or not disAbility-specific transition houses and services encourage women to leave an abusive relationship (and stay at risk);
7) If disAbility-specific transition houses and services were preferred, whether the woman and her children (if applicable) would leave their communities to access disAbility-specific services.

In the first phase of this research, the survey was sent to all members of Pacific DAWN as well as to members of the B.C. Society of Transition Houses. Recipients were asked to distribute the survey throughout their networks. The survey was also promoted at meetings for local disAbility organizations (such as the focus group for West Coast Legal Education and Action Fund). Respondents were sent a link to an online version of the survey and were also provided with the option to complete the survey by hard copy, over the telephone, or in person.

The results were that thirteen women completed our online survey, with an additional ten women having accessed and completed one or two of the demographic questions before exiting the survey. We believe that this high attrition rate (43 percent of those who began the survey) is in part due to the individual physical barriers faced by women with disAbilities as well as the financial barriers they face when trying to access computers and the Internet.

Findings

All survey participants identified themselves as having a disAbility. Four participants were born with their disAbility and nine were not; two of the nine women reported acquiring their disAbility after they were 40 years old. Four women indicated that they had acquired their disAbility as a result of abuse or violence.

In terms of type of disAbility, seven women had mobility issues, one indicated deafness, and another had communication and other hidden (or invisible) disAbilities. Three women reported visual and mobility disAbilities, while the others indicated a broad range of disabilities. While there are numerous types of classifications of disAbilities, the project team decided on the "major distinctive classifications" used by many in the disAbility community: mobility, deaf, communication, visual, psychiatric, developmental, learning, hidden, and other. The limited number of classifications does not allow for the broad range of abilities and barriers that each classification could encompass. For example, visual could include everyone from those who are totally blind to those who have no barriers if wearing prescription glasses.

The respondents were also asked whether they had children and whether they were the primary caregiver. Seven responded that they did have children, while six did not, numbers that may reflect the difficulties women with disAbilities have in becoming mothers (Track 2014). All respondents who had children reported that they were over the age of 21. For a woman with disAbilities, as for any woman, having and caring for children can have a great impact on her decision and ability to leave an abusive relationship.

In addition, respondents tended to be low income, with only one woman indicating an income greater than $30,000 per year. This is in line with national data, as Statistics Canada (2015) indicates 25 percent of people with disAbilities have a low income. Living in poverty can pose a significant challenge for women with disAbilities who have experienced violence, as challenges associated with poverty intersect with those associated with disAbility. Moreover, living in poverty is often correlated with violence against women (Barnett, Miller-Perrin. and Perrin 2005). It is extremely difficult for individuals to consider removing themselves from a violent living situation if they do not have sufficient income to live independently. This difficulty is often compounded for women with disAbilities, who may be living in poverty as well as relying on a partner to provide caregiver support. In addition, housing poses a significant challenge. Finding replacement housing adapted and suitable for their particular barriers can be almost impossible. Physical and financial dependence has the potential to drastically shift relationship power away from the dependent individual. One woman noted, "Although [I am] alone, the abuse continues financially as money affects my life. Sometimes I don't eat … [my] husband stole all [my food] and has not paid support."

Perhaps due to the types of relationships that are more commonly experienced by women with disAbilities — such as a caregiver or health care service provider — our results reflect a wide variety of perpetrators (Figure 10-1). Research consistently shows that women with disAbilities are equally likely or even more likely than able-bodied women to have experienced violence (Nosek et al. 2001). There are factors specific to women with disAbilities that increase their likelihood of experiencing violence, including an increased dependency on others for various aspects of care, a perceived or real inability to seek help when faced with violence, a lack of belief by able-bodied service providers, and social isolation (Nosek et al. 2001). Beyond the typical challenges and barriers that all women face in escaping violence, women with disAbilities have few options that are appropriate and accessible.

Figure 10-1 Relationship Between Woman and Abuser

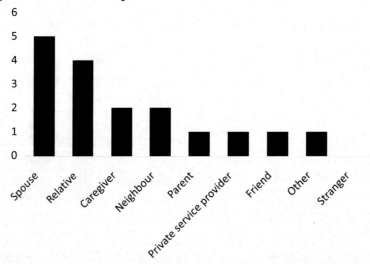

The personal experiences of the respondents and of Pacific DAWN members confirms that mainstream anti-violence services are often unable or unwilling to address caregiver or service provider abuse. Their mandates are often to provide services for women experiencing intimate partner or stranger sexual abuse. The hesitance to move beyond these types of abuse and consider vulnerabilities particularly associated with disAbility — for instance, caregiver abuse or neglect — is a service gap that can leave women with disAbilities who experience violence few options to find appropriate support and protection.

What a woman with disAbilities may also require is help in building up self-esteem and confidence, fighting negative thinking, and strengthening the tools to make decisions and communicate her needs effectively. In addition, a woman may have communication difficulties, which will require patience on the part of a service provider or counsellor and a longer time to allow her to share her experiences.

The responses to this questionnaire reveal dependence, frustration, fear, and low self-esteem. As one woman acknowledged, "Living on egg shells [is] better than putting my relationship with my caregiver and housing in jeopardy." There are multiple factors constraining the choices of women with disAbilities, and many women express feeling as though they do not have a choice at all because they depend on their caregiver to help meet their daily needs. For example, how does a woman press charges against an abusive caregiver, when the caregiver is the only helper she can afford to care for her personal needs?

Several survey respondents who reported living in rural areas of British Columbia specifically noted the challenges associated with accessing appropriate services that can accommodate disAbility. For example, one woman observed, "The Transition Society sends a counsellor once a month to this rural area … Help is a slow process." The women reported seeking help primarily through counselling services, support groups, and transition houses. While participants tended to find counsellors helpful, they discussed issues related to poor accessibility and availability. As one woman noted, "The counselling services were up two flights of stairs which was extremely challenging." This remark highlights key elements of basic accessibility for individuals whose disAbilities are mobility related. "Accessibility," however, goes far beyond wheelchair ramps and elevator access. In her struggle to communicate with counsellors (because of her communication disAbility due to living with Asperger's Syndrome), one woman described frustration at not being heard and frequently being told that the counsellor was "not available" (to her).

Several participants reflected on whether disAbility-specific services would encourage them to leave their abusive relationship, noting, "I would have better self-esteem now. All women with disabilities deserve to be safe." Research conducted by Nosek, Howland, Rintala, Young, and Chanpong (2001) supports these claims, finding that only 6 percent of 598 domestic shelters surveyed could handle the care needs of a woman with a disAbility. Though these findings are dated and from the U.S., there has been no comparable survey of domestic shelters in Canada. Shelters can self-report that they are accessible, though often the only phrase used to suggest accessibility is "women with special needs can be accommodated" (Public Health Canada 2008). In such instances, "special needs" usually means that the shelters can provide help for those who are addicted or that they have a ramp outside. This is not true accommodation.

Living with a disAbility can also be a very isolating experience, as one woman notes: "I continue to live in this [violent] situation because it is a very complex thing to figure out and I am terrified of discrimination outside my small known world." Consequently, nine of twelve women indicated a preference for services that are specifically designed for women with disAbilities. Nine women also reported that they would be encouraged and willing to leave their community and abusive situation in order to access these specific services. Key themes that emerged from this questionnaire included a desire to be "believed" by others about their experience and a need to be understood by "others like you." As one respondent explained, "Transition houses that are geared specifically for women that are disabled will help ease an already stressful situation because the houses will be equipped to meet their needs." However, one woman pointed out that "accessible and appropriate services" translates into more than simply meeting accessibility needs. In speaking about other experiences of discrimination, she expressed a desire for "a safe place specifically for ALL people with disabilities, regardless of race, religion, age or gender." When a woman's identity includes intersecting axes of oppression along the lines of disAbility, race, gender, or sexuality (among others), there are few safe places for her to turn.

Survey Limitations

Due to the small sample size and sampling methods, whereby a targeted sampling approach was used in order to obtain rich information from individuals with relevant lived experience, it is not possible to generalize the data to the broader population of women with disAbilities in British Columbia or beyond. In addition, there were numerous challenges to implementing the survey, including a lack of funding to hire interview staff or travel to speak with women from across the province. Seeking feedback from women with disAbilities has certain unique challenges, as these women do not necessarily belong to a cohesive community. For example, many women have disAbilities that are hidden, that they choose not to discuss or identify, or that they deny even exist (Ferri and Gregg 1998). It can also be very tiring for individuals with disAbilities to complete lengthy interviews by typing their responses online or responding to questions via telephone or in person.

Although only one woman indicated that she was Deaf, it is important to acknowledge that there is a distinct and well-organized Deaf community with its own culture, including a unique language, which makes it necessary to have a third party (interpreter) to communicate with the hearing world (Padden, Humphries and Padden 2009). Based on findings in the literature, it is possible that Deaf individuals might seek or need separate transition houses and anti-violence services that are more appropriately tailored to the Deaf community (Merkin and Smith 1995).

We acknowledge the difficulties that our limited number (nine) of disAbility classifications caused, but at this time there is no common set of categories to be used when listing the types of disAbilities. In order to ensure that our classifications resonated with potential participants, numerous discussions about Statistics Canada's 11 classifications (Statistics Canada 2007) were held with women with disAbilities. As difficulties with agility and pain can be a large part of other disabling conditions, it was decided not to use them. It greatly hinders any comparison of research done by others and often leaves us with little understanding of the true nature of the barriers an individual confronts. As research and knowledge expand, numerous categories have been further expanded; for example, currently the classification for those with issues related to their mental capacity has been expanded to include developmental, learning, psychiatric, and in some instances hidden or other. However, further research is required before any conclusions can be made such as the needs and desires of deaf women who have experienced violence and are seeking access to anti-violence services.

Moving Forward

Five key recommendations emerged from "What Women Want." Implementing these recommendations would immediately improve the access women with disAbilities have to anti-violence resources (such as transition houses and shelters), as well as to programs and services that are accessible and appropriate.

The first recommendation is to extend this survey to all disAbility organizations and then to all organizations and services that work with women in British Columbia. Expanding the research to include a broader range of organizations would result in a more comprehensive understanding of what women with disAbilities who experience violence perceive as the most effective way to meet their needs. Further, a similar survey should be conducted nationally. Though the first phase of the "What Women Want" survey was small, it showed clearly that services specific to women with disAbilities are essential. Yet, in British Columbia as well as nationally, the majority of human and financial resources are allocated to able-bodied anti-violence services. "What Women Want" also showed that such a shift must be done in consultation with women with disAbilities.

The second recommendation is that services currently available to able-bodied women leaving violent situations (such as transition houses), as well as organizations providing counselling and/or support groups, complete an in-depth physical accessibility audit. Such an audit should be extensive, reliable, and completed (if possible) by a woman with a deep understanding of living with various disAbilities. When asked if their facilities were accessible, one organization responded to a woman with mobility restrictions: "What do you mean? We have an elevator." Accessibility audits are particularly important in rural and remote areas with small populations where services are limited to begin with and there is a need to avoid a duplication of services. To prevent wasting resources it is felt it would be more efficient to set up special transition houses in three or four central locations around the province and provide women with disAbilities the opportunity to relocate to these houses.

In order to satisfy the need for specific services, our third recommendation is to develop and implement a model for transition houses specifically designed for women with disAbilities, initially, in at least three B.C. locations. This model should look to the Freedom House Domestic Violence Shelter in New York City (Ali, Mowry and Ho 2011). Its programming is innovative and unique, and Freedom House contains appropriate and accessible features to ensure that women with disAbilities feel more comfortable in their environment during what is a difficult and stressful time. For example, hallways are wide enough to accommodate two wheelchairs; bathrooms are large and contain transfer bars; light switches are lower on the wall; laundry machines are front loading; each room is equipped with an audio-visual intercom system in order to accommodate the ASL needs of deaf women or women who are hard of hearing; and occupational therapists are available. The transition house was designed using an inclusive and participatory approach with input from multiple organizations representing people with disAbilities. Support groups and counselling are also available, and Freedom House incorporates a trauma-informed approach to survival and safety. A trauma-informed approach is one that considers the impact of trauma in all facets of care delivery and encompasses an understanding of the impact that trauma can have on all aspects of an individual's life (Ko et al. 2008). Service providers using a trauma-informed approach strive to provide care in a way that prioritizes individual safety and choice and make a conscious effort to avoid re-traumatization (Harris and Fallot 2001). Overall, this model uses an empowerment approach to help ensure that spaces are inclusive and appropriate for all its clients. The creation at least of a similar transition house model in British Columbia would be a much-needed first step towards closing the anti-violence service gap for women with disAbilities.

Our fourth recommendation is to provide resources and training to help women with disAbilities create self-support groups in their communities. As our survey indicated, most women with disAbilities prefer and feel more comfortable with other women with disAbilities, and in the absence of such support they often forego appropriate services. Pacific DAWN, with the support of the Abuse Response Team at B.C. Women's Hospital and Health Centre, is currently working to adapt the hospital's existing programs and train individuals to facilitate anti-violence support groups for women with disAbilities in their community or in a transition house (inclusive of those with mental health and addiction issues). One goal is to enable these individuals, in turn, to train women with disAbilities to start support groups in their own communities. Facilitated and peer support groups have long been a part of the healing process for women who are able-bodied and have experienced violence. Peer support groups not only provide a venue to discuss our own experiences, but also provide information about other women's experiences with violence, thereby reinforcing the idea that they are not alone, that others have similar experiences. Though there have been a number of attempts in B.C.'s lower mainland to start peer support groups, current manuals and training materials are not inclusive of women with disAbilities, and, as mentioned previously, attempts to integrate into an able-bodied group have been shown to be insufficient.

Pacific DAWN's fifth recommendation is that organizations and individuals who help women leaving an abusive situation work to understand the environment and beliefs of the home in which a woman was raised; in so doing, they can better accommodate the needs of women with disAbilities. In other words, these organizations and individuals need training in cultural competency, defined as "the ability of individuals to establish effective interpersonal and working relationships that supersede cultural differences" (Cooper and Roter 2002: 554). Ideally, women with various disAbilities would deliver this training. Further, the need for accountability was noted by one of the respondents, who stated, "Training is useless without an accountability process because discrimination is most always the fall-back action when there is a shortage of services or workers are overworked and underpaid and underappreciated." A system of evaluation and oversight will thus be required to make sure that service providers are given the tools and training to help their clients. Over the last five years, Pacific DAWN has been providing orientation workshops with great success at Police Victim Services and the B.C. Society of Transition Houses conferences. We are concerned about the lack of any awareness training or materials for the majority of those who provide support groups or one-to-one counselling.

All of these recommendations address concern that anti-violence workers and service providers are not adequately trained to support women with disAbilities who have experienced violence (Lockhart and Danis 2010). Even disAbility organizations and advocates often have little knowledge about the issue of violence against women with disAbilities, beyond institutional violence. As one frontline worker from a disAbility organization stated, "We thought that the problem [abuse] would end when the institutions were closed. It hasn't … The abuse has just changed." The need for education about this issue is thus ongoing — and should be directed towards all disAbility organizations, frontline workers, and women with disAbilities themselves. Programs and relevant materials developed by a disAbility organization could provide information about the various aspects of violence experienced by women with disAbilities and address attitudinal barriers. As one respondent indicated, what is needed is a "special, deep understanding, [an] ability to relate, share and believe, be believed and accepted by those like you."

Appendix

1. Do you identify as having a disAbility? Not necessarily a medical diagnosis but do you believe you have a disAbility?
2. If you personally do not have a disAbility, what are your experiences or qualifications for completing this survey? Any comments?
3. What type of community do you live in: City, Town, Rural or Isolated?
4. Do you own or rent your home, or are you in some type of assisted living home? Any comments?
5. What income bracket most describes your situation:
   a. $0-9.999, $10,000-19,999, $20,000-29,000, $30,000-39,999, $40,000 or more.
6. Do you have children?
   a. How many do you have?
   b. What are their ages?
   c. Are you the primary care-giver?
7. What type of disAbility do you have? Mark as many as is applicable:
   a. Mobility, Deaf, Communication, Visual, Psychiatric, Developmental, Learning, Hidden or other
8. Were you born with your disAbility and at what age did you acquire your disAbility?
9. Is your disAbility the result of abuse or violence?
10. Do you have easy access to transportation? Own car, Driven by others, Bus, Cab or other.
11. Do you acquire assistance when traveling?
12. Are your friends and acquaintances comprised mainly of people with disAbilities? Any comments?
13. Have you been or are you currently in an abusive situation? Any comments?
14. How would you define the relationship between you and your abuser: Parent, Spouse, Stranger, Caregiver, Private Service Provider, Relative, Neighbour or Friend?
15. Have you tried to get help for your situation and from what type of agency: Transition House, counselling services, organization for People with disAbilities or other? Any comments?
    a. Were they helpful?
    b. Did you feel that they did not want you or screened you out of their services because you had a disAbility?
    c. What could they have done to make you feel welcome?

d. Did you continue in your abusive situation due to the services you approached not wanting to or being unable to accommodate your disAbilities? Did having a disAbility have something to do with you not seeking help? Any comments?

16. Have you reported the incident and/or ongoing incidents to police or RCMP?

16a Were they helpful?

a. Did you feel that they did not want or screened you out of their services because you had a disAbility?

b. What could they have done to make you feel welcome?

c. Did you have to continue in your abusive situation due to the police services you approached not wanting to or being unable to accommodate your disAbility?

d. Did having a disAbility have something to do with you not seeking help? Any comments?

17. Would you prefer to go into/use:

a. Transition House, Safe House or services that are SPECIFICALLY designed for women with disAbilities

b. Transition House, Safe House or services that are designed for all women?

c. Any comments?

18. If there was a Transition House, Safe House, or services built specifically for and use by women with disAbilities, would that encourage you to leave an abusive situation? Any comments?

19. Would you be willing to leave your abusive situation and your community in order to access a Transition House, Safe House, or services for women with disAbilities? Any comments?

20. Is there anything else you would like us to know?

References

Ali, A., R. Mowry and K. Ho. 2011. "Collective Action and Emancipatory Aims: Applying Principles of Feminist Practice in a Shelter for Domestic Violence Survivors with Disabilities." *Papers on Women and Girls with Disabilities.* <ncdsv. org/images/CWPS_llectiveActionEmancipatoryAimsApplyingPrinciplesFeministPracticeShelter_4-2011.pdf>.

Barnett, O., C.L. Miller-Perrin and R.D. Perrin. 2005. *Family Violence across the Lifespan: An Introduction.* Second ed. Thousand Oaks, CA: Sage.

Chang, J.C., S.L. Martin, K.E. Moracco, L. Dulli, D. Scandlin, M.B. Loucks-Sorrel and I. Bou-Saada. 2003. "Helping Women with Disabilities and Domestic Violence: Strategies, Limitations, and Challenges of Domestic Violence Programs and Services." *Journal of Women's Health,* 12, 7.

Cooper, L.A., and D.L. Roter. 2002. "Patient-Provider Communication: The Effect of Race and Ethnicity on Process and Outcomes of Healthcare." In B.D. Smedley, A.Y. Stith, and A.R. Nelson (eds.), *Unequal Treatment: Confronting Racial and Ethnic Disparities in Healthcare.* Washington, DC: The National Academies Press.

DAWN/RAFH Canada. 2007. "National Accessibility and Accommodation Survey." <dawncanada.net/resources/resources/national-accommodation-and-accessibility-survey/>.

Ferri, B.A., and N. Gregg. 1998. "Women with Disabilities: Missing Voices." *Women's Studies International Forum,* 21, 4.

Harris, M., and R.D. Fallot. 2001. *Using Trauma Theory to Design Service Systems.* San Francisco, CA: Jossey Bass.

Ko, S.J., J.D. Ford, N. Kassam-Adams, S.J. Berkowitz, C. Wilson, M.Wong, M.J. Brymer and C.M. Layne. 2008. "Creating Trauma-Informed Systems: Child Welfare, Education, First Responders, Health Care, Juvenile Justice." *Professional Psychology: Research and Practice,* 39, 4.

Lockhart, L.L., and F.S. Danis. 2010. *Domestic Violence: Intersectionality and Culturally Competent Practice.* Columbia University Press.

Merkin, Lewis, and Marilyn J. Smith. 1995. "A Community Based Model Providing Services for Deaf and Deaf-Blind Victims of Sexual Assault and Domestic Violence." *Sexuality and Disability,* 13, 2.

Nosek, M.A., C.C. Foley, R.B. Hughes and C.A. Howland. 2001. "Vulnerabilities for Abuse among Women with Disabilities." *Sexuality and Disability,* 19, 3.

Nosek, M.A., C.A. Howland, D.H. Rintala, M.E. Young, and G.F. Chanpong. 2001. "National Study of Women with Physical Disabilities." *Sexuality and Disability,* 19, 1.

Pacific DAWN. 2005. <http://www.pacificdawn.ca/index.html>.

Padden, C., T. Humphries and C. Padden. 2009. *Inside Deaf Culture.* Harvard University Press.

Public Health Agency of Canada. 2008. "Transition Houses and Shelters for Abused Women in Canada." <phac-aspc.gc.ca/sfv-avf/sources/fem/fem-dir-transition/index-eng.php#toc≥>.

Smith, J. 2009. "Bridging the Gaps: Survey Examines Accessibility at Women's

Shelters." *Canadian Women's Health Network,* 11, 2 (Spring/Summer).

Statistics Canada. 2007. "Participation and Activity Limitation Survey 2006: Analytical Report." Table 4 page 23. <http://www.statcan.gc.ca/pub/89-628-x/89-628-x2007002-eng.pdf>.

___. 2015. "Canadian Survey on Disability, 2012." <http://www.statcan.gc.ca/pub/89-654-x/89-654-x2015005-eng.pdf>.

Thiara, R.K., and A.K. Gill. 2012. *Domestic Violence, Child Contact, Post-Separation Violence: Issues for South Asian and African-Caribbean Women and Children: A Report of Findings.* London: NSPCC.

Track, L. 2014. *Able Mothers: The Intersection of Parenting, Disability and the Law.* West Coast LEAF. <westcoastleaf.org/wp-content/uploads/2014/12/2014-REPORT-Able-Mothers.pdf>.

United Nations. 2006. *Final Report of the Ad Hoc Committee on a Comprehensive and Integral International Convention on the Protection and Promotion of the Rights and Dignity of Persons with Disabilities.* United Nations General Assembly: Sixty-First Session, A/61/611. <daccess-dds-ny.un.org/doc/UNDOC/LTD/N06/645/30/PDF/N0664530.pdf?OpenElement>.

Yeo, R., and K. Moore. 2003. "Including Disabled People in Poverty Reduction Work: 'Nothing About Us, Without Us.'" *World Development,* 31, 3.

Index